Fire in the Soul

Reincarnation from Antietam to Ground Zero

JEFFREY J. KEENE

Fire in the Soul

ISBN: 978-0-578-32501-9

Preface

The first section of this book, Someone Else's Yesterday, was written as things revealed themselves to me over a period from roughly 1991 until the publication date in 2003. Section two, Phoenix Rising, updates happenings over the ensuing years and brings us up to the present. I have traveled many thousands of miles to get my story out. I have slept on couches, in my car, and on planes while traveling to lecture for no pay. I have done television shows on The Sci-Fi Channel, Biography, PBS, A&E, The History Channel, Discovery Channel and others that wanted to featured my tale of unending life... More than a dozen books, magazines and radio shows have carried my story. The Sci-Fi Channel's show, "Proof Positive," first airing November 2004, did an exceedingly thorough job. I spent six days with the film crew. With all the travel, lectures, magazines, TV and radio shows the single largest payment I ever received was a $250 "Honorarium" from one of the Hollywood production companies. But, I would do it all again. I have striven along the way to help others as much as possible with their struggles and conflicts arising from dealing with past life and reincarnation issues. I have been both student and teacher in this lifetime, as are we all. I hope that with my writings I can compel my readers to reach outward and inward, to raise up themselves and others, to understand and experience life to its fullest.

The second section, Phoenix Rising tells of people I have met along the way and discoveries I have made in my travel from time of the publication of Someone Else's Yesterday in 2003. One of the stories, The Phoenix, deals with a 9/11 survivor, not a physical survival but a non-physical one. 343 firefighters of the Fire Department of New York perished that day, but for one little boy, it was just a new beginning.

Contents

Foreword

THE PHRASE "NEW AGE" HAS been bantered about for so many years that it makes one wonder just when this "New Age" will come about. Well, stop waiting and start looking around. The twentieth century was chock full of technological advancements. We went from the infancy of air travel to flights to the moon and back. Communications went from crank operated telephones and primitive radios to mobile phones and televisions you can hold in the palm of your hand. We have come a long way here on Earth, but our spiritual advancement has not kept pace with our technical discoveries.

We are now witnessing the rebirth of spiritual seeking on a scale never seen before. One of the all-time great puzzles through the ages has been what happens after we die. Some people say, "There is only one way to find out: Die." There is an alternative way. This path involves studying the most recent cases involving reincarnation. Ever since 1952 when the Bridey Murphy story hit the media, people in the U.S. have seen a progression of reincarnation cases. Each decade has brought about stronger and stronger cases, including dozens of welldocumented histories of children who spontaneously rememberpast lifetimes.

At the turn of the millennium, a group of cases has emerged that demonstrates a common pattern in how reincarnation occurs. These cases show that facial architecture, personality traits, aptitudes, interests and writing style stay consistent from lifetime to lifetime. Symbols and synchronistic events related to past lifetimes have been observed. People are also found to incarnate in karmic soul groups. In my research, Jeffrey Keene's case is one of the first that I encountered, which demonstrates *all* of these principles of reincarnation. In his story, in which it is proposed that he is the reincarnation of Confederate General John B. Gordon, we observe the following features characteristic of reincarnation cases:

Similar Physical Appearance: Yes
Similar Personality Traits: Yes
Consistent Writing Style: Yes
Karmic Group Identified: Yes
Past Life Symbols: Yes (birth date, emergency room
                               visit)
Past Life Memories: Yes

To add to the credibility and feasibility of the conclusions drawn by Mr. Keene's belief that he had been General John B. Gordon is the fact that he bears markings on his face, in three places, that match wounds received by Gordon in battle. Once he was even rushed to a local hospital emergency room with pain that mimicked a wound Gen. Gordon received 115 years before. The photographic resemblance between Confederate General John B. Gordon and Jeffrey Keene is, to say the least, uncanny; some even say spooky. Jeff's story is a marvelous collection of hindsight and foresight. You will be carried through history from America's Civil War to the sorrowful aftermath of the terrorist attack on the World Trade Center, where Mr. Keene, a decorated firefighter himself, paid respects to America's fallen. It is a wondrous thing to travel along with someone who has not only seen the past, but who has felt it; someone who has witnessed a modern tragedy of historic proportions, who can also impart insights from past battles, which will help humanity grow beyond its recurring pattern of needless conflict and war.

If you listen closely, you may hear the guns of Antietam mixed with the sound of bagpipes echoing through the masonry canyons of New York. Let his story teach us and let wisdom emerge like a phoenix from the smoking rubble and our broken hearts.

Walter Semkiw, M.D.
Author of *Return of the Revolutionaries: The Case for Reincarnation and Soul Groups Reunited*

Introduction

A COMPELLING AND HONEST VIEW of one man's journey through history. How do you explain something you do not understand or necessarily believe in? This is an overwhelming story of Jeffrey Keene's walk through his past and present into a future that is still unfolding. I have known Jeff for a number of years and met him when the first edition of his story, "Someone Else's Yesterday," was released. From the beginning I was impressed with the simple honesty of a man telling a story he was living as it continued to unfold. This was an honorable man, an assistant chief with the Westport, CT Fire Department who would have a lot to lose just by relating the emotional story that began when he casually visited a Civil War Battlefield. Thus begins a journey that will compel Keene to question his purpose as he discovers that we have lived before and sometimes remember those events with clarity.

Keene remembers being a Confederate General, a military leader and a senator in his time. His was a time of division, conflict, slavery and deaths numbering over 600,000. In some ways, as tragic as our battles are today they pale in comparison, both in numbers and relevancy, to those historical battles. There are many details that unfold and become verifiable, to include scars on his body today that are the same scars of a wounded man from another time. Keene has been featured on television, various talk shows, and network news releases; he successfully passed a lie-detector test regarding his vivid memories. Interest in Keene's story has been nationwide and international in scope. In today's climate, there are ongoing conversations seeking to better understand our future by remembering, and embracing, the lessons of the past.

In some ways the intent of the conflicts in our current time is to erase our history with protest, riots, destruction and violence. No matter how bad our history was, we can't erase it by tearing down statues, or by defacing them. We should have already learned that 'protest' must become 'policy' if we are to become better stewards of the history we are creating. As Keene's eyes grow weaker at this stage of his life, his vision of the comparisons get sharper. Perhaps in remembering our history we begin to see our similarities and we will make better decisions. If we do not learn from our past, we are destined to repeat the same mistakes until we get it right. The only thing that is consistent is the inconsistency we walk through.

You will want to share this journey as Jeff's path takes him from a Civil War Battlefield, to the fallen towers of 9/11 and into the Black Lives Matter historical unfolding of today. You will share his inner conflict as he cannot turn away from his own truth unfolding. Of particular interest is the story of a young boy who was part of the crew that lost his life as the towers fell. Mr. Keene is not the only one who is remembering past lives, and it is interesting how their paths cross each other. Perhaps in remembering our history we begin to understand the similarities; we begin to understand that we are all the same, just on a different part of our journey. Mr. Keene releases his second edition with more details and a look into our unfolding saga. As his story draws closer to an ending in his lifetime, Keene now refers to his journey as "Fire in the Soul!" What can we learn from such a profound story...you be the judge.

Judy Goodman, CPC, CSRC, CRC
Author, Coach, Counselor, Speaker, Teacher
www.JudyGoodman.com   JudyKGoodman@aol.com

Someone Else's Yesterday

*The Confederate General
and Connecticut Yankee*

A PAST LIFE REVEALED

PART I

To my beloved wife Anna
for putting up with me,
and to Shannon and Samantha
for their belief in and love of their father

CHAPTER ONE

Not Yet

IT WAS A PEACEFUL QUIET DAY at the Bloody Lane, one of those beautiful days in May you would like to catch in a jar and save for winter. I walked down the fieldstone stairs into the old farm road. I had no idea of the series of events being put into action. Soon, in a few short steps, the line between past and present would become very blurred.

My wife Anna and I were on a vacation to hunt for antiques. Our travels took us through New Jersey, Pennsylvania and then into Maryland. While in Maryland, we stopped in Sharpsburg, where the battle of Antietam had been fought during the Civil War. I was not a student of the Civil War. For that matter, I had never even read a Civil War book. I had watched a couple of shows from the Ken Burns Civil War series on the local Public Broadcast System and, while we were in the area, felt compelled to visit this battlefield. Our first stop was at the section of the battlefield known as The Cornfield.

Anna and I walked around a bit, then drove a short distance to a parking lot near what is called the Sunken Road. Anna stayed in the car, having soon tired of looking at monuments and markers, thus ending her historical career. Walking over to the Sunken Road alone, I found myself the only visitor to this portion of the battlefield. Built into a stone wall was a piece of metal grillwork with a large button next to it with the word "Push." Much like Alice in Wonderland, my curiosity got the better of me and within a few seconds I was listening to a tape recording of what had transpired there during the battle. After listening to the tape, I walked down onto the road itself. I had only gone a few yards when something very strange happened, something the likes of which I hope will never happen again. A wave of grief, sadness and anger washed over me. Without warning, I was suddenly being consumed by sensations. Burning tears ran down my cheeks. It became difficult to breathe. I gasped for air, as I stood transfixed in the old roadbed. To this day I could not tell you how much time transpired, but as these feelings, this emotional overload passed, I found myself exhausted as if I had run a marathon. Crawling up the steep embankment to get out of the road, I turned and looked back. I was a bit shaken to say the least and wondered at what had just taken place. It was difficult getting back to the car because I felt so weak. I had regained most of my normal composure on the way back and said nothing to Anna about what had just happened. What could I say? How could I explain it to her? I did not have any answers, just questions. I would one day receive my answers, but not until more than a year later and then from a most unusual source.

On a day that is set aside for the unusual, I was soon to discover just how far from the commonplace a Halloween night could be. Life for me had become pretty routine, but that was all to change on All Hallows Eve 1992. Anna and I attended a birthday party for the husband of her friend who just happened to be born on Halloween. Anna's friend, Lourdis McBroom rented a ballroom at Roberto's restaurant in Monroe, Connecticut. I know what a few of you may be thinking. Halloween? McBroom? He's making it up. No, I am not. Lourdis's last name was McBroom. This name may conjure up visions of an old crone, but Lourdis was the farthest thing from it. She was petite and pretty, a firecracker of a redhead with a wonderful Spanish accent. Regretfully, I must use the past tense. Lourdis left us a short while back after a long illness. She is missed. Lourdis had decorated the place lavishly for her husband's party. On all the tables were bags full of masks, spiders, candy and the like. She had hired two people for the evening, one a cartoonist and the other a palm reader. Anna and

I had walked around for a while, then waited to have a caricature done.

While we waited, I watched the people having their palms read. The woman doing the reading seemed sincere and was not repeating anything she had said to others. People who had waited in line would sit down one at a time in front of this woman. Taking their hands in hers, she used a small flashlight to look at the lines in their palms. She talked about things like their personalities, travel and so on. When we sat for the caricature, the artist asked our occupations and hobbies. When he finished, he handed us the completed picture. The cartoon showed me wearing my fire helmet and sitting at a desk while Anna stood nearby cooking up a storm with a frying pan in one hand and a rolling pin menacingly close to my head in the other. The young artist was quite clever and talented. Anna and I returned to our table to eat.

With dinner finished, I asked Anna if she was going to have her palm read. She said, "Yes," and I said, "Me too." I had never had my palm read before. I put Anna ahead of me in line so I could hear what the woman said to her first. Before it was Anna's turn to sit, I told her to watch when it was my turn. She said "why?" All I could reply was, "I don't know, I just have a feeling." The line moved on. Anna sat for her reading. The woman proceeded to hit her personality right on the head. I was laughing and Anna said, "You better stop laughing, you're next." There were some pink sheets of paper on the table near the palm reader so I picked one up and it read:

> Hi! My name is Barbara Camwell. I am a Clairvoyant, Clairsentient and Clairaudient. As far as I can remember, I have been this way all of my life. What this means is that I may be able to see, hear or feel (emotionally) past and present issues for you, as well as some trivial and not so trivial information. I use palmistry as a tool. I will need both hands for this. What helps me? For you to think positively. Think of something good that has happened to you recently or something that makes you feel happy. This tends to make the reading clearer. Nervousness and anxiety tend to blur the reading.

Don't be afraid! I won't say anything to scare you! Honest! I don't believe in negativity, unless I can help you avoid it. So enjoy, and importantly ... HAVE FUN!

Well, after a good dinner, a few drinks, and laughing at my wife with the palm reader, I guess I was having fun already. Barbara told Anna that she would come into money within the next five years. She felt something about a little boy. She said she saw Anna surrounded by ocean and that she loved it. Anna told me later that she thought Barbara had been way off on this one. At the time I thought so too, as I knew Anna had a great dislike for water. Years later Anna stood on a black sand beach in Hawaii, the water swirling about her calves and tickling her legs as she watched giant sea turtles bobbing up and down in the surf. She had to confess Barbara had been right. Now it was my turn. I sat down and smiled at Barbara, and she smiled back. Barbara took hold of my extended hands and held them for a short while. (She did not use the small flashlight she had used on all of the others). Suddenly she dropped my hands and sat back in her chair. She said, "That is only the second time I have seen that." She told me she has a friend who has a simian line that crosses their hand and runs down the side. She said that mine was almost as long.

I asked, "Simian like monkey?"

She replied, "Yes." Barbara took my hands in hers. She started looking at my left hand. She said, "You have some real nasty stuff here. You have one line that you only see on insane people."

I chuckled and said, "I've been there."

"Your right hand shows that you have it under control; you are right-handed, aren't you?" I nodded yes. (I think that at that point, if I had been a lefty, I would have switched!) She said, "You are going to come into money within the next five years. I see ocean. You're going to take a trip to Sweden? Switzerland?" (At that point I informed her that my wife had been born in Austria and that was most likely the area). Barbara continued, "I see an accident, nobody is killed or hurt bad, it's just going to be a pain in the butt, so be careful. Do you play an instrument?"

I replied, "No."

"Did you ever play an instrument?" I said I had tried to play the drums, but it hurt my legs to do the bass. Barbara said, "You should play one even if it's only a hobby." There was a long pause as she studied my hands. She said, "You are very intelligent, very, very intelligent."

She suddenly dropped my hands and sat back in her chair. "You know what I mean by intelligent—you know about things like time and doors opening and closing, things like that?" I nodded. (Who was I to argue with someone who just finished telling me how intelligent I am?) "Do you believe in past lives?" she asked.

I said, "Yeah?"

She said, "There is a question mark there. I just take past lives for granted." I explained that I have seen and felt a few strange things in my life. She asked "like what?"

I told Barbara about the unusual thing that happened to me on our visit to the Antietam Battlefield. Barbara sat across from me nodding her head. "That's because you died there," she said.

"Oh, that's nice," I replied.

Barbara seemed deep in thought for a short time. She said, "When you were hovering over your body looking down, you were very angry and yelled NO!"

There was a pause, and I told her for reasons unknown to me, "Not yet!"

She said, "Yes, like not yet, but you hung around for a long time." Well, that was the end of the session, for others were waiting in line for their turn. I went back to our table with Anna. I asked her if she had been watching. She said yes, but she could not hear much. She asked why I looked so serious while talking to Barbara. I told her what Barbara had said to me.

I sat thinking over what Barbara had said. After a while, I returned to the line to see Barbara again because I wanted to ask her two questions. I sat down in front of Barbara, she sat back in her chair and said, "I have taken you as far as I can."

I said, "Just let me ask you two questions. Number one, are you sure that I was dead? What about wounds?"

She said "Oh honey, you had holes shot all through you."
Why the first question was important to me I did not know. Then
I asked her about something that had happened to me when I
was stationed in Florida during my hitch in the Air Force. I had
returned to my barracks at Orlando Air Force base hospital after
a long Labor Day weekend at Daytona Beach with some of the
guys. I was lying on my bunk starting to drift off to sleep when
I saw someone walk into the room. (The door was open and the
light in the hallway was on.) He walked over and stood at the
foot of my bed. I said, "Hey, what's happening." I wanted to get
him to talk so I could figure out who it was. There was no reply.
I boosted myself up on one elbow and leaned out so that the
upper bunk was not blocking my view. I started to say something
again when I noticed I could see the picture hanging on the wall
directly behind whoever this was. The problem was I was looking
right through him. I slowly brought my knees up to my chest,
pushed my feet out from under the covers and down to the floor.
I stood and moved rapidly to the door. The figure did not move;
he remained in the same position. All I could make out was black
hair combed back, dark sunken eyes and hollow sunken cheeks.
I heard a television on in one of the rooms, so I went in and told
them that I could not sleep. I watched television for a while not
saying anything to the other guys about what had just happened.
I sat in contemplation over what had been the most frightening
experience of my life. Did I have a hallucination, or was it just
that state that lies between asleep and awake? But why could I
still see him as I exited the room? Maybe I had simply overdone
it out at Daytona, or gotten too much sun on my head. After a
while, I decided to return to my room. I walked down the hall,
passed my door, turned around and made a beeline back to watch
some more television, for standing just inside the doorway was
the same man that I had seen earlier. I watched a lot of television
that night. I was awake, alert and confused.

Who was this apparition in my room? This was the second
question that I asked Barbara.

She asked, "Did he speak to you?"

I said, "No."

"Did you see a uniform?" she asked. Again I answered, "No."

"Well maybe it was someone from your past," she said. I thanked her and went back to my table. Over the years I have told many people about the story of the man in my room, and the best way that I could describe his looks was to say he was "Abe Lincolnish," when Lincoln was young, with sunken eyes, hollow cheeks and black combed back hair. On the way home from the party, Anna asked me, "What were you at Antietam? Just a soldier?"

I said, "I guess so."

The next day Anna went to work. I sat alone in my living room wondering about what had happened at the party. Was there anything to this past life stuff? Some curious thoughts came into my head. Here I am, a man in his mid-forties, and the only picture on my dresser for a long time was of my Great Grandfather, Lewis Knapp, 1st. CT. Heavy Artillery United States Volunteers. In the picture, he is wearing his Civil War uniform. Something else struck me as strange. When Anna and I were leaving the Sharpsburg area during our trip, we stopped in a gift shop. Anna wanted to buy some wine called Lake Anna, a local brew. I was looking around and picked up a bullet from the Civil War that had been found in the area. A magazine on the counter caught my eye, the *Civil War Quarterly* [Special Edition ANTIETAM]. I picked it up and took both the bullet and the magazine to the checkout counter and told Anna, "I want these." We left and returned to our home in Connecticut. Now the strange part. That magazine was the first Civil War book or magazine I had ever purchased. The bullet had been placed on my dresser next to my Great Grandfather's picture. The magazine had been placed in with our phone books. Our trip was taken in May of 1991. Here it was a year and a half later, and I had never read the magazine. I had come across it many times, every time I had used the phone books, but had never read it. As Lewis Carroll would put it, "Curiouser and Curiouser." The picture and the bullet on my dresser, the magazine I never read.

I was then aware that I had treated that magazine like no other I had ever owned. I figured it was time to read it. I turned to the section on the Sunken Road. A picture at the top of the page showed the road near the spot where I had that unusual experience I had told Barbara about. My eyes scanned down the page and stopped at a two-word quote. The hair on the back of my neck stood up. "Not yet," it read. That is what I had said to Barbara. I read on. "Not yet," John B. Gordon had told anxious members of the Sixth Alabama who requested permission to fire. "Wait for orders." "Closer and closer the Federals tramped, coming at last to the crest of the low ridge that fronted the confederate position. There they appeared in brilliant outline against the eastern sky, perfect targets less than 100 yards from the defenders. Shouted orders to 'FIRE' from the sunken road must have been audible to many of the attackers an instant before a tremendous volley struck them. In a moment the drill-like precision of the attack dissolved into chaos." I read on. "A huge volume of musketry spewed out from the sunken road. My rifles flamed and roared in the Federal's faces like a blinding blaze of lightning," wrote Gordon. "The effect was appalling. The entire front line, with few exceptions, went down in the consuming blast." Tears welled up in my eyes. I continued reading, and later in the account of the battle, I came across the wounding of Gordon. "On Rodes end of the line, John B. Gordon of the Sixth Alabama was hit in the left arm, the right shoulder, and twice in the right leg before passing out from loss of blood after receiving a wound in the face."[1] From what Barbara Camwell had said I figured this fifth wound was the one that Gordon would have died from. I turned back to the page with the picture of the sunken road, and on the page across from it was another picture. This time a chill ran through me and the hair on the back of my neck stood up again. The picture was of Brigadier General John B. Gordon. The face was not unknown to me. I knew it well; I shave it every morning. In the story they referred to Colonel John B. Gordon? He must have lived through his wounding to become a general. Was I going crazy? I wondered if I was imagining the likeness of the photo.

I read more of the magazine; a story called "Lee's Lost Orders." The story was about Special Orders number 191, the most famous orders General Lee ever issued. To capsulate, Special Orders number 191 were written at Frederick, Maryland, some forty miles northwest of Washington D. C. They were phase two of the first invasion of the north by the Army of Northern Virginia. Nine copies were written. Their fame is derived from the fact that one copy was lost in transit. The lost copy was found by some Union soldiers and upon discovering their significance, the orders made their way to General George B. McClellan, then commander of the Union Army. Now the Union Army had the game plan, whereabouts and dispersion of the Army of Northern Virginia. The result of receiving this information was the battle of Antietam, or Sharpsburg as it is known to Southerners. Now here we go with the chills and the hair on the back of the neck again. The date the orders were written? September 9, 1862. The date was well known to me, I would celebrate it every year. My birthday is September 9th. Let's backtrack now and see what we have so far from the time of the party. In one day, I see a palm reader, the first one I had ever talked to. I tell her about things that happened to me on an old battlefield. She tells me I died there. I have the picture and the bullet on my dresser. I read a magazine I have kept for one and a half years without reading. I read a quote that I said to Barbara, "Not yet." I see a picture that looks like me. I read about the orders that cause the battle and find that they were written on my birthday. Put yourself in my place. What would you think? What would you do? Oh yes, and one other thing. The picture of Gordon shows him wearing a double-breasted uniform with three stars on the collar. I am presently an assistant chief on the Westport Fire Department in Westport, Connecticut. My dress uniform is double-breasted, the rank insignia on the collar is three trumpets.

I needed another person's opinion on the picture (of Gordon), and did not want to impose my feelings on them. I took the magazine to work with me that night. I went to the dispatcher's room to talk to my good friend, Maria Macauda, who was working the night shift. I told her about the party and the palm reader. She listened to me about what Barbara had said. I told her about my reply of "Not yet." I placed the book in front of her and showed her the picture of the Sunken Road. I said not a word about the picture of Gordon. I stood back and waited. She read the part with the quote "Not yet." She said, "That's what you said to the palm reader." I nodded and remained silent. She looked over and saw the picture of Gordon and said, "Who is this?"

I said, "That's Gordon; it appears he didn't die from the five wounds."

She looked at the picture and up at me again. Sort of a double take. She said, "He looks like you!"

I said, "Thank you, now I know I'm not nuts."

What should I do now? What could I do? It would be very hard to forget all of this. The next day I decided to go to the library. I figured that if he was a Confederate General, there might be some information about him. I went to the Trumbull (Connecticut) library and looked up John B. Gordon in the index file. I noted that he had died in 1904. I found a copy of Who's Who 1903–1905, it read:

GORDON, JOHN BROWN (February 6, 1832 Jan. 9, 1904), soldier, statesman, was born in Upson County, Ga., although shortly before his birth his parents, the Reverend Zachariah Herndon Gordon and Melinda (Cox) Gordon, were living in Wilkes County, N. C. His great-great-grandfather, Adam Gordon, emigrated from Aberdeenshire, Scotland, about 1760 and settled near Fredericksburg, VA. Adam's son, Charles Gordon, moved to North Carolina and became prominent in the civic affairs of that state; and Charles's son, Chapman Gordon, was a soldier in the American Revolution. John matriculated in the University of Georgia and was a member of the class of 1853, but did not graduate. Studying the law privately, he was admitted to the bar and practiced for a while in Atlanta. The outbreak of the Civil War found him engaged in developing coal mines in the mountains of extreme northwest Georgia where the state touches Alabama and Tennessee. He was only twenty-nine years of age and his life up to this time had been without noteworthy events. Though destined to become the most important military figure in the history of Georgia, Gordon was wholly without training and experience in martial affairs when he was elected captain of a company of mountaineers. This company, the "Raccoon Roughs," was accepted by the Governor of Alabama and was soon at the front in Virginia. Gordon in September 1854 had married Fanny Haralson, of Lagrange, Ga. She went to the war with her husband and was his companion throughout the struggle. Under fire, Gordon's personality and genius for war speedily asserted themselves. He was promoted rapidly and in less than two years became a brigadier-general (November 1, 1862). In May 1864 he was promoted to major-general and near the end of the war he became a lieutenant-general, being one of the three Georgians to reach that rank. He commanded the II Army Corps and one wing of Lee's army at Appomattox. He participated in the battles of Seven Pines, Malvern Hill, Chancellorsville, Gettysburg, Spotsylvania, and Petersburg. In an official report, D. H. Hill spoke of Gordon as the "Chevelier Bayard of the Confederate Army." Returning to Georgia on the conclusion of the war, Gordon resumed the practice of law in Atlanta. He was still a young man, thirty-three years of age, and, with the prestige of his military record and his outstanding ability as a popular leader, naturally entered politics. (The book went on to say that Gordon became a one-time governor and a three-time senator of Georgia.) More than any other Georgian, Gordon fired the imagination of his native state. For nearly forty years he was the idol of the people. In physique, bearing, and manner he was courtly and impressive. From the organization of the United Confederate Veterans in 1890 to his death he was commander-in-chief…. In 1903 he published his Reminiscences of the Civil War. This volume gives a detailed account of the major battles in which he participated, but it is more notable because of its entire lack of sectional rancor and its uniform generosity and fairness toward friend and foe alike. Gordon died on January 9, 1904, at Miami, Florida.[2]

He wrote a book called *Reminiscences of the Civil War.* What would you do if you were in my place? Would you seek out the book? In the words of Sherlock Holmes, "Come Watson, the game is afoot!" By using the library computer I found that there was a copy of his book at the Fairfield library. I drove to Fairfield. In the library I found the book and turned to the section on Antietam. Gordon described the battle: "The Union forces numbered about 60,000, the Confederates about 35,000.

This battle left its lasting impression on my body as well as upon my memory." Well, now I know he had a sense of humor. He describes that sunny morning in September 1862 and the rolling farmland that surrounded him. Then the artillery of both sides opened fire; the battle had begun. The fighting off to the left of his position came to be known as the Battle of the Cornfield. Gordon wrote: "Again and again, hour after hour, by charges and counter-charges this portion of the field was lost and recovered, until the green corn that grew upon it looked as if it had been struck by a storm of bloody hail." The fighting had not commenced in the Sunken Road, which was the center of Lee's line. General Lee and General D. H. Hill rode by. They urged the men to hold the line at any sacrifice. Gordon writes: "I called aloud to these officers as they rode away. These men are going to stay here, General, until the sun goes down or victory is won. Alas! Many of the brave fellows are there now." Gordon went on to describe the Union soldiers' movements at the start of the battle over the Sunken Road.

> Drums, music and precision steps like a "holiday parade." Every act and movement of the Union commander in my front clearly indicates his purpose to discard bullets and depend on bayonets. He essayed to break through Lee's center by the crushing weight and momentum of his solid column. It was my business to prevent this: And how to do this with my single line was the tremendous problem which had to be solved, and solved quickly; for the column was coming. As I saw this solid mass of men moving upon me with determined step and front of steel, every conceivable plan of meeting and repelling it was rapidly considered.

Gordon shared his thoughts, which ended in a plan to hold their fire until the Union soldiers were almost upon them.

Now we come full circle to the "Not Yet" portion of the story that I described earlier. We continue from where we left off. "The entire front line, with few exceptions, went down in the consuming blast. The gallant commander and his horse fell in a heap near where I stood, the horse dead and the rider unhurt." Gordon tells of four successive charges in an effort to break through his line with bayonets. Speaking of the Union Commander, Gordon writes: "Finally, his troops were ordered to load. He drew up in a close rank and easy ranges and opened a galling fire upon my line. I must turn aside from my story at this point to express that I have never been able to ascertain the name of this lionhearted Union officer. His indomitable will and great courage have been equaled on other fields in both armies: But I do not believe that they have been surpassed." (Please remember this unknown Union commander for he enters into my story later on.) Gordon tells of his wounds:

> My extraordinary escapes from wounds in all the previous battles had made a deep impression upon my comrades as well as upon my own mind. So many had fallen at my side, so often had balls and shells pierced and torn my clothing, grazing my body without drawing a drop of blood, that some sort of blind faith possessed my men that I was not to be killed in battle. This belief was evidenced by their constantly repeated expressions: "They can't hurt him." "He's as safe one place as another." "He's got a charmed life." If I had allowed these expressions of my men to have any affect upon my mind the impression was quickly dissipated when the Sharpsburg storm came and the whizzing minies one after another, began to pierce my body. The first volley from the Union lines in my front sent a ball through the brain of the chivalric Colonel Tew, of North Carolina, to whom I was talking, and another ball through the calf of my right leg. Both sides stood in the open at short range and without the semblance of breastworks, and the firing was doing a deadly work. Higher up in the same leg I was again shot; but still no bone was broken. I was able to walk along the line and give encouragement to my resolute riflemen, who were firing with the coolness and steadiness of peace soldiers in target practice. When later in the day the third ball pierced my left arm, tearing asunder the tendons and mangling the flesh, they caught sight of the blood running down my fingers, and these devoted and bighearted men, while still loading their guns, pleaded with me to leave them and go to the rear, pledging me that they would stay there and fight to the last. I could not consent to leave them in such a crisis. A fourth ball ripped through my shoulder, leaving its base and a wad of clothing in its track. I could still stand and walk, although the shock and loss of blood had left but little of my normal strength. I remembered the

pledge to the commander that we stay till the battle ended or night came. I looked at the sun. It moved very slowly; in fact, it seemed to stand still.

Gordon tells of his movement over to the right side of his line where he saw a problem:

I was bloody and faint, my legs did not bear me steadily. I had gone but a short distance when I was shot down by a fifth ball, which struck me squarely in the face, and passed out, barely missing the jugular vein. I fell forward and lay unconscious with my face in my cap; and it would seem that I might have been smothered by the blood running into my cap from this wound but for the act of some Yankee, who, as if to save my life, had at a previous hour during the battle, shot a hole through the cap, which let the blood out. I was borne on a litter to the rear, and recall nothing more till revived by stimulants at the late hour of the night. My faithful surgeon, Dr. Weatherby, who was my devoted friend, was at my side, with his fingers on my pulse. As I revived, his face was so expressive of distress that I asked him: "What do you think of my case?" He made a manly effort to say that he was hopeful. I knew better, and said: "You are not honest with me. You think I am going to die; but I am going to get well." Long afterward, when the danger was past, he admitted that this assurance was his first and only basis of hope. General George B. Anderson of North Carolina, whose troops were on my right, was wounded in the foot, but it was thought, not severely. That superb man and soldier was dead in a few weeks, though his wound was supposed to be slight, while I was mercifully sustained through a long battle with wounds the combined effect of which was supposed to be fatal.[3]

As I thought of his wounds, a humorous parallel crossed my mind. It seems both he and I came close to departing this world under similar conditions. At the age of one, I spent a week in the Danbury Hospital in Danbury, Connecticut where I was born. I had a week of transfusions to save my life. The ailment?—lead poisoning. After reading this small portion of Gordon's book I believe what Barbara had seen when she said, "You were hovering over your body," then adding, "but you hung around for a long time," was not a death, but a near-death experience or N. D. E.

as they are called today. Now I understood why I went back and talked to Barbara that second time. And why I asked her, "Are you sure I was dead? And what about wounds?" When she said there were holes shot all through the body, I think that would be a pretty good depiction of Gordon on the ground after the fifth round hit him. We see Gordon himself questioning why he was spared from death, given the severity of his wounds and the medical practices of the day, he surely should not have survived.

I had a strange dream many years ago, strange for a few reasons. Back then I very seldom remembered my dreams, but this one I remembered and it was vivid although blurred. I was lying on my back in the dream with my head tilted back slightly. Not far from my face was a man, who was muttering and seemed to me to be cursing. I could not make out his face very well, but I thought he looked like one of the assistant chiefs I work with, John Gottfried (AKA Jocko). This man seemed to be doing something to my neck; there was a spurt of blood from the right side of my neck and everything went black. In the morning I told the dream to some of the men I worked with. I wondered if this was an omen of something to come. Was there to be some injury to myself and the only thing that would save my life was a tracheotomy? Does Jocko attempt doing one and end up cutting my throat? We had a good laugh. The right side of Gordon's face and neck had been blown apart. Did his good friend Dr. Weatherby work over him in despair, trying to stop the massive bleeding, swearing as he worked hard to save his friend's life? I wondered if he resembles Jocko. Maybe the dream was not a dream after all; maybe it had been a flashback to another time. As a young boy, I remember doing one of the Venus Paint by Numbers pictures of a Gettysburg scene, only it was the coloredpencil version. Once, when I was around seven or eight years old, I was playing at home using an old bench my grandfather had made out of logs. I turned it on its side, not realizing it greatly resembled breastworks I would see later in life. After a few rounds of pretend shooting at imaginary enemies, I was wounded. I remember crawling across the floor using only one arm and one leg. There is a little-known story about Gen. Gordon. I found it in an old interview where he tells of crawling and the strange feelings he went through after being wounded at Antietam.

I also built a fort with one of my friends—not an odd thing for children to do, but this fort was different. We dug a hole in the ground and then covered it with wooden planks. We then covered the planks with the dirt we had removed while digging the hole. Photos of Petersburg, Virginia, taken toward the end of the Civil War, show numerous forts such as the one built by myself and my companion, only they didn't call them forts; they called them "bombproofs" or "bunkers."

My friend, Dr. Ian Baillie (Ph.D.), called all this, "Spontaneous subconscious memory reenactment ... and at an early age before possible contamination from the media. " At the time I just called it playing.

One other thing: when my Uncle Joseph Knapp returned home from Korea, he gave my brother Jack and I some of his army helmets and army hats. One day I was wearing one of his old caps. I saw my brother playing near the road where we lived. I decided to sneak up on him and scare him. I crawled through the high grass, to a big tree where I could jump out and yell "Boo!" I jumped out from behind the tree and yelled, but I was the one who got the surprise. I was unaware that he was throwing rocks and one hit me square in the forehead. I ran home bleeding with the cap catching the blood. To this day my mother still remembers my coming in the house and handing her that army cap full of blood.

At the end of the chapter (about Antietam) in General Gordon's book, he reserves a spot for a very special person, Fanny Gordon.

> Mrs. Gordon was soon with me. When it was known that the battle was on, she had at once started for the front. The doctors were doubtful about the propriety of admitting her to my room; but I told them to let her come. I was more apprehensive of the effect of the meeting upon her nerves than upon mine. My face was black and shapeless so swollen that one eye was entirely hidden and

the other nearly so. My right leg and left arm and shoulder were bandaged and propped with pillows. I knew she would be greatly shocked. As she reached the door and looked, I saw at once that I must reassure her. Summoning all of my strength, I said "Here's your handsome (?) husband; been to an Irish wedding." Her answer was a suppressed scream, whether of anguish or relief at finding me able to speak, I do not know. Henceforward, for the period in which my life hung in the balance, she sat at my bedside, trying to supply concentrated nourishment to sustain me against the constant drainage. With my jaw immovably set, this was exceedingly difficult and discouraging. My own confidence in ultimate recovery, however, was never shaken until erysipelas, that deadly foe of the wounded, attacked my left arm. The doctors told Mrs. Gordon to paint my arm above the wound three or four times a day with iodine. She obeyed the doctors by painting it, I think, three or four hundred times a day. Under God's providence, I owe my life to her tender nursing through weary weeks and anxious months.[4]

The Sunken Road, from the time of the battle, was christened with a new name: Bloody Lane. The Battle of Antietam, to this day, holds the grim distinction of being the bloodiest single day in the history of the United States. Like Gordon, I too was to find what a lasting impression this battle was to leave on me.

CHAPTER TWO

A Helping Hand

ON THE PINK SHEET OF PAPER that I brought home from the Halloween party were some names and addresses of research and spiritual centers in the New England area. The papers were placed there just in case anyone wanted more information. After the events of the past few days, the party, the magazine, and the strange parallels from Gordon's story of Antietam, one word kept coming to mind—HELP! I called the nearest center in Branford, Connecticut and made an appointment for the afternoon of November 5, 1992.

Upon arrival, I met Jean Loomis, Director of the Aquarian Center in Branford. She's a professional psychic, astrologer and a certified clinical hypnotherapist. Jean is a lovely lady with dark hair, sparkling eyes and a sweet, soft style of speaking. Jean told me how she had gotten into her line of work. In 1975 she had a clinical death experience. The story was much like the neardeath experiences we hear about more and more every year. She said it changed her life and the direction of her life.

Jean looked at my palms and told me I have a long lifeline. She informed me that she had done my astrological chart (I had given her my birthdate information over the phone). Jean said I was in a phase, and had been for a few years, where I probably was getting little bursts, sometimes big ones, memories from other lifetimes (bleedthroughs she called them) and déjà vu feelings. She said I was a Virgo with Mercury in Virgo, so part of my mind must question it like crazy (it did). Jean told me how

34

she had spoken on a program with Edgar Mitchell, the astronaut. "Mr. Mitchell had said that, up until this generation (which began in 1980), scientists were able to predict the rate of changes which they judged by birth rate and population increase. Now, since 1980, the rate of population increase has kind of gone off the scale and their formulas don't work any more. They have gone back to the drawing board, questioning even the foundation of quantum physics. His point was that we are living in a time when the rate of change on planet earth is more rapid than at any other time in recorded history. There are more souls here, more energy and more information. The rules that our parents lived by, which they got from their parents and worked from generation to generation, no longer work."

Jean told me to trust my intuition. We talked about what had happened with Barbara Camwell at the party. Jean also explained that feelings and thoughts could carry over from past lives. She said I was in the profession I'm in as a result of some of those feelings I carried into this lifetime. We talked about the Civil War magazine quote, "Not Yet," and how Barbara said I was hovering over my body. Then she said, "It's not your only lifetime by any means; there's a whole past history here." Jean told me that, when these things start to come out, it's for a reason. They have some bearing on the present or the information wouldn't want to come up. It could be my career at the moment, or might be an expiation of killing people. She said afterward that, if there has been life in times of war, the soul says, "I don't want to kill any more, I want to save people." She felt there was a direct connection and probably more than one. I had been a medic in the Air Force, worked in a local hospital and now I am with the Fire Department. Maybe there was something to what she said.

Jean believed that a past life regression would be beneficial for a release of any emotion that had been brought up from my visit to Antietam. I showed Jean the picture of General Gordon. She thought the resemblance was amazing. I told her of the dream about someone leaning over me doing something to my throat. I

showed her some other pictures I had found of Gordon and again
she was amazed at the likeness Gordon and I share. Jean even
remarked on the set of the jaw (we will talk about the jaw later).
Jean asked me if there was any other more recent time period
that I felt an attraction to. At that time, the answer was "no."
I said that maybe because of my recent trip to Antietam. She
said that this Civil War period was what she called "the trigger
lifetime" for me—a lifetime that activates memories, ones that
we are deeply associated with. Jean talked about hypnosis and
meditation. She told me how the brain works:

> 5–10%   Conscious Reasoning Thinking
> 20%   Subconscious Storehouse of memories, past and
>   present lives
> 70–75% Unconscious Past life memories, psychic area

Jean recommended that we set up an appointment for the
following week, for a hypnosis session. She gave me some point-
ers on how to remember my dreams better, spontaneous writing
(if I lived before...), and meditation. During the coming week
Jean wanted me to meditate in the morning and again at night,
to quiet my mind and as a preparation for the next session. Jean
walked me through a meditation exercise. I was reclining in a
chair while Jean talked in a soft voice about things that were very
relaxing—blue skies and a field filled with flowers. She said, "If
you have a feeling or memory, it is okay, and if you don't, that's
okay too. When the meditation session ended, Jean asked me if
anything happened. I said, "Yes, a little." I told her I had felt as if
I was on horseback. There were woods off to my left. I was wary
of something in that direction.

The feeling of being on a horse brought back a memory of
something that had happened when I was stationed with the Air
Force in Florida, more than twenty-five years before. I told Jean
the story. One night I was in my barrack room and I heard a
bunch of the guys in the hallway. I popped my head out into the
hall and asked them where they were going. They said, "Horseback riding."

I said, "But it's 11:00 P.M." They said it was a midnight ride and asked if I would like to come along. I said "okay" and got dressed. When we arrived at the horse ranch, there were quite a few people there. The foreman looked worried, as if he was running out of horses. He came over to the group of us who were not yet mounted. He called out, "Are any of you experienced riders?"

I raised my hand and said, "I am!" I put my hand down and wondered to myself why I had said that.

The foreman came closer, cocked his head, squinted a little and asked, "Are you good?"

I replied without hesitation, "Yes, I'm good." He turned around and walked away in the direction of the barn. Now I was really confused by what I had said. I had been on a horse perhaps 3 or 4 times in my life. Once I had been in fear for my life. I was on my cousin's horse, "Blackie," when it decided to run at a high speed through a wooded area. We brushed trees; I dodged limbs, and yelled, "whoa," while pulling hard on the reins, but to no avail. My cousin Dave was on his mother's horse and when Blackie had caught up to them he slowed down his pace. My Uncle Harry had heard the noise and asked why I had been yelling. When I told him, he said, "Yelling won't help, the horse is deaf."

I said, "I pulled on the reins hard and he still wouldn't stop." My Uncle said, "You probably made him mad doing that." He explained that the people who owned Blackie before had left a training bit on him too much and he had a split tongue. Great, I'm flying around in the woods screaming at a deaf horse, yanking on the reins and making him mad. Now you can see why my reply to the foreman seemed inappropriate. He had not asked if anyone had a horror-filled experience while on a horse. The ranch foreman walked away from our group. As he did, he called to a man closer to the barn, "Bring out Rebel." My heart sank; what had I done? I had visions of a horse ten feet tall with smoke and flames coming out of his nostrils. A large grey horse was brought out to me. I carefully mounted. I patted the big horsey's neck saying in my mind, "Please don't hurt me." After a while I felt at

home, as if I was with a friend. I pressed my knees into the horse
slightly. He moved forward until I stopped.

When I turned my toe into his right side, he turned right in
place until I stopped. We repeated a left turn the same way. I
pulled back on the reins slightly and the horse backed up. The
ride wasn't much; we rode in line to an old gravel pit where we
stopped and drank warm soda that had been given to us by the
foreman before we left the ranch. Once during the ride as we were
passing through an orange grove, the automatic sprinklers came
on, scaring the horses. We had to dismount and lead the horses
the rest of the way out of the grove. At one point, Rebel's front
hoof came down on my right foot. I thought I would hear bones
crack any second but instead he just tapped the top of my shoe
and raised his hoof. I can't say much for the midnight ride, but I
guess the horse was memorable.

I asked Jean if she caught the name of the horse; she said, "I
got it," with a chuckle. "No accident," she added. When I have
told this story to other people, often their response is to say that
maybe the horse was well trained. My reply to them is "HOW
DID I KNOW WHAT TO DO TO MAKE THE HORSE ACT
IN THAT WAY?"

Jean ended by telling me to use meditation and the other tips
she had given me for the next week. She warned that I might get
feelings of being alone, but the more I learned, the more centered
I would be. The more centered I became, the better for myself,
my life and the people around me. Jean said because my face
looks so much like the face of that other lifetime, it tells her I'm
holding in my body structure a lot of the thoughts from that lifetime. She said the body tends to conform itself to our thoughts,
so the set of my jaw, my whole physique, tells her that I have
carried over a lot from that life. She said that going through this
regressive process can be a release of some negative emotions.

I left thinking about what Jean had said. It was up to me,
whatever I wanted to do. I returned home with my head in a
whirl. I had some answers but also more questions. More and
more things tied me to Gordon. Jean said to trust myself and that

I should be my own authority. Were all these strange things from a past life? How do you go about proving something like this? I decided the first thing I would do was to get a library card and check out Gordon's book, *Reminiscences of the Civil War*, and to follow Jean's tips. Little did I know that before a year was up, I would read more books than I had in all my life, travel thousands of miles, and visit many, many battlefields.

CHAPTER THREE

The Quest

I NOW HAD IN MY POSSESSION Gordon's book and the only portion I had read was Chapter VII, the one on the battle at Antietam. I decided not to read any more of the book for a while. I wanted to try meditation, spontaneous writing, and to see what my dreams would turn up first. I did not want to be influenced by the book. I've found that the periods just before sleep and just upon awakening are deep thought times. The day after seeing Jean Loomis, my thoughts lingered on what a complete turnabout the battle at the Sunken Road had been for Col. Gordon and his men. That day started bright and beautiful, even the approaching Union soldiers gave the appearance of being on parade. The Alabama 6th had repelled many charges without sustaining any casualties. By day's end the scene had changed dramatically. Gordon had been shot five times, the landscape was strewn with human wreckage, and the little roadbed now held many in a slumber that would carry them into history.

On the evening of November 6, 1992, I did my first solo meditation. It turned out to be very sad indeed. I remembered how Gordon had told of the mens' concern about him and how they wanted him to go to the rear to be attended. The last line of my meditation I wrote, "They are dying and they worry of me and my wounds, they cannot see the wound in my heart, it will never mend." I was too upset to continue. Upon awakening on November 7, many thoughts came to me: a stone barn, lying on straw, being thirsty, having difficulty swallowing and then there

40

were the men! What had become of them? I decided to get up. I went to the family room. It was clear to me that the process once begun would have to be played out to its conclusion (whatever that would be). It was 5 A.M. I got out a notepad to write down whatever came to mind. I played out the battle of the Sunken Road in my head. I would not fight the feelings nor end the meditation until it came to its own conclusion. It turned out to be one of the best things I have ever done for myself. It also turned out to be extremely draining. I had opened an emotional Pandora's Box. For over two hours I cried non-stop. Please bear in mind that I am 6 feet tall, close to 200 pounds. I have been a medic in the Air Force, worked in the operating room of a hospital, and have over 25 years experience doing fire rescue. I am not one who is prone to weeping at the drop of a hat.

Some of the things I wrote I will share with you, some I will not. They are mine alone. Since the first meditations I have discovered some strange facts:

I had written of a stone barn. Gordon had told of being taken to a barn but said nothing of its construction. On one of my trips to Antietam I inquired about where this barn may have been. I was told it was probably the barn on the Piper Farm to the rear of his line that day. From a window in the visitor center the roof of the barn was pointed out to me. I asked if it was the same now as then and was told, "It had been added on to." I asked what the barn was made of before and was told it was *stone*.

I had written of Gordon thinking: "We sure drew the short straw on this spot." Of all the places along the Sunken Road, the most shallow and least affording protection was the position of the 6th Alabama. Also, their right flank ended where the road made a 90degree turn to the right. On a ridge on the Union side the men could shoot straight down the length of the Alabama 6th and did so with deadly effect.

I wrote in my meditation about the Union officer that Gordon was never able to put a name to: "He holds his sword in his left hand, now there is a sign of the Devil." Not that many years ago the use of one's left hand was discouraged. Remember Gordon said he saw the officer and horse go down in the first volley of gunfire? "The horse dead, the rider unhurt." I found the name of that officer—it was General Max Weber. "On the receiving end the Federal Brigade of Brigadier General Max Weber, a 38 year old German trained officer. For five minutes, the Federals stood bravely. Then they fell back and took cover behind the crest. Weber was shot in the right arm. His brigade suffered an appalling 450 casualties." In the same book I found a picture of him with a caption that read, "he suffered a shattered right arm while leading the initial charge."[5] If Weber's right arm was shattered, he would have been forced to hold his sword in his left hand.

During my initial meditation with Jean Loomis I had that feeling of being on horseback. I decided to meditate and see if I could go back to that scene. Meditation of November 9, 1992— I was on horseback. I turned my head to the left and saw a rider approach from a wooded area. He saluted and held forward a piece of paper. I removed my gloves, took the paper and read it. I nodded to the rider and he rode off. The message said to bring the men to Gettysburg. I folded the paper and put it inside my shirt, something that I still do to this day. I don't mean put it in my shirt pocket; I mean unbutton my shirt and stick it inside. I called for an officer to pass the word to the other officers that we will stop to allow the men to cool off and talk over the orders I had just received.

When I came out of this meditation, I wondered if this was just my imagination. Ask anyone to name a battle of the Civil War, even someone who knew little about it (as I did at that time) and they would most likely reply "Gettysburg." What would Gordon be doing off by himself? As Jean Loomis said, "Trust yourself." I would later find a passage from a book on Gordon which read: "On June 30, Gordon marched his brigade from York to near Heidlerburg, where he received orders to move to Cashtown the following day. While on the march the next morning, new orders arrived; instead of turning west to Cashtown, Gordon was to continue south to a new destination—Gettysburg."[6]

Reading Reminiscences of the Civil War, I came across more areas where Gordon's life and mine touched. After helping to raise a group of men who were known as the Raccoon Roughs (because of their headgear and the Raccoon Mountain area from which they came), they headed off to war. They had wanted to go as cavalry, but cavalry was not needed at that time. Gordon writes: "We resolved to go at once to the front as infantry without waiting for orders, arms or uniforms." They were turned away.

After I had finished high school, I signed up for the Air Force. I was 17 years old. I passed the physical and was given a date to return for induction. The date was September 9, 1965. At the time I didn't think anything unusual about the date, but I do now. It was my 18th birthday. Why would I have consented to entering the service on my birthday? I volunteered, I was not drafted. Why didn't I stay home and party? I was sent home from the induction center that day to return at a later date. They took all the other men but not me. There was a war on and they sent me home! One hundred years after the end of the Civil War (1865) I spent my 18th birthday at the induction center and got sent away? I returned for induction at the end of September.

Gordon and the men went to Montgomery, Alabama and became part of the Alabama 6th. Some of the men, not having arms to fight with, were given "Joe Brown's pikes"—steel lances fastened to long handles (firefighters use these today on the hook-and-ladder trucks, the hooks are long handles with points on the end; they are also known as pike poles). The first part of my basic training was done at Lackland Air Force Base in Texas, the only place one could go after joining up. The second part of my training to become a medic took place at Gunter Air Force Base. Gunter at that time was located in Montgomery, Alabama. Now many people will say that all of this is coincidence, but at what point do things stop being coincidental? When you get a list of five things? Ten? Twenty?

Jean Loomis had picked up on the way my mind works. She knew I could be a hard nut to crack. She wanted to tell me some of what she had seen and felt about me, but did not want to lead me. It would be better to find out things for myself. Remember, Jean had remarked about the "set of my jaw." I have a pronounced jaw, something that has caused me some dental problems over the years. When I was in the service, I asked some dentists about my jaw. I was told it could be fixed, all that needed to be done was to remove a piece of bone from each side of my jaw and shove it back and wire my mouth shut until it healed. My face today remains in the same pristine condition in which God gave it to me. Gordon writes about his return to service: "It was nearly seven months after the battle of Antietam, or Sharpsburg before I was able to return to my duties at the front. Even then the wound through my face had not healed; but nature at last did her perfect work and thus deprived the Army surgeons of a proposed operation."[7] It seems military doctors like to play with people's faces.

One night many years ago, after a union meeting at Fire Headquarters, my brother Jack, a co-worker, and myself went to the local V.F.W. We had a few drinks and left shortly after midnight. In the parking lot I started getting a pain in the right side of my jaw down my neck and out to my shoulder. The pain grew steadily worse, so much so that I told my brother to drive me to the hospital. Having been a medic, I knew the pain might be a sign of a heart attack, even though I was not having chest pains. At the Norwalk Hospital emergency room they ran some tests, E.K.G. and such, and could find no cause. I remained there for an hour or so and the pain slowly subsided and then vanished altogether. I remember the date that this all happened ... at the stroke of midnight; it was September 9, 1977, my 30th birthday. Gordon's fifth wound at Sharpsburg was the bullet that entered just below his left eye, traveling through his face exiting the right side almost severing the jugular vein. This is the same area where I had the pain. At the time Gordon was wounded at the Sunken Road, September 17, 1862, he was 30 years old.

During some of my meditations, things surfaced, things not connected with Gordon. Leather armor, a rifle with a scope and words like Tamerlane and Mara Poso. I telephoned Jean and told her I needed to see her, that it was a special day. On the afternoon of November 11, 1992, I drove to Branford, Connecti-

cut once more. I told Jean what had happened and the parallels I
had found during the past week. I told her about being hit so hard
emotionally. She explained that the process I was going through
was a cleansing of "body and mind, spirit and emotion." She
said, "I needed to remind myself that I was an innocent child of
God. It is the mind that makes us guilty. Whatever I had done in
the past, I did the best I could at that moment. Guilt comes in
retrospect; it is not in the moment of the doing."

I told Jean about asking Barbara Camwell if she could identify the man that entered my barrack room. Barbara couldn't, or
I feel now, wouldn't answer my question. I had found the answer
myself. I had obtained many pictures of Gordon and in one he
didn't look quite himself; he looked rather haggard and worn. I
covered up the portion from the nose down and bingo, he was the
man in my barracks. I called a couple of my men at the firehouse
into my office one at a time, as they happened by. I covered the
lower portion of Gordon's picture and asked, "If you had to guess
who this is, what would you answer?" They replied "Abe Lincoln."
I had always described the man in my room as looking "Abraham
Lincolnish." Now, around 25 years later I had an answer to my
question of who it was ... John Brown Gordon. I told Jean that
I was going to read the rest of Gordon's book and that I bet he
worked to help the veterans after the war. She caught the significance of what I had referred to as a special day. She said, "It's
Veterans Day, bless your heart." Instead of a regression session,
Jean gave me another meditation for a "wider spiritual frame-
work." I had asked her how I could protect myself, because many
things that I came across during my meditations were nasty. I left
Branford more at ease.

In my quest for information I became a sponge. I'm told that
there are over 60,000 volumes written on the American Civil
War. I was to find many that spoke of General Gordon. There
are quite a few magazines for Civil War buffs. There are people
known as Reenactors, who dress in authentic reproductions of
uniforms and use weapons and accoutrements (some authentic)
and recreate battles of the Civil War. In the movie *Gettysburg*,

most of the soldiers used as infantry, artillery and cavalry were
from re-creation organizations.

I wanted a photo of General Gordon, not a reproduction, but
a real one. I saw an ad for photographs from the original plates.
In the list of people available, I found John B. Gordon among
them. Upon receiving the photo I was surprised how clear it was.
I took it to a local camera store. I asked a salesman if I could have
a copy made. We walked over to a machine that looked like an
ordinary copier. This machine could take a photo of a photo and
develop it in all different sizes. The salesman said he had just
finished changing all the solutions in the machine and if I didn't
mind waiting, he wanted to run through all the sizes. He said he
would only charge me for the one copy. How could I refuse a deal
like that? When I left the store I had eight copies of varying sizes.

When I arrived home I checked the photos out. Ever after
from the time of being shot, Gordon was always photographed
from the right side because of the deep scar under his left eye
(the entry point of the bullet). Anyone who knows about bullet
wounds knows that the damage becomes greater as a bullet travels through flesh, striking bone, expanding and fragmenting as it
goes. The photo was a 3/4 view. One of the copies was an enlarge-
ment of Gordon's face. You could just make out the indentation
under his left eye. You could see where the right side of his face
had been blown out. There was an area from his right cheekbone
down to his jaw and back to his ear that had seen better days.
Then something caught my eye, a line that started at mid-ear and
zigzagged across his cheek, almost like a lightning streak.

I walked into the bathroom and stood before the mirror, photo
in hand. I remembered my friend Maria doing the double take;
now it was my turn. On the right side of my face starting at mid-
ear is a scar, light but discernible. It moves across my cheek in a
zigzag pattern. Under my left eye there is an area about the size
of a quarter, indented a little with a jagged line outlining most
of it. I looked at the photo again and did a second double-take.
The mark on the left side of my face was in the same place as the
entry wound under Gordon's eye. I was not only receiving con-

firmation of a past life; I was being beaten over the head with it.

Thinking back over the years, I cannot for the life of me recall receiving any injuries that would explain these markings on my face. (Author note: I have a small cluster of spider veins on my right calf and a larger one higher up on the thigh of the same leg. Gordon said during the Battle of Antietam that he was shot through the calf of his right leg and later was shot "higher up in the same leg." My left forearm bears a scar at the point where I had a blood clot removed. When I asked the doctor how I got the blood clot, he said, "It just happens." I have been unable to find medical records that indicate the exact location of the wound to Gordon's left arm, but find it odd that the bloodclot scar *just happens* to be in the same general region. The spider veins on my right leg are the only place on my body where they occur.) I decided to continue reading Gordon's book. Gordon tells a story about a horse, one he had a problem with. He received the horse from the quartermaster in exchange for one of his own.

> He was an immense horse of unusually fine proportions and had behaved very well under the cannonading; but as we drew nearer to the blue line's front, and their musketry sent the bullets whistling around his ears, he wheeled and fled at such a rate of speed that I was powerless to check him until he had carried me more than a hundred yards to the rear. Fortunately, some of the artillerymen aided me in dismounting and promptly gave me a more reliable steed, on whose back I rapidly returned in time to redeem my reputation.[8]

Gordon describes the animal: "He was solid black in color and dangerously treacherous in disposition." I thought back to my ride of horror and to my cousin's horse Blackie.

About the battle of Malvern Hill Gordon writes:

> A great shell fell, buried itself in the ground, and exploded near where I stood. It heaved the dirt over me, filling my face and ears and eyes with sand. I was literally blinded. Not an inch before my face could I see; but I could think, and thoughts never ran more swiftly through a perplexed mortal brain. Blind! Blind in battle!

Was this to be permanent? Suppose there should be an assault upon my command from the front? Such were the unspoken but agonizing questions which throbbed in my brain with terrible swiftness and intensity. The blindness, however, was of short duration. The delicate and perfect machinery of the eye soon did its work. At last came, also the darkness for which I longed, and under its thick veil this splendid brigade was safely withdrawn.[9]

Anyone who has lost their sight even for a short period knows how Gordon felt. I know because it happened to me. A motor vehicle accident, on South Compo Road in Westport, left a car hanging sideways on an embankment. The occupants were trapped in the car. The first thing that needed attention was stabilizing the car. Only then could work begin on removing the people. The Hurst Tool, AKA the Jaws of Life, was set up to force open the driver's door. It was at this point that I walked over behind the two firefighters using the tool. As I stood there, something hit me. It felt as if fine sand had been thrown in my face. My eyes started to burn and there was a taste on my lips. Hydraulic fluid! There was a pinhole leak in the hose line for the Hurst Tool and I had been sprayed in the face with a corrosive liquid. My vision started to blur. I went to the closest fire engine and opened one of the outlets. I used the water from the tank carried on the pumper to flush my eyes. The water was not very clean, but it helped to take away some of the burning sensation. Many of the thoughts that went through my mind were the same as Gordon's at Malvern Hill. Quickly I washed my eyes out as best I could with the rusty water. An ambulance took me to Norwalk hospital where they flushed my eyes out for fortyfive minutes. Both of my eyes were covered with tiny scratches caused by the rust in the tank water. Thankfully, I fully recovered my sight.

In a book called *Lee's Dispatches*, I found this interesting letter to Jefferson Davis from Robert E. Lee:

Head Qrs. Army No. VA. 26th May 1863
His Excy Jeffn Davis President Confed. States.

   MR. PRESIDENT.
Since my letter of the 20th inst. which I stated that I would assign
General Gordon to the command of Rodes' old Brigade, I have
received the enclosed petition of all the commissioned officers of
Lawton's Brigade. I respectfully submit it to your better judgement,
whether it will not be best, if General Lawton is still unfit for the
field (as it would that he is from a late letter I have received from
him) to keep General Gordon in his present position where he is so
acceptable, and where he is entirely willing to remain, being a Georgian by birth. If you decide that this is best, then a brigade commander will be necessary for Rodes' Brigade. In reference to this I
enclose Genl Rodes' letter upon that subject/ Col. Morgan is highly
spoken of by General Rodes. He formerly commanded an Alabama
Regiment of Infantry, but retired before the reorganization. Col.
O'Neal is the Senior officer in the brigade, and commanded it in
the late battles, and had been one of the three officers mentioned
by General Rodes, but would recommend the appointment of Col.
O'Neal as perhaps the most fit-as he has been identified with his
regiment and the brigade by long service as lieut. Col. and Colonel.

I am with great respect, Your obt. Servt. (Sgd.)
R. E. Lee General[10]

The mention of a petition brought a memory of a similar incident. I did not get on the Fire Department on the first attempt,
but on the third. The first test I had taken was good for two years.
Two years and one month later, another test was given. Two men
had been hired, leaving two people remaining on the first test list,
myself being one of them. Instead of hiring us for two new open-
ings, they had waited for the test to run out. I fared no better on
a second attempt. A third test was completed and the marks were
posted. Now they were required to pick from the top three. My
brother Jack, a Firefighter at the time, was working as dispatcher
the day the Chief posted the test results. Jack saw the list and
called me. He told me "Come on down here, you won't believe
this." I went to the firehouse and my brother showed me the

posted results of the test, I was in 4th place, which put me out
of the running. Truly though, I was tied for second place. What's
the old saying? "I smell something rotten." My brother said he
asked the Chief about the results and was told that the State of
Connecticut had broken the tie. The Union President called the
state office that administered the test. He was upset that they
had broken the tie. They responded that the state had done no
such thing and that they would send an amended copy to the
town. To make a long story short, the results were changed to
my being in a tie for second place. It was apparent that someone
lurking in the background did not want me on the department.
I went to the VFW and told my story about the tests and the
tie-breaking. I told them my father was a retired firefighter and
my brother was currently on the department. I was informed by
a member of the Veteran's Council (made up of members of the
VFW and the American Legion) that my grandfather was one
of the first volunteer firefighters in town, a fact of which I was
not aware. They told me they would see what they could do. So,
thanks to these fine gentlemen and others, I became a member
of the Fire Department. I feel that one of the biggest contributing factor for my getting the job was that all the firefighters had
signed a petition saying they believed I should be the one to fill
the vacancy.

The things that we do today in the fire departments are much
like what is done in combat during wartime. Instead of rifles, we
use nozzles or deluge guns. We use offensive and defensive modes,
but instead of riding horses we ride in big red fire engines. Many
of the same thoughts go through my mind during the course of
my duties as those that must have been of concern to Gordon. At
Wrightsville, Pennsylvania, Gordon had a taste of my job. Union
troops had set fire to a bridge so that it could not be used by the
advancing confederates. Gordon writes:

> With great energy my men labored to save the bridge. I called on
> the citizens of Wrightsville for buckets and pails, but none were to
> be found. There was, however, no lack of buckets and pails a little
> later, when the town was on fire. The bridge might burn, for that

incommoded, at the time, only the impatient confederates, and these Pennsylvanians were not in sympathy with my expedition, nor anxious to facilitate the movement of such unwelcome visitors. But when the river's banks, and the burning lumber fired the town, buckets and tubs and pails and pans innumerable came from their hiding places, until it seemed that, had the whole of Lee's army been present, I could have armed them with these implements to fight the rapidly spreading flames. My men labored as earnestly and bravely to save the town as they did to save the bridge. In the absence of fire-engines or other appliances, the only chance to arrest the progress of the flames was to form my men around the burning district, with the flank resting on the river's edge, and pass rapidly from hand to hand the pails of water. Thus, and thus only, was the advancing, raging fire met, and at a late hour of the night checked and conquered.[11]

The following is a letter that I wrote to the Chief of the Westport Fire Department. It may give you an idea of what it is like to be in charge of an emergency scene and how I feel about my men:

Incident #200-752 On Saturday, May 30, 1992 at 1451 hours a call was received by dispatch of a propane line severed and propane gas leaking at 87 Maple Avenue South. My vehicle was the first on the scene at 1455 hours. The owner of the house and her friend were waiting by the road. I was informed that there were two leaking gas cylinders at the rear of the building. All the other apparatus had been advised to stand off from the scene to avoid all possible ignition sources. After a short conference with my driver (an ex-fire inspector) we determined it was two 100-pound propane tanks leaking. Firefighter Eugene Maloney donned full gear and headed towards the rear of the building, while I gathered more information from the owner. While trying to place the apparatus, I lost use of my portable radio, which forced me to return to my command vehicle. During that period Firefighter Maloney (with no portable radio because he had the presence of mind not to take a possible ignition source with him) with only the protection he was wearing, sized up the situation and reacted. At great risk to himself, he turned off the valves to both tanks, stopping the leak which reduced the problem. After finishing that task he reported his actions to me. With my radio restored, manpower and apparatus were brought in and put under the guidance of Acting Lieutenant

Christopher Ackley. While setting up a plan of action, Lieutenant Ackley displayed good common sense, knowledge, training and a deep concern for the safety of the firefighters under his command. A large amount of gas had entered the structure by way of an open window. Though we tried to remove all possible sources of ignition, we were able to remove all but two. The owner informed us that the house contained an oil-fired furnace and a hot water heater. There was no way to shut them off from the inside or outside. I made Lieutenant Ackley aware of the situation (I need not explain the destructive force propane gas in a confined space represents). Using metering devices, a positive pressure fan and by opening and closing windows the hazard was removed. When reading fire reports, they don't tell the whole story; they list things like ladders raised, amount of hose used, etc. Recognition is usually reserved for the saving of a life and not often enough given the fire service personnel for placing their lives in jeopardy. It is my recommendation that a well deserved WELL DONE be given to all involved; paid, volunteer, and Dispatcher Maciver (Dispatcher Maciver re-routed Engine #4 to report to Headquarters after I had put them in service. This gave us a centrally located engine and someone to man Rescue #8 in the absence of the Truck #1 driver). It is my feeling that special attention should be paid to the actions of Firefighter Maloney and Lieutenant Ackley. Anyone passing that house five minutes after we left would not have known that anything had happened there. If I were given the chance to explain the situation to them they undoubtedly would not appreciate the courage and selflessness I saw displayed for that one-hour period.

Respectfully submitted,
Assistant Chief, Jeffrey Keene

The homeowner mentioned in the letter asked me a question as we stood in the roadway in front of her house. She said, "Is this a dangerous situation?"

I replied, "Did you see those men go into your house?" (She nodded) "I love those guys and they could be gone in a heartbeat."

She said, "You don't look nervous."

I said, "I'm not supposed to, but you can't see me on the inside, can you?" She looked at me a little puzzled. I returned to the job at hand.

In Gordon's book, one of the few moments he stops to give some insight into what it's like to be in command, is at the wounding of General Robert Emmett Rodes at the 3rd Battle of Winchester.

> As the last words between us were spoken, Rodes fell, mortally wounded, near my horse's feet, and was borne bleeding and almost lifeless to the rear. There are times in battle—and they came often—when the strain and the quick shifting of events compel the commander to stifle sensibilities and silence the natural prompting of his heart as cherished friends fall around him. This was one of those occasions. General Rodes was not only a comrade whom I greatly admired, but a friend whom I loved. To ride away without even expressing to him my deep grief was sorely trying to my feelings; but I had to go. His fall had left both divisions to my immediate control for the moment, and under the most perplexing and desperate conditions.[12]

What I had gone through during the first meditations, the ones that had drained me emotionally, were some of the feelings deep inside Gordon and myself—feelings that we do not have the luxury of purging at the moment they arise. The job comes first, the feelings must await a later time. The General and I share much more than a physical resemblance; we share a common heart. I had found Gordon, or I should say, he found me. We did not meet that day I opened that Civil War magazine, nor when I read his name or saw his picture. Long before the Halloween party, palm reader or library books, we knew one another. We were never strangers. We met again when our hearts touched, a reintroduction at a place called Bloody Lane.

CHAPTER FOUR

Back to the Front

I DISCOVERED A BOOK WRITTEN about Gordon. It was on a list of books my mother had sent me. I called and ordered it right away. In a few days I had the book in my hands: *John Brown Gordon: Soldier, Southerner, American* by Ralph Lowell Eckert. In the first chapter he tells of John Gordon's early years:

> John was fourth of twelve children born to Zachariah and Malinda Cox Gordon. Although successful in Upson County, the reverend moved his family to Walker County in northwestern Georgia around 1840. He settled about ten miles from Lafayette, on property he dubbed Gordon Springs because of the great abundance of mineral water that flows from twelve main springs in the space of a quarter of an acre.

The author continues with,

> Ironically it was in the peaceful fields and valleys surrounding the Gordon homestead in northwestern Georgia, over which John roamed during his adolescence, that the Battle of Chickamauga— one of the Civil War's bloodiest struggles—would later rage.[13]

The book also told of Gordon's education:

> Gordon's early education differed little from what the sons of most small planters received at the time. He attended rural schools until his father became dissatisfied with the quality of instruction in Walker County. The reverend established a school on his own and assumed responsibility for securing and paying a good teacher. He

also provided housing, at a nominal cost, for neighborhood boys who attended the institution.

The author tells of Gordon's entry into College.

> After finishing his father's school, Gordon ventured to Lafayette, where he entered Pleasant Green Academy, reputedly "one of the best schools in all northwest Georgia." The reputation was evidently well deserved, because when Gordon completed his studies there near the end of 1850, he enrolled at the University of Georgia in Athens as a second semester sophomore.[11]

I picked up the phone and called my mother, one of the sweetest souls ever put on earth. This is not just my opinion, but that of many others who know her. My mother had recently sold her home in Florida and bought a house with my sister Joy. The house was in the northwestern corner of Georgia, Walker County. The name of the town? *Lafayette*. While talking to my mother, I asked if she ever heard anything about John B. Gordon. She said there was a Gordon Mill and that in a local church there was a stool or table which had been used by a John Gordon. She asked, "Why do you ask?" I told her about the palm reader and so on and, when I finished, there was a short pause and she said, "You're nuts, Jeff." Now, is this any way for a mother to talk to her son? My mother was planning to come up north for the summer and my sister was getting married. I had never visited my mother and sister in Lafayette and barely remembered the name of the town. I decided to drive down and attend the wedding, then drive my mother back to Connecticut. It was a good opportunity to stop at some of the places I had read about. I planned my route and left a few days before the wedding, to give myself time to stop a while on the way. Civil War battlefields run the scale from large tracts of land with visitor centers and hundreds of monuments to tiny areas where you need a local inhabitant to point it out. Most saddening are the ones under tract housing and shopping centers, gone forever. I drove on I-95 to just outside Washington D.C., then turned inland across Maryland to

my first stop, Monocacy National Battlefield. It is located just
three miles south of Frederick, Maryland. The battle was fought
on July 9, 1864 and is known as the battle that saved Washington, D.C. On the confederate side was Lt. General Jubal Early,
and on the Union side was Major General Lew Wallace (who
would later pen *Ben Hur*). Early and his men were en-route to
Washington. Wallace wanted to stop them, or at least stall for
time, so that reinforcements could reach the Washington area.
Gordon's division was assigned to Major General John C. Breckinridge's command. (Breckinridge had been Vice President of the
United States under Buchanan.) Gordon wrote, "The battle of
Monocacy which ensued was short, decisive and bloody."[15] I have
visited Monocacy twice. On the first visit, I stopped at the visitor
center in the old Gambrill's Mill. The mill was used as a hospital
during the battle. I asked some questions about a stream I had
read about in Gordon's book. The park ranger said she was not
sure which one was the one in question. She was surprised at my
knowledge. She asked how long I had studied the Civil War. At
that time it had been six months. The ranger looked puzzled and
asked, "How did you get interested in it?" I walked over to a
book on one of the shelves, removed it and skimmed through the
pages, until I came to a picture of Gordon. I handed the book to
her and pointed to the picture. She looked at the picture and
then at me. I said nothing. She looked at the book again and said,
"Just how closely related are you?"

"About as close as you can get," I replied. I thanked her for
her help, walked to a container near the entrance and put in
some money to help preserve the park. Through a little research,
I received my answer about the stream.

On a return trip to Monocacy with my mother, we visited the
visitor center and near the road in front of it runs the little stream
I sought. Why the search for the stream? Gordon's men pushed
back the first Union line to a second line. Gordon writes:

> The Union lines stood firmly in this second position, bravely
> defending the railroad and the highway to Washington. Between

the two hostile lines there was a narrow ravine down which ran a small stream of limpid water. In this ravine the fighting was desperate and at close quarters. To and fro the battle swayed across the little stream, the dead and wounded of both sides mingling their blood in its water; and when the struggle was ended, a crimsoned current ran toward the river. Nearly one half of my men and large numbers of the Federals fell there.[16]

A local authority put this stream moving across the Thomas property, running down to Bush Creek and Gambrill's Mill. As my mother and I walked near the little stream, she found a small glass bottle with a metal top. She was talking about it to me, but my mind was elsewhere, back to when this pretty little creek ran red. An idea came to me. I asked my mother if I could have the bottle; she complied. I carefully climbed down the steep embankment to the water. The water was cool and clear. It trickled over stones and sticks, causing it to make little bubbly sounds. I dipped the bottle into the water, tilting it so it would fill. The bottle full, I capped it and we returned to the car. I put the bottle in a bag and we drove on through the rolling hills and green fields. At home I transferred the water to an old perfume bottle and glued the top on. I mounted the little bottle, along with other mementos and photos, in a large frame. There is a small brass plate under the bottle engraved with one word: MONOCACY.

In a book by John H. Worsham, a Confederate veteran, he tells of coming across General Gordon during the Battle at Monocacy. "There was Gordon—I shall recollect him to my dying day—not a man in sight—he was sitting on his horse as quietly as if nothing was going on, wearing his old red shirt, the sleeves pulled up a little, the only indication that he was ready for the fight."[17] I have seen a painting of the battle. In part of the picture Gordon is on horseback wearing a double-breasted red shirt. In a earlier phone call to my mother I asked, "Mom, do you remember that red shirt I had as a kid?"

"Red shirt?" she said.

"Yes, a double-breasted one," I said. It was one of my favorite shirts and I remembered it very well. Many years ago, a boy in the old neighborhood had thrown a match at me while I was wearing my double-breasted red flannel shirt. The match stuck to the front; a second later a flame started licking up toward my face. My brother Jack and the boy beat on my chest to put out the fire.

My mother replied "A flannel shirt? Vaguely, why?" I told her about the quote and painting. I do not recall any other kid having a red double-breasted flannel shirt, not then and not now.

At the visitor center at Monocacy, I had picked up a small map on the shortest route to Antietam Battlefield. The route went through Middletown and over South Mountain. On the directions it read, "at the top of South Mountain you will find several Civil War markers." These were markers for the Battle of South Mountain. Colonel Gordon and the 6th Alabama held the left flank at Turner's Gap. "Brigadier General Rodes reported that on South Mountain, September 14, Gordon had handled the Sixth Alabama 'in a manner I have never heard or seen equaled during the war.'"[18] Division Commander D.H. Hill, in his official report, styled Gordon "the Chevalier Bayard of the army."[19] I looked up Bayard in the encyclopedia. "Bayard, Pierre Terrail, Seigneur de (c1473-1524) French Commander famous for his bravery, who became the epitome of French chivalry. He first distinguished himself in French campaigns in Italy. Later at Mezieres in 1521, with only 1,000 men against 35,000 he held off an invasion of central France by the emperor Charles V."[20] This was high praise indeed.

Shortly after the battle of South Mountain was the battle of Antietam, which we spoke of earlier. I stopped at the Antietam visitor center. It was at this time that I had inquired about the barn to which Gordon had been taken after his wounding. I visited the Sunken Road once again. There were no strange feelings this time. I guessed I was finished with that aspect, and the deepest emotions had been purged. I walked the old road and stood where the Sixth Alabama was placed to defend Lee's center. Looking around, it appears much the same as during the fighting there. Following a tradition I had started for battlefield visits, I said a prayer for the souls who had given their lives. I returned to my car and drove away, catching myself glancing in the rear view mirror as the little hill on Bloody Lane became smaller and smaller.

I drove to Winchester, VA. Winchester changed hands more than seventy times during the Civil War. I followed signs for General Jackson's Headquarters, but found it closed. I headed east out of town on the Berryville Pike to find the site of the Third Battle of Winchester, fought on September 19, 1864. I continued for a while, but saw no markers or signs indicating where the battle had been. It seemed to me that I had driven too far, so I turned and headed back. Stopping at a small store, I asked about the Battlefield and was directed to a local woman who worked in the store. She told me about a marker across the street, but that was the only one she knew of in the area. Across the Pike, set way back off the road was a small marker. No wonder I had missed it on my first pass. Standing on a little rise and gazing north, I could see the fields where Gordon, Rodes and Ramseur formed their line of battle. It was there that Rodes fell with his mortal wound. Sweeping the field from right to left, my eyes followed the path of the battle as the Confederates were pushed back into Winchester. In Winchester at that time was Mrs. Gordon. She had come close to being captured that morning by Federal Cavalry; only with the help of General Rodes and his men did she escape such a fate. Gordon writes about finding Mrs. Gordon in Winchester:

> To my horror, as I rode among my disorganized troops through Winchester I found Mrs. Gordon on the street, where shells from Sheridan's batteries were falling and Minie balls flying around her. She was apparently unconscious of the danger. I had supposed that, in accordance with instructions, she had gone to the rear at the opening of the battle, and was many miles away. But she was stopping at the house of her friend, Mrs. Hugh Lee, and as the first Confederates began to pass to the rear, she stood upon the veranda, appealing to them to return to the front. Many yielded to her entreaties and turned back—one waggish fellow shouting aloud to his comrades: "Come, boys, let's go back. We might not obey the

general, but we can't resist Mrs. Gordon." The fact is, it was the
first time in all her army experience that she had ever seen the Confederate lines broken. As the different squads passed, she inquired
to what command they belonged. When, finally, to her question
the answer came, "We are Gordon's men," she lost her self-control
and rushed into the street, urging them to go back and meet the
enemy. She was thus engaged when I found her. I insisted that she
go immediately into the house where she would be at least partially protected. She obeyed; but she did not for a moment accept
my statement that there was nothing left for her except capture
by Sheridan's army. I learned afterward that her negro driver had
been frightened by the shells bursting about the stable, and had not
brought out her carriage and horses. She acquainted some of my
men with these facts. With the assurance, "We'll get it for you, Mrs.
Gordon," they broke down the fences and brought the carriage to
her a few moments after I had passed on. She sprang into it, and,
taking her six-year-old son Frank and one or two wounded officers
with her, she was driven rapidly away amidst the flying missiles
from Sheridan's advancing troops and with the prayers of my brave
men for her safety.[21]

I drove back to Winchester and headed south to a route that
would take me to my next destination, Fredericksburg, VA. It
was late afternoon when I arrived. I drove around to familiarize
myself with the area, then checked into a motel and had dinner.
I went to my room to plan for the next morning. There are four
battlefields all within a short distance and in some cases they
even overlap one another: Fredericksburg, Chancellorville, The
Wilderness and Spotsylvania Court House. I was tired from the
long drive of the day and fell asleep before I knew it. I awoke
early—too early. It was still dark outside. Unable to return to
sleep, I showered, packed my bag and checked out. Soon I was on
Marye's Heights, overlooking the city of Fredericksburg. Marye's
Heights is now a National Cemetery. During the Civil War, the
Heights played an important part in many battles. In April 1863,
less than seven months after being wounded at Antietam, Gordon took command of one of the largest brigades in the Confederate Army. Gordon's first task, as commander of this unit, was
to retake Marye's Heights during the battle of Chancellorville. It

was during this fighting that Gordon came into possession of his favorite battle horse. The horse Gordon was riding had become partially disabled. At this time, a Union officer had been shot from his mount's back. The horse galloped

into the Confederate line and Gordon was quickly upon her. He named her Marye after the hill. "Her courage was equal to her other high qualities. She was afraid of nothing. Neither the shouting of troops, nor the rattle of rifles, nor the roar of artillery, nor their bursting shells, intimidated her in the slightest degree. In addition to all of this, she seemed to have a charmed life, for she bore me through the hottest fires and was never wounded."[22]

As I stood on the heights overlooking Fredericksburg, the blacks and grays of night slowly turned to the blues and greens of dawn. The sun peeking over the horizon transformed the stone markers of the cemetery to a light warm pink. The flow of sunlight moved slowly down the hillside coming to rest on the wall near its base. This was the infamous wall of Fredericksburg. It was here during the Battle of Fredericksburg (December 11–13, 1862) that General Burnside, in an attempt to take Marye's Heights, sent brigade after brigade across four hundred yards of open ground, all the while under well-placed artillery fire. After running the gauntlet of shellfire, the Union soldiers came up against the riflemen behind the stone wall. Tongues of flame licked out at them from behind it. Wave after wave of the blue-clad fell. From midday until dark they kept up their assault. Not a man finished the journey. Approximately eight thousand men lay in front of that wall. Many remained there for days before help would reach them. Some of the wounded froze to death in the cold December air. Burnside's decision to attack this area became one of the biggest blunders of the Civil War. What a scene it must have been as the cannons and muskets fell silent, the smoky curtain rising to reveal the brave men who followed their orders and now covered the scarred earth with their twisted forms. It must have seemed as if they had been scorched by dragon's breath. The Union men were not soon to forget the wall, and in many battles afterward the men would go into the fight with remembrances of Fredericksburg on their lips.

I drove on to Chancellorsville. Near the visitor center is a monument marking the spot where Stonewall Jackson was mortally wounded. The Confederacy would never recover from the loss of Jackson. His tactics are taught to this day in the military schools. Some said his name alone was worth a division in battle.

Not far from the Chancellorsville visitor center is the Wilderness Battlefield. It is well named, for there are few open areas. Tall trees and a thick growth of smaller trees, tangled bushes and other assorted flora cover most of the land. In much of the area it is difficult to see ten yards ahead. Many units on both sides became lost or disoriented, often resulting in heavy casualties or capture. On May 5, 1864, two divisions of Ewells II Corps came under attack. The division commanded by General Rodes was to the South of the Orange Turnpike. They had been hit so hard that the center units were falling back. At this time, General Ewell rode to the rear where he found Gordon. With a yell, Gordon's men counter-attacked with such force that what happened next even caught Gordon by surprise. The Union soldiers in his front had been pushed back so fast as to cause Gordon's men to come into line with the Union troops on the left and right. If Gordon's men moved forward, there was a good chance of them becoming surrounded. Gordon halted the men, and while some of the men held the front, the others were divided and turned to face to the right and left. Gordon writes:

> This done, both these wings were ordered forward, and, with another piercing yell, they rushed in opposite directions upon the right and left flanks of the astounded Federals, shattering them as any troops that were ever marshalled would have been shattered, capturing large numbers and checking any further effort by General Grant on that portion of the field.[23]

I found a marker that showed the area where this maneuver took place. I marveled that it was done in a place with such thick growth. I drove back to the Orange Turnpike and found a visitor shelter. There were maps of the battlefield and a walking trail. A box had been placed at the beginning of the trail; big letters spelled out "Gordon Flank Attack Trail" on a pamphlet. On May 5, Gordon's men were shifted to the far-left flank. Scouts returned and told Gordon that the Confederate line overlapped the Union flank. More scouts were sent out, and then Gordon went himself. He could not believe their good fortune in placement. On the morning of May 6th, Gordon approached Generals Ewell and Early with a plan for a flank attack on the Union right. He awaited orders, but none were forthcoming. Many attempts were made by Gordon that day to get the Generals to act on his plan. Shortly before sundown on the 6th he was given the go ahead.

> He struck the enemy's flank fairly and squarely. The surprise was complete, and the panic very great. The Federal officers endeavored to draw out brigade after brigade, division after division and form at right angles to the breastworks, so as to check the impetuous attack. But Gordon's men were upon them before they could beproperly placed in the new position. He met with no check until sometime after dark, when in the confusion attending all night attacks, one or two of his regiments on the right faltered and gave way. But the other troops pressed on until the enemy's lines had been captured by Gordon's one brigade for more than a mile, nearly 1,000 prisoners taken, including Brig. Gens. Seymour and Shaler, and a complete disorganization effected in a large portion of the Sixth Corps of Grant's army.[24]

I walked the trail to where the flanking movement had occurred. Even though the sun was out, the canopy of trees above filtered the light, giving the surroundings a dusk-like appearance. Rills in the ground showed where entrenchments had been placed. The thick underbrush hindered sight, limiting it to a few yards in some places. The area had changed little; the confusion of the terrain nearly cost Gordon his life. On the night of May 6th, General Gordon rode with a courier by the name of William Beasley to check on pickets that had been sent out.

There was no moonlight, but the night was cloudless and the stars

furnished enough light for us to ride without serious difficulty
through the woods. It was, however, too dark for us readily to dis-
tinguish the color of uniforms. Before we had proceeded far we rode
into a body of men supposed to be the troops whom I had sent out
on picket. There was no sort of deployment or alignment, and I was
considerably annoyed by this appearance of carelessness on the part
of the officer, to whom I had given special instructions. But before I
had time to ascertain what this indifference to orders meant, my
trusted courier, whose sight was clearer than mine at night, said to
me in a whisper "General, these are not our men; they are Yankees."
I replied, "Nonsense, Beasley," and rode on, still hoping to ascertain the reason for this inexcusable huddling of my pickets. Beasley,
however, was persistent, and taking hold of my arm, asserted in the
most emphatic manner, "I tell you General, these men are Yankees,
and we had better get away from here." His earnestness impressed
me, especially as he strengthened his assertion by calling my attention to the fact that even in the dim starlight the dark blue of the
uniforms around us presented a contrast with those we were wearing. I cautioned him to be quiet and keep close to me as I began
to turn my horse in the opposite direction. Meantime, and at the
moment we discovered our alarming position, we heard the startling
calls from Union officers close by us, who were endeavoring to dis-
entangle the confused mass of men: "Rally here, New York." "Let all
the men of the__ Regiment of Pennsylvania form here." Up to this
moment not the slightest suspicion seemed to have been contained
by these men that Beasley and I were Confederates; and, apparently for the sole purpose of ascertaining to what Union command
we belonged, an officer with his sword in hand asked in the most
courteous manner to what brigade we were attached, evidently hoping to aid us in finding it. Both Beasley and I were, of course, deaf
to his inquiry, and continued to move on without any reply, turning our horses' heads toward the gray lines in which we would feel
more at home. Either our strange silence or our poorly concealed
purpose to get away from that portion of the Wilderness aroused
his suspicions, and the officer called to his comrades as we rode
away from him. "Halt those men!" His orders were scarcely uttered
when the "boys in blue" rushed around us, shouting, "Halt, halt!"
But the company in which we found ourselves was not congenial and
the locality was not at that moment a good place for us to halt. We
had to go, and go instantly, back to our own lines or to a Northern
prison. I instantly resolved to take the risk of escape, though we
might be shot into mincemeat by the hundreds of rifles around us.

Beasley was well mounted, and I was riding a thoroughbred stallion, the horse General Shaler rode when he was made prisoner a few hours previous. Both Beasley and I were fairly good riders. Instantly throwing my body as far down on my horse's side as possible, my right foot firmly fixed in the stirrup, my left leg gripping the saddle like an iron elbow, I seized the bridle-rein under my hoses's neck, planted my spur in his flank, and called, "Follow me, Beasley!" This courier had intuitively followed the motion of my body, and was clinging like an experienced cowboy to the side of his horse. As the superb animal which I rode felt the keen barb of the spur, he sprang with a tremendous bound through the dense underbrush and the mass of startled soldiers. It seems probable that the Unionmen were in almost as much danger from the hoofs of our horses as we were from the Union rifles.[25]

Beasley and Gordon were lucky that night, while the luck of others had run its course. Fires caused by the fighting erupted in the dry woods. Whipped by brisk winds they moved across the battlefield, consuming the dead and wounded who were unable to move out of the path of the flames.

I continued along the trail and emerged back into the sunlight near the visitor's shelters. Returning to my car, I headed to my next destination, Spotsylvania Court House. I drove the winding country roads, following the signs for the Spotsylvania battlefield. Turning into the Battlefield Park, I did not bother to stop at the information signs. A short while later, I looked to my left and my mind said, "Mule Shoe, I'm at the Mule Shoe."

At dawn on May 12, Grant sent Hancock's men storming out of the fog and misty rain in a massive surprise attack on the so-called Mule Shoe Salient at the center of Lee's lines. They overran the defenders, as a Southerner recalled, "like a swollen torrent through a broken milldam."
The Yankees swept up twenty guns and thousands of prisoners, including two general officers and most of the famed Stonewall Brigade, but success so disorganized the Federals that a slashing counterattack by John B. Gordon's division knocked them back to the first line of captured trenches. They held there, and what followed was the most vicious struggle of the Civil War.[26]
No printed page, no cold type can convey to the mind the reali-

ties of that terrible conflict. The results were appalling. The whole
engagement was practically a hand-to-hand contest. The dead lay
beneath the feet of the living, three and four layers deep. This hith-
erto quiet spot of earth was devastated and covered with the slain,
weltering in their own blood, mangled and shattered into scarcely a
semblance of human form. Dying men were crushed by horses and
many, buried beneath the mire and mud, still lived.
Some artillery was posted on high ground not far from the apex of
the salient, and an incessant fire was poured into the Confederate
works over the Union lines, while other guns kept up an enfilade of
canister along the west of the salient. Until three o'clock the next
morning the slaughter continued, when the Confederates sank back
into their second line of entrenchments.[27]

Driving around a corner, my eye caught a street sign. It read
"Gordon Drive." This road runs along the remains of the second
line that the Confederates fell back to after the long battle of the
12th of May. Between this road and the apex of the Mule Shoe,
there is a marker alongside what remains of the foundation of the
McCool House. Gordon tells what happened here on the morning of the 12th:

I was at the centre of that line when General Lee rode to it. With
uncovered head, he turned his face toward Hancock's advancing
column. Instantly I spurred my horse across Old Traveller's front,
and grasping his bridle in my hand, I checked him. Then, in a voice
which I hoped might reach the ears of my men and command their
attention, I called out, "General Lee, you shall not lead my men in
a charge. No man can do that, sir. Another is here for that purpose.
These men behind you are Georgians, Virginians, and Carolinians.
They have never failed you on any field. They will not fail you here.
Will you, boys?" The response came like a mighty anthem that
must have stirred his emotions as no other music could have done.
Although the answer to those three words, "Will you, boys?" came
in the monosyllables, "No, no, no; we'll not fail him," yet they were
doubtless to him more eloquent because of their simplicity and
momentous meaning. But his great heart was destined to be quickly
cheered by a still sublimer testimony of their deathless devotion. As
this first thrilling response died away, I uttered the words for which
they were now fully prepared. I shouted to General Lee, "You must
go to rear." The echo, "General Lee to the rear, General Lee to the

rear!" rolled back with tremendous emphasis from the throats of my men; and they gathered around him, turned his horse in the opposite direction, some clutching his bridle, some his stirrups, while others pressed close to Old Traveller's hips, ready to shove him by main force to the rear. I verily believe that, had it been necessary or possible, they would have carried on their shoulders both horse and rider to a place of safety.[28]

While walking the Mule Shoe, my thoughts returned to those days of the struggle between the blue and the gray. It was hard to conceive that at this spot so many had fallen. It is such a beautiful landscape of rolling fields with tiny streams zigzagging across them, trees standing as silent sentinels keeping watchover the tall grass gently waving in the wind. It is hard to believe that this gift to the eyes had seen so much horror. My heart felt heavy. The sky, now filled with birds, was then clouded with iron and steel— tempered in brave men's blood and mothers' tears. All those men, gone, but were they gone? The ground had been soaked with their blood; it had seeped into the earth, around the base of the trees and the roots of the grasses. Suddenly, I realized those brave men were still there. The mingling of their blood with the soil had made them part of it and therefore a part of everything else. They are in the grass, trees and in the animals that live off the land. No, they are not gone, but live on in a different form. My eyes searched the ground for a sign of something, anything from that time so long ago. It had recently rained and there were tiny rivulets of water running everywhere. Walking on, a flash caught my eye, off to the right near the edge of the woods. It happened again, just about eye level. It came from a medium sized tree about five inches in diameter. As I approached it, it happened once more, a bright sparkle from the area of a knothole. A knothole—could there be something stuck in the tree? A bullet? I wondered. No, the tree is too small; it wasn't even here one hundred and thirty years ago. Could it have picked up something in the ground as it grew? It deserved a closer look. I walked to the tree and examined the knothole. My finger probed inside. Moss, just moss, but why had it sparkled? I guess it was just wishful thinking that I would find anything. Disheartened, I lowered my head and my eyes focused on the ground an inch in front of myleft foot. I blinked my eyes and focused again. I was looking down on a pile of old wood. It might have been a log or a stump,but time and weather had turned it to the consistency of sawdust. A dark brown spot stood out in the top of the pile, washed into view by the recent rain. I stooped and took hold of the brown object; it yielded itself willingly. Convex on one side, concave on the other, made of heavy metal—a cannonball, it was part of a cannonball! I cleaned it off a little more. Never had it even crossed my mind that I would make such a find. I realized that at this place, on this day, under these conditions an unseen hand had guided me. I had been manipulated, but in a pleasant way, to be at that spot at that time.

I drove to Spotsylvania Court House and visited a museum there. I asked for directions to my next destination, Petersburg, 25 miles below Richmond. Following the directions I had been given, I soon found Interstate 95 and was on my way south. It was not a very long ride. Just outside Petersburg, signs appeared for the National Battlefield. I took the exit for the Battlefield and drove to the Visitor Center, parked, and went inside. The gift shop and information desk area of the center was filled withshelves of books and souvenirs. The pretty girl behind the counter said, "The movie on Petersburg will be starting soon." Isaid "thanks, but I'm in a hurry." She said, "It's a short film." I told her I was pressed for time but could use a battlefield map. My request was granted with a smile. Upon reading the map, my eyes came across the words I sought, Fort Stedman. I will give you a bit of information, so you will understand my interest in Fort Stedman. Fort Stedman was named after Col. Giffin Stedman of the 11th Conn. Vol. Regiment, who was killed August 5, 1864 on Hares Hill, where the fort still stands. Petersburg was the longest siege in American warfare; it lasted nearly ten months. Approximately 2 A.M., on a bitterly cold February night in 1865, General Lee sent for General Gordon. Gordon rode to the commanding general's headquarters in a house on the outskirts of Petersburg.

As I entered, General Lee, who was entirely alone, was standing at the fireplace, his arm on the mantel and his head resting on his arm as he gazed into the coal fire burning on the grate. He had evidently been up all the previous part of the night. For the first time in all my intercourse with him, I saw a look of painful depression on his face. Of course he had experienced many hours of depression, but he had concealed from those around him all evidence of discouragement. He opened the conference by directing me to read the reports from the different commands as he should hand them to me and to carefully note every important fact contained in them. The revelation was startling. Each report was bad enough, and all the distressing facts combined were sufficient, it seemed to me to destroy all cohesive power and lead to the inevitable disintegration of any other army that was ever marshalled. I was not prepared for the picture presented by these reports of extreme destitution—of the lack of shoes, of hats, of overcoats, and of blankets, as well as of food. Some officers had gone outside of the formal official statement as to numbers of the sick, to tell in plain, terse, and forceful words of depleted strength, emaciation, and decreased power of endurance among those who appeared on the rolls as fit for duty.[29]

In the reports the number of Confederates fit for duty was put at 35,000, around and nearby Petersburg. Grant had approximately 150,000 well-fed and well-equipped troops. General Lee sat down across the table from Gordon, and posed a question to him. He asked his opinion on what he though best to do under the conditions stated in the reports. Gordon answered:

"General, it seems to me there are but three courses and I name them in the order in which I think they should be tried: First, make terms with the enemy, the best we can get. Second, if that is not practicable, the best thing to do is to retreat—abandon Richmond and Petersburg, unite by rapid marches with General Johnston in North Carolina, and strike Sherman before Grant can join him; or, lastly, we must fight, and without delay."[30]

Gordon asked Lee for his feelings on the matter. Lee replied "Certainly, General, you have the right to ask my opinion. I agree with you fully." Lee returned from the conferences in Richmond and informed Gordon that peace talks or abandonment of the capital were not viable issues at that time. There was but one option left, fight. Gordon writes: "This was the prelude to my assault upon Fort Stedman on March 25, 1865—the last confederate attack on Grant's lines at Petersburg."[31]

> As the solitary signal shot rang out in the stillness of the early morning, the Confederate pickets, who had crept close to the Union sentinels, silently sprang upon them and killed or captured them without the discharge of a single Federal alarm. Simultaneously, the fifty axe-men sprang over the parapets and with swift blows, slashed down the Federal obstructions. Close behind followed the selected three hundred men and after them the main body of the infantry.

The battle escalates:

> Up to this point success had exceeded Gordon's fondest expectations. The Confederates had succeeded in cutting through the heavy Federal obstructions and had taken Fort Stedman and several works on either side, besides capturing nine heavy cannons, eleven mortars, and nearly 1,000 prisoners, including General McLaughlin, who commanded Stedman.

Things seemed to be going well:

> Select officers and men in Stribling's battalion had charged the enemy's breastworks and turned the four light 12's of Fort Stedman upon the Federals. The guns of Battery No. 10 were brought into action against them. According to Freeman, Gordon had "anticipated in miniature by fifty years and more the tactics of the breakthrough."

Gordon makes a report to Lee:

> From the Fort, Gordon sent word to General Lee, who was on a hill in the rear, that the Confederates were in the works and the 300 select men were on their way to positions behind the Federal lines. Anxiously Gordon received a message from General Lewis that he had passed the Federal lines with no difficulty, but had lost his guide and could not find the fort.

Thing start to turn bad for the Confederates.

Presently similar reports came from the other two advance columns. Daylight was coming, and faintly Gordon could see the gathering preponderance of Grant's overwhelming forces. He could make no further advance and found it necessary to draw in his forces toward Fort Stedman, where they could presently be subjected to a heavy fire of artillery from both flanks.

Without reinforcements there is no chance of success:

There was no hope of reinforcements, as Lee had already warned him that the arrival of Pickett's division was doubtful. Accordingly, Gordon notified Lee that his men could not reach the rear forts and that the advance had been halted. Gordon was not long in realizing that tenure of Stedman was impossible.

The fight disintegrates:

His men had not been able to capture Battery 9, though they had come within 500 yards of it only to be fired upon so hotly that they had to seek shelter in a depression of the ground. Here they were held under fire of canister until most of them surrendered. As soon as the haze of the morning cleared away, thirty pieces of artillery opened a concentrated fire upon and around Fort Stedman.

The end draws near:

By 7:30 a.m. Federal forces had regained Batteries 11 and 12 and had drawn a cordon of troops around the Fort and Battery 10. Most of Gordon's men were driven back into these works, where they suffered heavy casualties from the artillery on both flanks as well as from the reserve batteries in the rear.

Hope disappears.

By 8 AM. confusion increased and became general throughout the Confederate ranks. At about this time General Lee sent orders to evacuate the captured works.[32]

I left the visitor's center and slowly drove the short distance down the twisting little road through the battlefield. Parking near Fort Stedman, I found only one other vehicle occupying a space.

Two gentleman walked nearby. [Let me pause here and explain a
few things to the reader. It does not come easy to me, this book
writing. I know from my own readings that you are most likely
waiting to see what I find or feel of a tangible nature on my visits
to these historic places. I, too, approach them with anticipation.
I understand your anticipation and hope I do not disappoint you.
But, be forewarned, not all of my stops were as rewarding as the
Mule Shoe. Be aware also, that I refuse to fabricate anything
purely for your enjoyment or just to make a good story. Maybe
at these places there were no psychic events or deja-vu feelings,
but I never left empty-handed. Just being there has an effect on
anyone who has knowledge of what transpired on these hallowed
grounds. Point made, we return to the parking lot at Fort Stedman.] Exiting my car, I walked the path through the remains
of the fort. Now not much more than dirt breastworks remain,
covered with grass and a few cannons placed here and there, its
passive facade belying the fact of its violent birth. The two men
walking on the sidewalk returned to their car and drove off. I
was now alone on this portion of the battlefield, something I
prefer, but which rarely happens. Near the fort is a monument to
the 1st Maine commemorating the greatest regimental loss in a
single action of the Civil War. I walked across the open field to
Colquitt's Salient from where the Confederate attack had orig-
inated. It was here during the retreat that, once again, General
Gordon was wounded, in his leg, but it was not serious. Stroll-
ing unimpeded and unencumbered on the short cut grass to the
salient, it was an enjoyable trip this time. Blue sky, birds chirping
and squirrels scampering to and fro. I stood for a while, looking
over the field to Fort Steadman and then made the short return
trip. I realized, upon my arrival at the fort, that by transecting
the field as I had, I had traveled exactly opposite to the trek
of March 25, 1865. I thought back to a picture I had seen in a
book. It was of a 14-year-old boy, a Confederate, lying dead in
the bottom of a trench in Petersburg. He was ragged and barefoot. A small mark on his chest indicated where a bayonet had
penetrated. Petersburg is another case of a pretty place with sad

memories.

The battle of Fort Stedman was one more example of things that could have gone one way or the other, but swung in favor of the Union. Gordon was involved in a few such conflicts: the Wilderness and Petersburg, as I have mentioned, and Gettysburg and Cedar Creek, which we will cover later. Here is something to ponder—remember the picture of my Great Grandfather, Lewis Knapp, that sits on my dresser? As a Union soldier, he was at the siege and fall of Petersburg, with the 1st Connecticut Heavy Artillery. Day after day, they lobbed shells into the city and surrounding fortifications. Could it be that I came under fire from my own Great Grandfather?

The sun moved lower in the sky. I headed to the west in the direction of Appomattox Court House. It was approximately 90 miles away and I wanted to get there before the park closed for the evening. I traveled west on Rt. 460, pretty much paralleling the course taken by the Army of Northern Virginia. Gordon's last official report written on April 11, 1865 gives some insights into the condition of the Confederate Army. Gordon's men acted as rear guard during the retreat—moving, fighting, and moving again. Men already pushed to the edge were now being pushed over it. Lack of food, physical exhaustion and sleep deprivation continued to take its toll. Unable to reach supplies, and continually harassed by Federal Troops and Cavalry, the men in grey kept moving on by not much more than willpower alone. There was an added woe for Gordon on the night they left Petersburg. He had given the order to fire the bridges after the last troops had crossed. He did this with the knowledge that Fanny and his newborn son, John Brown Gordon, Jr., must remain behind. I spotted a sign that read Sayler's Creek Battlefield 6 Miles. Not having time to turn off, I would have to return another day.

Arriving at Appomattox Court House, I had about 45 minutes before they closed the visitor's center. I hurried up the walkway from the parking lot. I was struck by the charm of the little village. Buildings of many different construction types, wood frame, brick and log were scattered around the central feature, which was the courthouse itself. Fences of all descriptions, split rail, zigzag and picket among them ran along the country lanes and around some of the structures. The Old Richmond-Lynchburg Stage Road bisects the settlement leading up to and circling the Court House where the visitor center is located. I entered the courthouse and took a pamphlet, and then promptly headed for the McLean House (both the McLean House and the Court House are reconstructions). The McLean house has two outbuildings and is surrounded by a white picket fence. I walked through the gateway, passed the well-house and walked up the porch stairs to the front door. Just inside to the left is a parlor, with its furnishings set up as closely as possible to how it looked on April 9, 1865. A park guide stood near the front door and answered questions as they arose from the visitors. I hurried through the house and back to the Visitor Center. Heading to the second floor, I climbed two or three risers at a time (I would do this more often in my youth, but less after hitting the big 40). The upstairs contains a small theater that shows a slide program (closed because of the late hour). A small gallery of artifacts and pictures surround a small theater enclosure. One item in particular caught my attention—a wooden tabletop. To work out the details of the formal surrender, a commission of three officers from each army was formed. The names of the men picked by Grant and Lee were carved into the tabletop that stood before me. For the North, Grant sent Generals Griffin, Merritt and Gibbon. For the Army of Northern Virginia, Lee appointed Generals Longstreet, Gordon and Pendleton. I moved on and returned to the staircase. Over the landing hung some flags, one was all white except for the canton, which was the well known St. Andrew's Cross design of the Confederate battle flags. Gazing at the flag while descending, my mind said, "That's the flag that was used at the time of the surrender." Near the base of the stairs hung a print called the Last Salute depicting the formal surrender of the Army of Northern Virginia. Generals Joshua Chamberlain and John Gordon were in the center, sitting astride their horses, facing each other. Gordon's mount's head bowed, his sword pointed to the toe of his boot. Behind Gordon were the remnants of the Army of Northern Virginia, with one man holding a flag almost furled. Something caught my eye; this flag was the same as the one in the stairwell with one exception. A red bar ran across the end he held in his hand. It just did not look right to me. Looking back over my shoulder, I saw a park ranger standing near the information desk. I asked him if he could answer a question for me. "If I can," he replied.

Pointing to the flag in the stairwell I asked him, "Wasn't that the flag that was used in the surrender ceremony?" Then motioning to the print, I said, "The one in this print has a red bar across it?"

He stood there in his immaculate brown uniform, with a surprised look in his eyes. "You're right," he said. "The flag in the print is the third National Confederate flag. That was the official flag at the time of the surrender, but it had not been issued to the troops in the field yet." Turning toward the stairs he continued, "The flag over the stairs is the Stainless Banner. That's the one used at the surrender." I had surprised myself. How did I know about the flag? In a book I was to read long after my stop at Appomattox, there was another confirmation about the flag that was used. The book was written by Joshua Chamberlain. The title of the book: The Passing of the Armies. Major General Joshua Lawrence Chamberlain, Hero of Little Round Top and Congressional Medal of Honor winner, Chamberlain survived being wounded many times during the war. Later in life, he became Governor of Maine and President of Bowdoin College (of which he was a graduate and professor). Chamberlain is the protagonist in the Pulitzer Prize winning novel, Killer Angels, by Michael Sharra. General Grant picked Chamberlain for the honor of receiving the formal surrender of the Army of Northern Virginia, though many other generals outranked him. His counterpart on the Confederate side was John Gordon. I left the Courthouse and walked down the road to the Peers House. The House sits on the summit of a hill overlooking the Appomattox River. The Richmond-Lynchburg Road runs down the hill past the House and across the nearby river. Two small lanes run into the Richmond-Lynchburg road to form a large triangle in front of the Peers House. This area is

known as the surrender triangle. I moved down the road near the
Peers House and took a few pictures. More than one person has
said to me, "I bet if you could go back in time, you'd like to go
back to the Civil War." Or "Why don't you become a re-enactor?"
To the latter, my standard reply is, "I was there the first time."
Followed by a grin. To the former I explain that I do not think
anyone who knows what the Civil War was like would choose to
return to it. As an example, in the three-day period during the
battle of Gettysburg, North and South suffered more than 50,000
casualties, killed, wounded and missing. Approximately 5,000
horses lay dead on the fields in the summer heat and the wagon
train carrying the Confederate wounded southward stretched
almost 17 miles. Not exactly a stroll in the park. I have changed
my mind though; I would go back, but to one day only—April 12,
1865, in front of the Peers House at Appomattox Court House.
The reason I would return to that day is based on what transpired
there. Chamberlain would do something that morning for which
he would be criticized for the rest of his life. His actions have
stood the test of time to become one of the most eloquent events
in our Nation's history. I hope his critics lived long enough to
read his book, Passing of the Armies, and his account of that day.
General Chamberlain writes of a dejected Gordon riding at the
head of the surrender column and tells of his response to a most
gracious salute by the Union soldiers.

> At the sound of the machine-like snap of arms, General Gordon
> started, caught in a moment of significance, and instantly assumed
> the finest attitude of a soldier. He wheeled his horse, facing me,
> touching him gently with the spur, so the animal reared, and as he
> wheeled, horse and rider made one motion, the horse's head swung
> down with a graceful bow and General Gordon dropped his sword-
> point down to his toe in salutation. By word of mouth the gen-
> eral sent back orders to the rear that his own troops take the same
> position of the manual in the march past as did our line. That was
> done, and a truly imposing sight was the mutual salutation and fare-
> well. Bayonets were affixed to the muskets, arms stacked, and car-
> tridge-boxes unslung and hung upon the stacks. Then, slowly and
> with a reluctance that was appealingly pathetic, the torn and tat-

tered battle-flags were either leaned against the stacks or laid upon the ground. The emotion of the conquered soldiery was really sad to witness. Some of the men who had carried and followed those ragged standards through the four long years of strife rushed, regardless of all discipline, from the ranks, bent about their old flags, and pressed them to their lips. And it can well be imagined, too, that there was no lack of emotion on our side, but the Union men were held steady in their lines, without the least show of demonstration by word or by motion. There was, though, a twitching of the muscles of their faces, and be it said, their battle-bronzed cheeks were not altogether dry. Our men felt the import of the occasion, and realized fully how they would have been affected if defeat and surrender had been their lot after such a fearful struggle.[11]

In my opinion, Chamberlain's clear vision, wisdom and heart were much greater than that allotted to most men. I was later to find that Gordon and Chamberlain had much in common. Both men were civilians before the war, both attained the rank of Major General and both would become Governor of their home states. Even stranger was the fact that each had received wounds that were believed to be fatal but survived, and both Generals' wives shared the name "Fanny."

I walked back past the Court House and turned down the road leading to the parking lot. When I arrived at my car, there was a man leaning against his car staring at the village. I struck up a conversation with him. He told me he had felt drawn to Appomattox. His wife and kids were off in a nearby city, but he had been compelled to drive to the battlefield. He asked me if I had ever been there before. I laughed and said, "Yes, but that was almost 130 years ago." He didn't run away, so I gave him a capsulized version of my story and showed him a picture of Gordon. He stood there and listened intently. He told me he was not sure about reincarnation but knew strange things happen, like his attraction to this place. We shook hands, I got in my car and drove off to Rt. 460 once more. No more battlefields for a while, there was a wedding to get to and many miles between Georgia and me.

CHAPTER FIVE

You Can't Go Home Again, Can You?

OVER THE BLUE RIDGE MOUNTAINS and into the Shenandoah Valley I went. Stopping at Roanoke for the night, I got an early start the next morning. The drive from Roanoke to the Tennessee line on Route 81 was nearly 100 miles. I had not eaten anything before I left the motel and now my tummy was craving a good old-fashioned southern breakfast. Just over the line near Bristol, Tennessee, my eye caught a sign. I can't remember exactly what the name of the place was, something like Mama's Country Kitchen. Exiting the highway and driving up a hill, I parked near the front door. Inside, the motif was sort of country cutesy, but I wasn't there for the scenery; I was there to eat. A hostess showed me to a table and gave me a menu. Upon perusing the bill of fare, I could see that I had made a good choice in restaurants. I ordered four eggs over easy, Virginia ham, grits, toast, sausage gravy with buttermilk biscuits, coffee and orange juice. The waitress asked if someone was joining me. "Nope, it's all for me," I replied. Entertaining myself with a game that had been placed on the table for just such a purpose, time passed quickly and the food soon arrived.

My breakfast was placed on the table in front of me. I quickly devised a plan. The egg yolks stared up at me like a couple of frightened Siamese twins, who knew they would go first. I ate two with the ham. Then, the grits were poured on the plate and the remaining eggs put in a place of honor on top. They too would succumb to my hunger, but not nearly as fast as the others had. I cut the eggs in a crisscross manner and blended them together with the grits. This mixture was soon consumed along with the intermittent pieces of toast, a little O.J., and then it was time for the sausage gravy and biscuits. When finished I sat back and sipped my coffee. The waitress approached the table, her eyes scanning the empty plates. "I can't get you anything else, can I?" she asked. "Not unless you want to pick up the pieces!" was my answer. I paid the bill and waddled out the door, southbound once again.

I followed Interstate 81 to Knoxville, where I caught Rt. 75 South. The undulating hills rolled by and before I knew it, I was in Chattanooga. As Rt. 75 turned due South, I could see Lookout Mountain to my right. It loomed above the city, dwarfing its surroundings. A few miles later, a sign announcing the Georgia State line came into view. Following my mother's directions, I transferred to Route 27 for the last leg of my journey. Route 27 takes you straight through the middle of the Chickamauga Battlefield. Georgia had been hit with record snowfalls that previous winter and many trees bore the scars of the heavy snows. Branches and whole trees lay scattered along the roadway. The scene looked much like what the artillery damage must have been after the battles fought there. There are wooded areas broken by open fields all through the park. It is not uncommon to see deer feeding at the edge of the woods. I had never seen a battlefield park with so many monuments— every size and shape, from small tablets to towering sculptures, from the plain to the ornate. They are well placed and the spacing does not intrude on the scenic beauty, but enhances it by reminding the viewer of the deeper meaning of their surroundings. Shortly after exiting the park, a few miles down the road, something strange happened. A feeling, one I had learned to pay attention to, a subtle, dull pressure at the bridge of my nose and up to my forehead, much like being struck on the nose but without the pain. I looked around, and as I gazed out of the car to the right, I was struck by a most beautiful sight:

a large expanse of fields stretched from the roadside to the base of a distant mountain ridge. Sunlight shone through the clouds, illuminating the grasses with its golden light. A stream snaked its way across the landscape. All this was framed by the contrasting colors of the blue mountains in the distance and the green trees along the roadway. It was not just the beauty that hit me, but a familiarity, like meeting a friend after a long absence.

I continued my drive until I found myself on Main Street in Lafayette, pop. 6,313. Finding my mother's and sister's house, I pulled into the driveway. After a round of hugs and kisses, I settled in, tired from my long drive. The next day was my sister's wedding, at a lodge in Tennessee. With that behind me, I could rest, visit with family and explore the area.

My youngest brother, Joel was up from Florida. It was especially good to see him, because our meetings are usually many years apart. Joel directed me to John B. Gordon Hall, a few blocks north of my mother's house. It is reported to be the oldest standing brick schoolhouse in Georgia. Set back from the roadway and surrounded by mature trees and plantings, it can easily escape detection in the casual drive down Main Street. The schoolhouse was built in 1836 from bricks made from the local Georgia clay. The two-story structure is a simple Georgian style, with one large room on each floor. At the Lafayette library I came across Allen P. Tankersly's book, *John Brown Gordon, A Study in Gallantry*, written in 1955. In the beginning of the book, he tells of John and his brother Chapman attending this school and boarding at the Marsh House just North of Gordon Hall. They would stay in town for the week and return to Gordon Springs on Friday evenings. In front of the school is a walkway lined with tablets marking this historic spot. A large pyramid of cannonballs was centered in the walk and a tall, slender stone monument crowned with a Confederate soldier, standing guard near the edge of the road. What tales this red brick schoolhouse could tell if it was given the power of speech, for it had stood as a witness to the comings and goings of generations of local children.

In 1863, Confederate General Braxton Bragg used the hall

as headquarters and mapped out the battle plans for the conflict with Union Troops at Chicamauga. The great oak tree, under which Bragg and his staff devised their strategy and tactics, stood until struck by lightning in the early 1920s. In 1864, the Hall once again became an Army headquarters, only this time under Union control during the Battle of Lafayette. What a strange mixture of echoes the walls of this school must retain, the rattle of muskets and the moans of wounded men intertwined with the laughter of school children.

I walked around snapping pictures, then paused a while to ponder an inscription at the base of the stone monument. "It is a duty we owe to posterity, to see that our children shall know the virtues and become worthy of their sires."

I feel it would be beneficial for all generations to study the lives of their forefathers (and mothers): to know the struggles and trials they endured, to give one a sense of whence they came and a deeper foundation on which to base their own identity. Walking around the school, I tried to get a look inside. The only windows not blocked by bushes were five feet or more off the ground, so there I stood or should I say hopped, up and down like a kangaroo. My attempts to see what the interior looked like were futile. I would have to settle for the view outside. At that time, the Hall was not open to the public.

The Marsh House is a private residence so I could only admire it from afar. Like the schoolhouse, the Marsh House was built in 1836 and the structure is of the style known as "Plantation Plain." The house shares much of the same history as the school. After the battle of Lafayette, stories were told of soldiers on horseback riding in the north door, down the central hallway and out the south door, leaving the walls smeared with blood and the flooring imbedded with their horse's hoofprints.

I took a few more pictures and then was on my way. Doing more research at the library, I came up with a map of Walker County from 1893. The map showed Gordon Springs, near Taylor's Ridge, not too many miles away. I was off again. I set the odometer on my car to zero. From Tankersly's book and other

sources, I knew I needed to travel about ten miles. Driving along
the base of the ridge, I watched the odometer snap to the ten-
mile mark and at almost the same time I spotted a marker setback
in the woods.

I parked the car as best I could, because this country road did
not have much of a shoulder; it was more like a ditch. I walked
with camera in hand to the marker. "Gordon Springs Gap," the
tablet announced with a brief history after. This was the beginning of the old road east through a gap in Taylor's Ridge to Gordon Springs. The road was used by many in the Army of the
Cumberland; "General Hooker in person" stated the sign. The
road was no more; it had returned to nature.

Now the hillside was covered with dense woods. I felt much
like a prisoner looking through bars. I had found Gordon Springs
but I was on the wrong side of the ridge. Night was approaching
and I would have to wait until the following day to visit Gordon
Springs. I headed back to the main road to return to Lafayette.
Upon approaching the main road, I was greeted with the same
view that had struck me so hauntingly on my way into town. I
wondered how many times a young John Gordon was blessed
with this lovely panorama after emerging from Gordon Springs
Gap? I turned left and drove to Main Street with a warm feeling
in my chest.

The next morning, along with my mother, we embarked once
more on the quest to find Gordon Springs. Over the ridge we
went, following the twisting roads until we reached an area near
Taylor's Ridge at around the ten-mile mark. Stopping at a store,
I asked the owner where Gordon Springs was. He gave me directions to a small country road. When I say small, I mean one of
those roads that you worry what you will do if you were to meet
another car coming from the opposite direction. We scanned the
area for any remnants of Gordon Springs; none were found. A
few houses and structures of modern construction dotted the
countryside. I was forced to be content with the stories John
Gordon told of this area. It was here that Gordon became an able
horseman. In a boyhood sketch he wrote for "Youth's Compan-

ion" magazine, he tells of "fox chase with packs of carefully bred hounds and in the exhilarating pursuit of wolves when these ravenous beasts would steal from their hiding places into the sheep fold at night. There were few Southern boys who did not become, through these experiences, expert riders before they were fifteen years old."[34] With a hint of sadness, Gordon tells of days gone by, of "Fourth 'o July barbecues," "Christmas times" and "corn shucking." He told of events shared by whites and blacks; good times enjoyed by all. John Gordon laments in his post Civil War writing that, "only picturesque memories remain." It was in his youth while attending the school set up by his father, that John would develop his ability as a orator, a seemingly natural gift that would serve him well both in war and peacetime politics. Leaving Gordon Springs behind, we traveled back to Lafayette ("LaFet" as it is pronounced by the local inhabitants.)

Back at my sister's house, I was talking to Joy in the kitchen. Her best friend was on the telephone in one of the bedrooms, chatting with her ex-husband, Trey. She called me to the phone to speak with him. It turned out that Trey is very much into the Civil War and relic hunting. I talked with him, telling him that I was interested in John Gordon. Trey really caught my attention when he spoke about a friend of his who had been using a metal detector around a house once owned by Gordon. This treasure hunter had found an old watchback with the letters J.G. stamped in it. Trey gave me the relic hunter's name and phone number. I called him and asked him about the watchback. He didn't seem interested in parting with it so I gave him my name and number, just in case he ever wanted to sell it. I hung up and sat there, a little discouraged. I had always hoped to come across something that had belonged to Gordon and what could be better than a personal item that he carried with him? I filed away the man's name and phone number with the hope that some day I might receive a phone call from him.

I mapped out a route that would take my mother and myself back up north. I planned to stop at some places I did not have time to visit on my way down. It was a beautiful day for driving when we left. We drove over the mountains of the Chattahoochee National Forest and caught Interstate 75 South. In Atlanta, we stopped at a used bookstore. When we were ready to leave, I asked for directions to the Capitol Building, for there was something I very much wanted to see. We found the CapitolBuilding with little effort. There, on the corner, stood a statue ofGordon on horseback, a sight that neither Gordon nor I had seen before. The Gordon Monument had been unveiled May 25, 1907, years after his passing. The artist that sculpted Gordon astride his horse Marye was Solon H. Borglum. I was later to find some interesting facts about Borglum. Solon was born in 1868 in Ogden, Utah. His brother Gutzon sculpted Mount Rushmore. He studied under his brother (John) Gutzon de la Mothe Borglum and Rebisso. He was a member of the Cincinnati Art Academy, National Academy of Design (1911), and The Silvermine Group. He also created the Sailors and Soldiers monument in Danbury, Connecticut. He is the Founder of the School of American Sculpture in New York Cityand served as YMCA Secretary in World War I were he was awarded the Croix de Guerre for courage under fire. He died in Stamford, CT, in 1922 from war injuries. Two things stood out when I read this. I had once taken an oil painting class at Silvermine School of Art and many times admired the Sailors and Soldiers Monument (not being aware of the creator's name)in the city of my birth Danbury, Connecticut.

I rounded a corner adjacent to the statue and parked the car. I told my mother to stay with the car in case it needed to be moved. I looped the camera strap around my wrist and bounded across the street to the base of the statue. It was gorgeous and surrounded by beautiful trees and plants. I am told, although I don't know if it is a fact, that it is the only equestrian statue in Atlanta. Click, click went the camera and back I went to the car before I got a ticket. Not far away we found Oakland Cemetery, the last resting-place of John B. Gordon. I asked some workmenif they knew where he was buried and they directed me to the visitor's center. At the center I picked up some pamphlets. Margaret Mitchell, who wrote *Gone with the Wind,* rests here along with

2500 Confederate soldiers and five General Officers: Gordon, Evans, Iverson, Gartrell and Walker. They all rest in the shade of old oaks, magnolias and dogwood trees. I received directions to John Gordon's grave and then asked where the family plot was. I was told there was no family plot. I had a strange feeling that there was a family plot so I posed the question again. "Just Fanny buried with John," the woman at the desk replied with a stern voice and cold stare. I dropped thesubject. My mother and I walked to Gordon's grave, a modest stone monument about three feet high, six feet wide and about two and a half feet thick. One side simply read GORDON, the other

John B. Gordon
Feb. 6, 1832–Jan. 9, 1904
Fanny Haralson
Wife of John B. Gordon
Sept. 18, 1837–Apr. 28, 1931

"Wife of" somehow did not seem fitting. It should read "The other half of John B. Gordon"—sweet Fanny, who followed Johnall over the countryside through most of the major battle campaigns of the Army of Northern Virginia. Her presence and tender nursing had saved John's life at Sharpsburg. Gordon writes:

General Early was a bachelor, with a pungent style of commenting on things he did not like; but he had a kind heart and was always courteous to women. As might be expected, however, of a man who had passed the meridian of life without marrying, he had little or no patience with wives who insisted on following the army in order to be near their husbands. There were numbers of women—wives and mothers—who would gladly have accompanied their husbands and sons had it been possible for them to do so. Mrs. Gordon wasone of the few who were able to consult their wishes in this regard.General Early, hearing of her constant presence, is said to have exclaimed, "I wish the Yankees would capture Mrs. Gordon and hold her until the war is over!" Near Winchester, as the wagon trains were being parked at night, he discovered a conveyance unlike any of the others that were going into camp. He immediately called out to his quartermaster in excited tones: "What's that?" "That is Mrs. Gordon's carriage, sir," replied the officer.

"Well, I'll be ——! If my men would keep up as she does, I'd never issue another order against straggling."

Mrs. Gordon was fully aware of the general's sentiments, and had heard of his wishing for her capture; and during a campdinner given in honor of General Ewell, she sat near General Early and good-naturedly rallied him about it. He was momentarily embarrassed, but rose to the occasion and replied: "Mrs. Gordon, General Gordon is a better soldier when you are close by him than when you are away, so hereafter, when I issue orders that officer's wives must go to the rear, you may know that youare excepted." This gallant reply called forth a round of applause from the officers at table."[35] In wartime and peace, she was always by his side.

> After Gordon entered politics in 1868, she was of great assistance to him in his campaigns and in his study of current questions. She generally accompanied him on speaking tours, and when he could not remember the name of an old veteran who came up to greet him, she whispered it to him. The veteran, flattered at being recognized by his old commander willingly gave his political support.

Fanny Gordon helped her husband stay up to date.

> When the duties of public office did not afford him time to read the newspapers, she read for him and marked or clipped items that she thought he ought to see. She discussed the news with him and advised him in his political decisions. But Mrs. Gordon spent most of her time being a good wife and mother. Had her husband lived ten months longer, they would have celebrated their golden wedding anniversary.

Their love affair was called legendary by many.

> As long as he lived, he was romantically in love with the woman whom he had married on her seventeenth birthday and he was never too busy to think tenderly and sentimentally of her.[36]

She is by his side still and always will be.

A small tablet rests in the ground nearby, placed by the Alfred Holt Colquitt Chapter of the United Daughters of the Confederacy. It tells a condensed story of Gordon's life:

JOHN   BROWN   GORDON
1832–1904

A native of Upson County, Georgia, and a Major General, Confederate States Army, was one of General Lee's most trusted officers. He brilliantly led his devoted men in every engagement in which the Army of Northern Virginia participated and was severely wounded at the Battle of Sharpsburg. He led the war's last charge and following the Appomattox surrender, returned to Georgia.

Idolized by the populace, he served his state three times as U.S. Senator and as Governor 1886-1890. He was Commander-in Chief of the united Confederate Veterans from its inception until his death—a fitting tribute to a gallant gentleman.

I stood there a while, just looking at the gravesite. I asked my mother to take some pictures of me by the stone. The camera was a Polaroid, so in a few minutes the pictures had developed. I looked them over and started laughing inside. I said, "Hey Mom! You know that old expression—He was beside himself?"

She said, "Yes."

I smiled at her, while holding up the pictures that she had just taken, saying "Now I have a picture of it." She gave me one of those patented mother looks, as if trying to remember how many times she dropped me on my head.

A short stroll downhill from Gordon's plot, I found the grave of General Clement Evans, a good friend of John's and the General that replaced Gordon in brigade command when Gordon advanced to a Major General position. Down the hill a little farther, stands a stone obelisk. When this monument to the Confederate dead was unveiled in 1874, its 65-foot height made it the tallest structure in Atlanta. We walked back to the car. Oakland cemetery has a large grid-work of roads; I drove a little, turned right, drove a little more and then turned right again. As we started up a small incline, my mother said "Hugh Haralson Gordon." I hit the brakes and brought the car to a sudden stop. "Where did you see that?" I asked. "Right back there, on your side. Why? Who is he?" she asked. "Gordon's son," I replied as I shifted the car into reverse and backed down the hill. The woman at the visitor's center had been wrong, there was a family plot. Of all the roads we could have taken, we took the right one. If my eagle-eyed mother had not been with me, I would have driven right by, my mind still on Fanny and John. We got out of the car and walked to the small cluster of headstones. The three nearest the road were John's son Hugh, his wife, Caroline and their daughter, Mary. I walked over towards two headstones that were at the rear left of the small enclosure, one small but with ornate scrollwork, the other tiny and plain. The larger one of the two read:

John B. Gordon, Jr.
Son of John B & Fanny H. Gordon
1865-1884

This was the boy who had been born to the sound of guns at Petersburg. He died from typhoid fever at the age of 19. My eyes moved right to the tiny marker. My heart sank to the ground like an express elevator. A thought flashed through my mind—"My little girl, my poor little girl." My eyes started to well up, but I fought back the tears. My mother didn't need a 200-pound sniveling idiot on her hands. The tiny marker read:

INFANT DAUGHTER
OF
John B. Gordon and Fanny Haralson Gordon

No dates, for none were needed, as the baby had not survived long enough to even receive a name. It had not dawned on me at the moment it occurred, but now as I stood there it hit me. The word "MY," not "poor little," but "MY poor little girl." It had flowed so naturally and the effect had been swift and immediate.

Had I not been with my mother, I might have had a replay of what happened at the sunken road in Sharpsburg. I busied myself with taking photos of the headstones and then told my mother it was time to leave. My mother said, "Are you going back to tell that woman she was wrong about the family plot?"

"Not me," I said. "Besides, who else would ask the where-abouts of the Gordon's family plot?" We left the cemetery and worked our way through traffic to the interstate. Next stop—Richmond, Virginia.

Just south of Richmond, we turned off the Interstate onto Route 156, a road that would take us to an area south and east of the old Confederate capital. In 1862, Union General George B. McClellan's peninsular campaign was launched in an attempt to capture Richmond. We followed the twisting roadway to our first stop, a large clearing of sloping farmland. I drove the car into a small parking area and walked over to an information shelter near a row of cannons. "Malvern Hill" read a sign. The battle here had been fought on July 1, 1862. I was standing at the position where the Army of the Potomac had rimmed the crest of the hill with more than 100 pieces of artillery to hold back the Confederates and allow McClellan's men to withdraw from the peninsula. It was here, on the slope of Malvern Hill, that Gordon was blinded for a short time by dirt thrown into his eyes by an exploding shell.

Looking downhill across the green fields to the woods beyond, it was sad to think that when the southern troops fell back, they left behind over 5,000 casualties lining the slopes.

> Colonel Gordon had the butt of his pistol carried away by a Federal bullet, and his canteen was pierced by another, while his coat was torn open by a third. Hill had promised Gordon reinforcements, but they came too late. Finding his brigade isolated from the rest of the army, Gordon halted his men and ordered them to lie down and fire upon McClellan's flank.[37]

After darkness fell, Gordon and his men were then able to make a safe return to their lines.

We drove off following Route 156, passing the White Oak

Swamp and through Seven Pines. Tankersley's book on Gordon
tells of the fighting in the area:

> The Confederate losses were appalling. More than sixty per cent of
> Gordon's entire command were killed or wounded. His lieutenant
> colonel, major, and adjutant were all shot down. As he rode at the
> head of his regiment, he saw his own brother, Captain Augustus M.
> Gordon lying wounded and bleeding profusely, but he could not
> stop to help him.

Somehow Gordon escaped being wounded.

> The Colonel's clothes were pierced by three bullets, and his horse
> wounded but still able to carry him. He was then the only mounted
> officer left, but he rode so close to the Federal lines that his men
> distinctly heard Union officers command: "Shoot that damned Col-
> onel!" Finally his horse was shot from under him, and he was forced
> to command afoot for the rest of the battle.

The terrain was not much help to the men fighting in it.

> Fighting in water several feet deep, the Confederates formed a detail
> to prop the wounded against trees and stumps to prevent their
> drowning. Of the 600 in Gordon's command, more than 300 were
> killed or wounded; yet the Colonel stood at his post till the end
> of the action, unhurt and unshaken. For his conspicuous gallantry,
> he was put in command of Rode's brigade while the latter recovered
> from wounds received in the battle.

Gordon was a bit uneasy about his elevation.

> Because of his inexperience and youth, Gordon found his new
> position "unwelcome and extremely embarrassing," but, as he later
> wrote, his brother officers "did everything in their power to lessen
> my embarrassment and uphold my hands."[38] Gordon's part in the
> battles around Richmond had not been inconspicuous. Before the
> battle of Seven Pines he was hardly known outside of his regiment.

That was all to change.

> One month and two days later his valor had secured the attention

of the whole brigade and even Division Commander D.H. Hill. He was now the veteran of three hotly contested engagements, and was acting commander of a brigade. If he could maintain his fine record, he might reasonably expect a brigade of his own.[19]

Entering Richmond, I drove to 1201 East Clay Street, the home of The Museum of the Confederacy. I enjoyed the museum, with all its beautiful galleries filled with paintings, prints and photographs. Relics from the Infantry, Cavalry and Artillery fill the building's displays: tattered Southern battle flags, weapons of all types, including revolvers belonging to General Beauregard and Jackson, now lying silent in their showcases. I stood for a long time in front of one display in particular; it was filled with items that had belonged to General Lee. The display was a tent set up as if it were sitting on the edge of a battlefield. On the left side was a small metal camp bed with a blanket. Placed on the bed were the General's frock coat, leather gauntlets and sword belt. Next to the bed stood a tall pair of black riding boots. At the rear of the tent was a wooden camp chest with assorted utensils on top. To the right, was a small table with a square top. On the table rested a gray hat, field glasses and a model 1851 Colt revolver. One other item on the table caught my eye. It is the smallest thing on display but without question, the most powerful, the pen used to sign the surrender at Appomattox Court House.

We left Richmond heading North until we reached Fredericksburg, Virginia. I gave my mother a quick tour of Marye's Heights, the stone wall and Visitor's Center. Once more I followed Route 3 to Chancellorsville. The roadway became narrower and started to undulate like a small rollercoaster. Houses and stores became fewer and farther apart, strip malls gave way to fertile farm land and patches of aged trees. We paused briefly at the small Visitor's Center and viewed the monument where Stonewall Jackson fell. A short drive later and we were at the Wilderness. Driving here and there, I explained to my mother about the battles that had transpired on this splendid landscape of small fields and thick woods. We returned to Route 3 and headed back toward Fredericksburg, but there was one more place I wanted to stop. On my first pass through this area, I spotted a store called Stars and Bars Military Antiques. I had been on the road so early that it was not yet open. I had made a mental note to stop on the way back. The lady who runs the store greeted us as we entered. The place was filled with a wide range of items from World War I, II and Vietnam and of course, the Civil War. My mother talked to the woman as I scampered about the store looking for anything to do with the battle of the Wilderness. Inside a glass case I spotted some small items and asked if any had been found on the Wilderness battlefield. The woman went through the cases turning over each piece to read the description on the sticker on the back. Very few had been recovered from the area that I had requested. But there was one I really liked, a round Union breastplate with an eagle on it. I asked to see it. It was in pretty good shape and still had a small amount of brass coloring in some of the little nooks. I turned it over and read the sticker: "Found Wilderness Battlefield." Under that was the price. I handed it back to her and asked if she had anything less expensive that was from the Wilderness. She checked a little more, but came up empty handed. "Why do you want something from the Wilderness? Did you have a relative there?" she asked.

I looked at my mother and then back to the woman. "Yes, I guess you could say that," I replied.

"What regiment was he with?" she asked. "He was with General Gordon," I replied. "What regiment?" she asked a second time.

I looked back at my mother again. My mother said, "Go get the picture." The woman looked puzzled as I walked out the door to my car. I returned with a picture of Gordon and placed it on the counter in front of her. She looked at it and said "I know who that is, it's General Gordon. He was a gentleman." I told her the story of what had happened to me at Antietam, about the cannonball, Halloween party and the story in the magazine. She listened to me intently. She told me some of her thoughts on the subject of reincarnation. She didn't put much store in it; she felt that there might be some sort of a genetic remembrance passed down, like you might retain some of your relative's memories. I told her that as far as I can tell I am no blood relation to Gordon, so, in my case, her theory didn't apply. We talked more and she said reincarnation went against her religion, so that is where we left it. I thanked her for her help and started for the door. I stopped and turned to face her once more. "Let me leave you with this thought" I said. "I heard you tell my mother that you were born in Chattanooga, Tennessee on the anniversary of the Battle of Chattanooga and look at where you are now." I left her standing there with a strange look on her face as she gazed around the store. I would return to this store while on another trip South, and when I did, it would be her turn to tell me a story.

It was not a very long ride back to Connecticut, but it gave me time to think about my first trip to Lafayette, Georgia, about the battlefields I had stopped at along the way, and the strange and unexpected things that had happened to me. This was my first quest into the past. It would not be my last.

CHAPTER SIX

Insights and Wonderments

I WANTED A COPY OF GORDON'S BOOK, Reminiscences of the Civil War, so before leaving Lafayette, I had called a book dealer and ordered one. A few days after my arrival home, the book arrived. It was not the same as the 1903 edition I had borrowed from the library; it was the 1904 Memorial Edition published after John Gordon's death. An introduction by General Stephen D. Lee (Gordon's replacement as Commander-in-Chief of The United Confederate Veterans) and a memorial account by Frances Gordon Smith had been added. There, in the center of this book, I came across a drawing of Gordon. It was done from a daguerreotype taken when he was twenty-two. This was the first time I had seen Gordon's face without his mustache, only a close cropped beard covered his chin. I looked at his mouth and was reminded of something that I was told years ago. Sitting across the kitchen table from my then mother-in-law Bette Brennan, she remarked that I have a cupid bow mouth. I said, "I have a what?"

She said, "Your mouth is shaped like Cupid's bow." I had never heard this description used for anyone's lips before and just filed it away in my memory bank. Now, while looking at Gordon's youthful face, I turned the book sideways and sure enough, there was a cupid bow mouth if ever I saw one.

It took several attempts to read the memorial sketch by Gordon's daughter, Frances. So moving was this tale of a nation's grief, I found myself halting every paragraph or so to wipe my eyes and swallow the lump in my throat. Words like "beloved" and "loved" were used unsparingly. It was not the outpouring of love for him that impressed me, so much as the realization of how much he must have loved, for I'm a big believer in you get back what you give out.

It seems Gordon and I share not only physical features, but

also mannerisms. I have a habit of standing with my arms crossed. When people ask me to sit, I usually decline the offer and explain that I prefer to stand, and when I stand, I almost always have my arms crossed in front of me. In a book called *Their Tattered Flags*, I found a quote that brought home to me something that I had overlooked. It was a description of General Gordon that read "John Brown Gordon, he of the hitched shirtsleeves and fiery eye."[40] Well, I don't know about the fiery eye part, but I realized that in three or four of the pictures I had seen of General Gordon, he has his arms crossed. This pose carried over to civilian photos taken after the war. I guess you could say even our bearings have a bearing.

Ever since the time of the Halloween party, I had alternated between reading about reincarnation and books on the Civil War, sometimes reading one of each at the same time. I would walk through bookstores, stopping in the History and New Age sections. I felt guided to certain books; they would stand out from the others, sometimes lying alone on the top of a counter. The books seemed to come to me in the order that I should read them. Not just books, but people too. I have learned not to fight these occurrences and to go along with the flow of things. One of the first books to come my way was titled *Many Lives Many Masters*, written by Dr. Brian L. Weiss, a graduate of Columbia University and Yale Medical School.

I had made a perfect choice in picking this book, if indeed it had been my choice. The first few lines sum up my feeling exactly. "I know that there is a reason for everything. Perhaps at the moment that an event occurs, we have neither the insight nor the foresight to comprehend the reason, but with time and patience, it will come to light."[41] Dr. Weiss had been skeptical when it came to past lives. All that was to change during his

treatment sessions with a young woman. While under hypnosis, past life memories surfaced and times between lives emerged.
The woman gave information to Dr. Weiss about his family—
information, which she could have had no way of knowing. Later
on in the book, Dr. Weiss expressed something that he was going
through.

> Doubts would surface. It was as if my mind, when not focused,
> tended to drift back into the old patterns, belief and skepticism.
> But then I would remind myself—this actually happened! I appre-
> ciated how difficult it is to believe these concepts without having
> personal experience. The experience is necessary to add emotional
> belief to intellectual understanding. But the impact of experience
> always fades to some degree.[42]

Well said. I know the feelings. A few times I had started to
doubt the conclusions being drawn by the events in my life,
much like a dazed prizefighter rising from the canvas in disbelief
after being floored. I have had my conclusion reinforced, many
times, by the equivalent of a jarring right to the head. Things
can be strange or frightening to us, especially if we are unfamiliar with them. The key lies in knowledge. Words like "occult"
or "psychic" for some, conjure up visions of things supernatural
or satanic. Occult means "hidden or secret" and psychic simply
means "of the soul." There are more than a few people who may
have just cause to fear having a soul. One of the universal laws
I have read about, and have seen in action, goes like this: "You
reap what you sow." Albert Einstein once stated, "God does not
play dice with the universe." I believe he is right; I believe that
there is lawfulness at work around us. Einstein also was of the
view that a man was not capable of knowing the full results of his
actions. We can see the truth in this in our lives today. If, within
the family unit, we teach hatred or violence to our children, that
pattern may continue for generation after generation. The same
would apply to children taught love and respect for others.

I attended a week-long school for Fire Officers, held just
outside Boston, Massachusetts. One day the instructor set up a

problem for us on the blackboard. There was a fire that involved a large tank of propane gas next to an apartment house. We were told the backgrounds of all the occupants. One was a Nobel Prize winner, another a wino, a child, a pregnant junkie and so on until we knew the history of all the occupants in the building. The instructor said, "The gas tank will explode in exactly five minutes. You can only save one person. Who do you save?" I raised my hand and was called upon. "You are asking us to make a value judgment on the people in the building and that cannot be done. They are all humans and their value is intrinsic." He stood there with a look on his face as if I had caused a cloudburst over his parade. Maybe he was looking forward to spending the whole class in chatter about the fictional residence. I could feel the predicament he was in. I added, "I know who the firefighter would go for—the kid." The loss of a child in a fire has a devastating effect on firefighters. They take it personally. Once, before I was on the department, I walked into Westport Fire Headquarters to inquire how a fire had gone. "We lost two kids," was the reply. This normally raucous group became hushed and milled about doing their tasks in silence, but the tracks of the tears down their soot stained cheeks spoke for them. By my adding that they would try to save the child, the room came to life with banter and a smile returned to the instructor's face. As far as I was concerned, class was dismissed. There is another law, "Judge not." We are all here for a purpose although we may not be aware of what it is. There could be many reasons; to learn lessons, pay back debts to other souls or to serve as an example for others. The list has no end. I believe I am performing one of my requirements at this very moment by writing this book. If we are not aware of our own purpose, how can we presume to judge others? What yardstick do we use to measure the deeds of our fellow humans? It can become difficult and subjective. You may say something is for the greater good. Whose greater good? Yours, your family, your town, your country or maybe even the world? You can see the dilemma, much like someone asking you which is more beautiful, a painting by Monet or a child's smile? Our time would be better spent on learning about ourselves rather than judging others.

What have I found out about myself? Many things. I am an ordinary man, no better or worse than anyone else. I find many of my favorite things are in-betweens. I love sunrises and sunsets, those times just between night and daylight. I enjoy the songs of the birds as they greet a new day or bid the old farewell.I was once treated to a beautiful in-between, as I traveled acrossthe Piedmont area of Virginia. The sun was setting in the West,causing half the sky to turn an azure blue, while long finger-like clouds took on a bright pink color. The other half of the sky to the East, from horizon to midpoint directly overhead, was filledwith dark clouds. Right in the middle of these clouds was an opening, with a large full moon shining very brightly against thedark background. If you were to stand facing North, on your leftwas day and on your right was night sharing the same sky, perfectly divided. I find I am never more aware than during thatperiod just before falling into a complete slumber or just before becoming fully awake. I have found many answers in those landsof transitions, answers to problems, sometimes insights, sometimes messages and gifts. Past, present and future collide to form one continuous stream, a confluence that forms the river of life,a river that defies all laws of our world and flows back to its source. I have found that I have lived many, many times before.One life in particular, Gordon's, proved that to me, and if one past life, why not more than one? I had wondered why this pastlife person had turned out to be a historical figure, but how elsewould there be information enough for me to find all the photosand parallels of our lives. Edgar Cayce claimed that most souls make their greatest advancement while living obscure, normal, everyday lives. He also stated that it didn't matter how famous or important you once were in one lifetime, but it was very important that you live a decent life in the present one.

There is a store called the Tabergerie, which my good friend Tony Esposito and his wife Sandy own. Tony is the local tobacconist, and upon entering the store, one is greeted with the aromas of the pipe tobaccos. Exotic odors of perique and latakia waft through the air mixing with sweet Cavendishes to become a smorgasbord for the senses. The clientele is mostly male and the store has become a gathering place, much like the general stores of old. Stools line the front of the tobacco bar and behind it sits Tony, ready to hold court. One never knows what the topics of discussion will be at any given time; it could run the gambit from cabbages to kings. Many of the world's problems have been solved in less than a day at that little counter. It was here that I met Jim Lomuscio, a reporter/correspondent for the Connecticut Post newspaper. We shook hands and he told me that Tony had mentioned I was writing a book. I was having some difficulty with my novice attempt, so I asked him about ghostwriters and possible places to get technical help. As we talked, the smoke from our cigars rose to a point just below the ceiling, then flared out across the room. Jim seemed to be only mildly interested in my tale of reincarnation.

Months went by before our paths would cross again. When we saw each other again, not much more was said about my book. But then, one day, all that changed. I strolled into Tony's store on a warm June morning to find Jim sitting at the tobacco bar. I selected a Macanudo cigar[43] from the humidor and took up my customary spot at the left-hand side of the bar. Jim seemed deep in thought and was gazing out the window. Suddenly, he swung around on his stool to face me and said in a louder than necessary voice, "Hey! How would you like me to interview you for a newspaper article?" I jumped a little, biting down on my cigar, thankful it wasn't my tongue. This was a big change, from no interest to being all over me, like a mudslide. Jim was talking about calling his editor and getting a photographer. I thought for a moment and figured that the timing must be right, based on Jim's enthusiasm. I agreed to do the interview. Jim disappeared out the front door. A short time later, he returned. He said he had called his editor and that he liked the story. We set up a meeting time for the interview. The day of the interview, I gathered up some things that I would need to show Jim, including the rough draft of the first two chapters of my book and some photos.

On the way to meet with Jim, I kept in mind the fact that he was a reporter. I had dealt with reporters many times at emergency scenes. More than once, I had read articles written about incidents where I was present, only to wonder if the reporter telling the story had been at the same location. I entered Tony's store to wait for Jim. I resolved to think twice and speak once, while answering his questions. When Jim showed up, we took our normal positions at the tobacco bar. I showed Jim some photos and gave him the first two chapters of the book. I asked him to read it while we waited for the photographer. By reading the chapters it would save me rehashing the story and allow him to ask questions as he read. He had not read far when he raised his head and through slightly squinted eyes asked, "What proof do you have of reincarnation?" I love this question. My reply had the same effect on him as it has on most people; it stopped him cold, as if he were teetering on the edge of a cliff. "What would be proof to you?" I said. There was a long silence and then he said, "I don't know." He returned to his reading.

Enter Patrick Whittemore, the photographer. He was not the man Jim was expecting. Pat was filled in on the storyline. He roamed around the store a little shaking his head and muttering "No, no, too dark." Pat and I talked a short distance from where Jim sat reading. Pat asked me if I had a Civil War uniform.

I said, "No."

"How about a sword?" he said.

My answer again was "No."

"How about a Musket?" he said.

"Sorry," I said, "but I don't play dress-up."

Jim piped in and said "He's an Assistant Chief on the Fire Department." Jim went on to explain the similarities of my dress uniform to Gordon's.

Pat's eyes lit up. "That's great! You can wear that for the shot!" he said.

"No," I said. "I want to play down the Fire Department aspect of the story." Back and forth went this discussion. Pat wanted me to wear my uniform. I told him I didn't want to bring the spotlight onto the Fire Department.

He said, "That's okay." Jim took my side in the debate.

Pat turned to me and said, "Don't listen to him, all he needs is paper and pencil." I tried once more to explain my feelings about the department and not wanting to wear the uniform for the picture. "That's okay," Pat said. "The uniform will be great in the photo." I could see I needed a different approach to this seesaw battle.

I said, "I'll tell you what, I will talk to the Deputy Chief and the Chief and ask them if they think I should wear my dress uniform or not."

Pat's face took on a dejected look. He said, "They'll both say no."

I said, "Well, I guess the vote is three to one in favor of the nos." Pat finally gave in. He told me there was an old cemetery in Westport with some headstones from the Civil War.

Jim said, "Jeff's great grandfather was in the Civil War and he's buried in Branchville."

Jim looked at me and asked, "Is there a chance that your great grandfather and Gordon were at any of the same battles?"

"Yes, Petersburg." I said. Pat's face brightened a little. I gave him directions to the cemetery. He took my phone number and was off to check things out. Jim said he needed the photo to go along with the story, so we would wait to do the interview. I left the rough drafts with Jim to read at his leisure. As I was leaving, I asked Jim if he caught the crack that Pat had made about all he needed was a piece of paper and a pencil." He had. "It seems he is an artist and you're shit," I said. We laughed at what appeared to be Pat's high opinion of himself or his low opinion of Jim.

Later, I would receive a dose of Pat's medicine, the only difference being I would refuse to swallow it in silence. I drove home and had hardly been in the house ten minutes when Pat called. He said he had found the grave and the light was good "Right now." Could I be there in twenty minutes? I said that at that time of day, with commuter traffic, it would take me at least thirty minutes. He told me what colors to wear and to bring some of the photos I had of Gordon. I dressed, grabbed three different colored sports jackets and was out the door. Thirty minutes later I found Pat at the gravesite. He had set up his camera on a tripod facing the headstone. I emerged from my car and held up the three coats for his approval. "The blue one," he said. I put on the jacket. Pat picked out a photo and we walked over to the grave. He had me lie down in front of the stone marker, placing a photo of Gordon in my hands. Back to his camera he went. "Raise the photo up." "Bring your left knee up more." "Tilt your head more to your left." On and on he went, until I was in a very uncomfortable position. I told him I was having trouble holding the pose because it was not natural. I should have saved my breath. "That's okay," he said, without even looking up from his camera. Click, click went the camera. Pat walked over and told me we had to mark the spots on the ground where my elbow and knee had rested so I could get back in the same position. Up and down I went, first with me in the picture then out. Once, while lying in front of the tombstone, Pat kept telling me to move back. I was back as far as I could go, because there was the stump of a rose-bush sticking into my back. I told Pat about my predicament, to which he replied, "That's okay." When would I learn to keep my mouth shut?

A short time later, while I stood nearby, I saw a large St. Bernard lumbering up the road behind Pat. "There is a big dog coming up behind you," I called to Pat.

"That's okay," he said.

I said, "No, we're talking big, like Cujo," referring to the monster dog from the Stephen King thriller.

"That's okay," was again Pat's reply. The big dog just waddled past Pat and headed in my direction, frothing and drooling as he came. He stopped right next to me and started swinging his big, fat head so that slobber flew everywhere. I moved away to avoid being covered. Then the fuzzy oaf walked over to my great grandfather's tombstone and started lifting his hind leg. I chased him off before he could complete what he had started. I knew what Pat's reply would be if I protested about reclining in dog urine. It was quite warm, and the hairy beast was puffing like a freight train as he wandered off. I got down into position once more, making sure I was on my marks. I heard the huffing and puffing growing louder and louder somewhere behind me. Pat looked up from his camera. "The dog laid down right behind the headstone," he said.

I saw an opening and took it. "That's okay," I said.

"No, it's not," he said, with anger creeping into his voice. I said, "If he looks good in the picture, take it."

Pat said, "No, he doesn't look good in it." Pat commenced yelling at the dog to go away. Dummy dog arose and headed over to Pat, thinking that he was calling him. Around and around the camera they went. Finally, Pat was successful in his attempt to drive off the beast. I was glad that the camera's position had not been upset. I did not really want to go through a whole session of ups and downs and ups and downs again. We continued with the photo shoot.

A while later, I heard a woman yelling. Scanning the cemetery, I saw a woman with a small dog under her right arm, walking backwards over the cemetery plots. Her left arm was extended in front of her and in it she held a lit cigarette. A short distance from the cigarette the St. Bernard was plodding along after the woman. I yelled to her, "He's big and stupid and you're not going to stop him." She put her tiny dog in her car and closed the door. She yelled some more at the furry mountain that stood nearby. She turned in my direction and yelled, "You're right, he is stupid." I said, "Yes, but he's big too, so he thinks he can do whatever he wants."

We finished with the picture taking and Pat was loading his equipment into his car while I put my things away. Pat started to get into his car, but instead turned and walked over to where I stood. He said "For what it's worth, I believe that you believe in this story you're telling." I said, "Let me get this straight. You believe that I believe in this story I am telling?" He nodded his head in affirmation. I looked him straight in the eyes and said "For what it's worth, I don't give a shit what you believe!" I went on to give him a short lesson in history. How many people had died because others tried to force their beliefs on them? I explained that in my book all I ask is that the reader keeps an open mind, and comes to his or her own conclusions. When I was finished, Pat said, "That's a good attitude to take." Pat walked back to his car. He must have thought about the remark he had made to me and tried to recover a little by telling me he would call me later, and when he did, I should ask about the strange thing that happened at his mother's house. It's all right if people don't believe my story. It's fine if they say they don't know or are not sure. But I refuse to stand silent, while being patronized and patted on the head like the village idiot. As we drove along the small road through the cemetery leading to the main road, a large hairy mass stood defiantly in the center of the roadway. It was old fuzzy nuts making one last attempt at being a total pain in the butt. No amount of horn blowing or revving the engine could make him move. Pat carefully drove around him and I followed. As I passed around the St. Bernard, a thought crossed my mind that some day that dog would try something like this with a tractor-trailer with bad brakes. Then he will be in for one big surprise. After we had passed around him, he wandered off the road and disappeared into the cemetery.

Over the next few days, I talked to Jim on the phone. He had what there was of my book, so it was not necessary for us to meet for him to write the story. I received one last call from Jim. He asked a few questions and then told me the story would run on the front page. I asked, "What section?" He said "Front page, front page, there is only one front page, Jeff." Jim said the story was all set for Friday, in all editions and would run statewide. On the way home from Thursday's nightshift, I stopped at a store to get a copy of the Connecticut Post. There I was on the front page. The photo was a double exposure of me in repose, a ghostly image holding a picture of Gordon. You could see the headstone right through my body. I have to admit Pat did a great job. My wife said it was the best photo of me she had ever seen.

I read the article. The story flowed along pretty well. Jim told how I had held a picture to show him the likeness. He wrote, "Except for the Southerner's beard, the resemblance was strik-ing." I read on and was pleased to see pretty much the same storyline as in the two chapters I had given Jim. Three quarters of the way through, I came to a paragraph that started "Over the past couple of years Keene has been undergoing regression with Jean Loomis, a certified hypnotherapist." I could not believe it. I had made a point of telling Jim that I had never been hypno-tized and my reasons for declining hypnosis. It's not that I don't believe in it, it's just that in all my reading of past life studies the first questions they ask potential subjects was, "Have you ever been hypnotized?" If the answer was yes, they were dropped from the study. "Many people believe that a hypnotist can lead a person or plant things in their minds, such as a thought or sug-gestion. I did not want this stigma placed on me. I made all this very clear to Jim. I had two sessions with Jean Loomis, one week apart in November of 1992 and had never been hypnotized. I was amazed at one other thing in the article. Jim had talked to Anna on the phone, but she would not tell me what she said to him. She said, "You can read it in the paper." What the paper said was that because of my research, she now believes in reincar-nation. I asked Anna about this and she confirmed it. This was the first time she had expressed her belief in the subject and I had to find it out from the newspaper. I was pleasantly surprised by the feedback I received from the article—pleased by the fact that most of it was positive.

I caught up to Jim at Tony's store a week or more after the story came out. He entered the store and scurried over to the humidor. "How did you like the article, Jeff?" he asked.

I said, "Jim, can I talk to you a minute?" He walked over to where I stood. I said, "Jim, didn't I make a point of telling you that I had never been hypnotized? Now I read that I've been going for hypnotic regressions for two years."

He just looked at me a while and then asked, "Aside from that, how did you like the article?" What could I say?

During my daily meditations, many amazing things would

come to me. Fragments like faces, symbols or just eyes. At other times, short scenes of a minute or less in duration would unfold. These tantalizing tidbits beckoned me to press on in my search for my true identity, or should I say my other selves—the many pieces that make up the whole. It is very important to stay in the present and not fall prey to the problems of the past life personage. Each life carries with it its own set of problems and lessons to learn. If one gets too involved with past lives, one runs the risk of being incapacitated in the present and is likely to fall short in this life's lessons and goals. I do not put a large amount of stock into what I receive during my meditations, unless they are reinforced or validated in some way. One recurring image was that of a soldier. The first time I came across him, he was crawling through leaves that were covering the ground. He carried a rifle with a very long tube on top. I took it to be a scope. It occurred to me that the leaves could be friend or foe—friend in the fact that they could conceal and foe because of the noise they make as one makes his way through them.

I have only had one auditory episode. It happened as I was parking my car at the grocery store. While waiting for someone to back out of a parking space, I noticed a car behind me waiting to park also. A short distance up the line another car was backing out of a space. I figured I would take the farthest one and let the car behind me have the space in which I originally intended to park. (This gives you an idea of where my mind was.) I pulled into the space and shut off the motor. Just then I heard one word—"Fusilier." It was a strong voice, emanating from behind me, over my left shoulder. I looked around but saw nothing. I surveyed the area around the car and found no one in the immediate vicinity of my car. The windows of the car were closed because of the weather. The voice had been loud and very clear, as if someone were calling to me. I rested my head on the steering wheel. What was going on? What was the meaning of this strange word? Later that day, I stopped at the Trumbull Library. In the Oxford Dictionary I found the word "fusilier." "Originally, a soldier armed with a fusil. (A light weight musket or fire-lock.) In the British Army, the designation of "Fusiliers" is still retained by certain regiments which are distinguished from the other regiments of the line only by wearing a kind of busby and by some small peculiarities of costume." Further down, it read: "All officers belonging to fusilier corps have two epaulets." Now the voice started to make sense. If someone had knowledge of British uniforms, upon approaching a fusilier from behind and seeing the two epaulets on his shoulders, all they had to do was call out "Fusilier!" If the person did not know the soldier's name or rank, but saw the double epaulets, he may do just that to get his attention.

Now I had a name for the crawling soldier of my meditation—not a proper name, but a regimental designation, Fusilier. The Fusilier has played a prominent role in my meditations.

His episodes were the longest in duration. I have kept a log and will recount them for you as they occurred.

First came short bursts, like flash cards, a diamond shape on an epaulet, brown uniform and the word "tam." Symbols and insignia like a small crown, torch and wings with a dark border around them, popped in and out of view (I would make drawings of these images). Other times, names like Gwendy (Gwendolyn?) Daily and Becky McCall would come to mind. Once, I found myself in the company of another man. We were on a hill, looking down on a city street through field glasses. The man I was with said a three-word phrase in French. I wrote the words down phonetically (I do not speak or write French). The man then handed me the glasses and through them, I could see two men walking down the street. I repeated this phrase to a local storekeeper, who was born in France. I asked, "What does it mean?" He said, "It sounds like you are saying 'the two passing,' as if you were talking about two people passing in the street." I was surprised for this went along with my vision perfectly.

There was a view of a large city, with a fire raging at its center, a huge column of smoke rising into the sky. All these were a prelude to small vignettes. It was remarkable how abruptly most of these started. As I lay on the couch one day, a very loud noise to my right caused me to jump. It was the sound of a very powerful airplane engine, popping and sputtering to life. The sound was then repeated to my left. I was standing in the middle of the fuselage of a plane, facing toward the front. Above me, I could see the head and shoulders of the pilot and copilot. Directly ahead of me, on the same level I could see the transparent nosecone, metal bracing running through it.

A short time later, there were bright flashes, possibly from bombs, because of the low level we were flying at, or maybe from flack exploding near the plane. It may even have been from both sources. I remember thinking, "I'm not part of the crew, they don't even know who I am or what I am. All they know is they are dropping me over Germany. I am going to France by way of Germany. I get the impression that the crew had been warned not to talk about me or the drop zone, even among themselves. To do so may cause them to spend the remainder of the war in a cell."

One day in a bookstore, I saw a book on WWII airplanes sitting on top of the bargain book pile. I skimmed through it. There, in a short section on bombers, was the plane I had seen in my meditation. The nose was just as I had drawn it after my meditation. It was a "Martin Marauder," a fighter-bomber. There was one large engine on each wing. The American forces primarily used them but I was to soon find that some were also used by the British.

Beautiful photos accompanied the story. The pictures were of the only flying Martin Marauder now in existence. I had to laugh when I read who owned it—The Confederate Air Force. The name on the plane also stood out to me—"Carolyn." One of John Gordon's daughters was named Caroline. The daughter that died in infancy, had she survived, was to be named Carolina.

The next in the Fusilier series of meditations brought forth a scene of two women. It was a lovely day, blue sky and no clouds. The woman nearest in my vision was wearing a large hat with a brim that curved down front and back. It had a domed top with a wide band encircling it. She wore a suit-type jacket with wide lapels and squared off shoulders, and carried a dark clutch purse under her right arm. Her outfit was finished off with a mid-calf length skirt and clunky looking high-heeled shoes. She had dark hair and was very pretty. The second woman had long blond hair, slightly curled. She had a nice figure and was wearing a light colored floral print dress. I couldn't make out her face because she was holding one hand over her eyes to shield them from the sun. Both appeared to be looking at something, an airplane. They were at an airfield. I get the impression they came to see me off, then the scene fades to black. I lay there on the couch quietly for a few minutes. All of a sudden, there is a pop, a loud rustling noise and a sudden jolt, all in rapid secession. I find myself looking up into a fully deployed parachute. It is night, but I can tell the chute is dark gray in color. I understand that it is this color so it won't be easily seen. Everything fades to black again.

The next thing I know, I am on the ground. I feel that the chute has been hidden or buried and there has been a change of clothes. I have a compass in my hand, it is open and there is a slit in the top. Using the slit, I sight in on a church steeple in the distance to get my bearings, the meditation ends.

Before starting my next meditation, I asked to know more about the Fusilier. Instead of a meditative state, I fell asleep. This is a risk you run when you put yourself into a relaxed state. Upon awakening, I heard the words, "He clung tenaciously to life." I took this to mean he did not survive the war. This would make sense because the Fusilier's lifetime was between Gordon's and my own, which leaves a period of only 43 years.

The Fusilier was not to reappear again for two months, but his reappearance was sudden and dramatic. I grabbed at the couch on either side of me to steady myself. I was now standing on the bow of a fast moving ship. The ship was cutting through the water like a knife. I was facing the stern. There was a gun turret at my level and above it, a bridge. I think "battleship?" The word "Korvette" pops into my head followed by a large, red letter "E." Something is very menacing and ominous about the "E." Walking to the side of this ship I gaze up and see some numbers painted on the side. Only seeing the top two thirds, it seems to be the number 113. When the meditation was over, I drew a picture of the ship, as I viewed it from the bow. The gun turret I saw had very dark areas on each side of the barrels where they move up and down. I talked to a firefighter who had been in the Navy. I asked him about Korvettes and he said that they are a type of destroyer escort used by the British Navy. He later produced a photo of a Canadian Korvette and it was just as I had drawn, dark lines on the gun turret and all. I then queried him about the menacing letter "E." He said, "Maybe you mean a Eboat." I asked, "What's that?" I was told it was the German equivalent of a PT boat. It seems that E-boats were given the duty of patrolling river and coastlines. I talked to my driver, Gene Maloney, who is well-versed on WWII subjects. From the things that I told him on the Fusilier's exploits, he said, "It sounds like he was SAS." SAS stands for Special Air Service, an elite commando unit of the British Army. All the meditations now made sense in light of what I had learned from the two firefighters.

What better way to carry a commando behind enemy lines than in a fast fighter-bomber under cover of a bombing run. Once the mission was complete, though, he needed some way to be extricated. The most logical scenario would be to make his way to the coast and meet a submarine or maybe a fast ship, like a destroyer escort. If leaving on board a Korvette, I doubt very much that they would enjoy running into a German E-boat. I know for a fact that such a run-in would prove unpleasant for the Fusilier. The last vision I had of him was short and intense. I was sitting next to another man on a narrow metal bench attached to the metal side of a ship (I took to be a Korvette.) Large rivets held the pieces of metal together. We were drinking coffee as the ship moved quickly through the water. There came the sound of bullets striking the side of the ship followed closely by reports of rapid gunfire. The pattern of bullets moved across the ship from my right where the other man sat and continued toward the bow of the ship. It all happened so fast that neither of us had a chance to move. My companion was struck and a millisecond later, I was hit. Both my hands went up and grabbed my left chest area as I was slammed back against the bulkhead. I turned my head to the right and saw the man next to me had been caught mid-swallow as a bullet struck him. I remember thinking that he shouldn't even bother to swallow as I watched his jaw slacken and the coffee run out of his mouth and down the front of his brown uniform. He slumped over dead. Our ship was making a sharp left hand turn as some of the crew members ran over to me and asked something to the effect of how badly was I hit. One man took my hands away from my chest. As I looked down, I saw a large hole in my left breast and heard a horrible sucking sound. All went black after that.

Many things have come to me during meditations, names of places like Glen Kerry, Cork and the University of Edinburgh. Strange things like leather helmets, breastplates and unusual saddles and stirrups. Once, I saw a beautiful black horse with a white diamond shaped blaze on its forehead. Another time, a shield of red with a white band at a forty-five degree angle across it. Inside the band there were three red Bottony Crosses (I later found out that this band is know as a "Bend Sinister.") Other visions brought forth a large black dog, a panther and a bird of prey landing right on my arm.

Once there was a very deep sounding horn that would send chills up my spine. Another time a very beautiful oriental woman with emerald green eyes and jet black hair (I call her the pearl because she was holding a large pearl between her thumb and forefinger.)

One meditation was very short; I could see date palms and sandy, rocky hills. Two words came to mind, "Dark Remembrance." That was the extent of it, I didn't press this one, the message had been clear.

Many of these experiences from my meditations would fall neatly into place. Sometimes, their arrangement (or alignment) would be supplied from books, at other times by people. I never knew where nor when it would happen, but I did know it was just a matter of time.

CHAPTER SEVEN

Psychic Insights

ON A BRIGHT, SUNNY SEPTEMBER MORNING, I picked up my daughter Samantha. We were spending the day together and I was not sure what we would do. While driving, Samantha spotted a sign for a psychic fair being held that very day. I asked if she would like to go and she said "sure." She had never attended a psychic fair before. The fair was held at the Westport Inn in a conference room on the lower level. After paying the admission, we read the schedule we had been given. There were lecturers on Astrology, Numerology, Dreams and so on. Under a heading "Today's Readers" was a list of names broken down into categories such as Clairvoyants, Tarot Cards, Past Lives and Palms. What you do is pick a name under the desired topic and then pay for a session with that person. The cost varies with the time one wishes to spend. I asked Samantha, "Who do you want to see?" She wasn't sure. I said, "Did you ever have your palm read?" She said, "No." So I paid for thirty minutes with a palm reader named Alberta.

A flier on one of the tables caught my eye. I had seen this ad before at a local bookstore. I had meant to write down the telephone number before leaving the store, but had forgotten. The ad was for a woman name Yvonne Smith. Yvonne is a clinical hypnotherapist, hypnologist, regression therapist and master hypnotist. Yvonne is also a member of the International Association of Counselors and Therapists and The National Guild of Hypnotists. One of her areas of expertise is past lives. She lectures on the subject and does past life regressions. I was informed by the gentleman taking the money that Yvonne was booked up. While this attested to her popularity, it also ended my hopes of seeing her that day. I paid for a session with another psychic. This turned out to be uneventful for me. Psychics are like any other profession; some are good and some are not so good. Psychics can have bad days just like the rest of us, or they may not be able to tune in on the person sitting before them. Some deal with generalities while others can be frighteningly specific. Samantha had fared better on her maiden voyage into the world of the paranormal. As we walked across the parking lot, she was looking at her palm. "How do they do that, dad?" she asked. I said, "Do what?" She said, "How do they read the lines in your palm; who teaches them to do that?" I said, "I guess it may be a gift they have. What did she tell you?" Samantha explained how Alberta looked at her hands and said, "Your parents divorced about five years ago, when you were eleven years old." She also told her, "You broke up with your boy friend about three weeks ago and you have been together recently, but just as a friend." All this was right on the money. We drove through the beautiful autumn scenery. Every once in a while, I would catch Samantha glancing at the lines in her palms, a quizzical look furrowing her brow. I knew the feeling well.

A week later, there was another psychic fair in Danbury, Connecticut. I asked Samantha if she would like to go. She said yes and asked if she could bring her friend Lara. I was anxious to go because Yvonne Smith was to be there. Maybe this time I would get to talk to her. The three of us left early in the morning for the twenty-mile drive. I wanted to arrive, as close to starting time as possible so I would have a better chance for a sitting with Yvonne. We zipped along the winding country roads and arrived in time for me to make a triple appointment (three fifteen-minute slots running consecutively, for a total of fortyfive minutes). I waited for my turn while the girls were off doing their own thing. The appointed time came and I walked over to Yvonne's table. I said, "I've finally caught up with you." She gave me a strange look. I explained how I had seen her advertisement and how I was unable to see her at the last fair. I said "You're all mine for the next 45 minutes" as I handed her the three tickets.

Yvonne sat with her hands on the table in front of her. She reminded me of one of Raphael's cherubs only with a large shock of blond hair and pendant earrings. I will tell you one thing, whether Yvonne was right on or not with what she told me, the time spent with her was well worth the money for the sheer entertainment value. Yvonne had a marvelous sense of humor. She asked me, "What would you like to know?" "Past lives, just past lives," I said. For the next 45 minutes that is exactly what I got. I told her a little about John Gordon, but that I was interested in other lives. She reached her hands across the table palms up. I placed my hands on top of hers. Yvonne closed her eyes and sat up straight in her chair. I asked, "Just how far back do I go?" There was only silence for a few seconds after my query, then she spoke one word, "Tribes." Again, there was silence. What followed next was a cast of characters that spanned years, centuries, and even millenniums. I did not have a tape recorder with me and it was impossible to take notes because Yvonne was holding my hands. Upon my return home, I wrote everything down. The following is, to the best of my recollection, the conversation that transpired between the two of us. When a long period of silence was finally broken, Yvonne spoke. "You're a strange one, you have been following family lines. You have been reincarnating very quickly, I see the longest period between the lines as one time of 100 years." One hundred years may seem like a long time here on earth, but in the big scheme of things it's less than a nanosecond. Yvonne said, "You had a powerful influence over people." Then she asked me if I studied history and I said, "Just recently, the Civil War period because of John Gordon." She said, "You might want to ask yourself why you're in Connecticut."

Yvonne said she saw an "oriental monk, a round little guy with a bald head." Another monk showed up only this time a "Franciscan" who lived in a "cloistered order." "He had not taken a vow of silence," she said. "He was tall and thin and enjoyed working in flower gardens." This, she said, was a "happy lifetime." (As I sat writing this last sentence, Anna walked over and put three flowers in front of me, one purple, one pink and another a pretty salmon color. I guess the monk lives on still.) Yvonne picked up something about Manchuria. "Many battles, many killed." I asked, "Was he Samurai?" She said, "Yes, a very ugly man with a big hair knot on top of his head." She went on to say, "He was close to the Emperor and the Emperor found him entertaining. When he was young, he was very cocky until some elders put him in his place." She told how he would put on tournaments and taught martial arts. From my meditations and other events in my life I waswell aware of the Samurai. I was also aware of a woman from that time period that seemed to be out of his reach (a different class or something to that effect). I asked Yvonne "Do you see any women?" She said, "There were many women. There was one in particular but she was *forbidden.*"

Yvonne picked up an Irish lifetime; A pert redheaded girl named Margaret (Peggy). A lifetime as a girl, it struck me odd until I thought about it a while. If we are here to learn lessons and grow, why would we be restricted to one gender? How could we possibly understand things like motherhood or childbirth unless we went through it ourselves? She said, "There was a lifetime in Atlantis; you were with a pretty woman with black hair." She told me that we were very devoted to each other. Yvonne sat quietly across from me. I started to ask her a questionuntil she shushed me saying, "Quiet!" "I'm into some X-rated stuff and I don't get out to the movies often." She was smiling abig smile as she sat with closed eyelids. Well, I was glad she was enjoying herself, but I was starting to get the feeling that maybe she should be paying me.

The next person to show himself was from the 1700s, a barrister. This barrister, she said, was friends with George Washington and Benjamin Franklin. "He had pushed Washington towards the presidency. He knew Franklin very well, all his affairs and projects." She said, "He's mentioned in one of Franklin's diaries." I asked her if she got the name of any town or city and she replied "Jamestown." Yvonne went on to tell of his death. " He was murdered on the docks. It was not a planned killing but rather like a robbery. He was stabbed in the back." I said, "Where exactly in the back was he stabbed?" As Yvonne replied, I mouthed the exact same words, "Right between the shoulder blades." Now when someone links you in history with two heavyweights like Washington and Franklin, you should take it with more than a grain of salt. I did, but curiously, some things struck home. (1.) Several times, for no apparent reason, a sharp pain between my shoulder blades has taken my breath away. (2.) I have in my possession a large copper button with the inscription, "MEMORABLE ERA MARCH THE FOURTH

1789." The button is from Washington's inauguration in New York City in 1789. (3.) The button had belonged to my Grandmother, Grace Keene. It was given to my mother after my grandmother's death. My mother gave the button to me after my father passed on. My grandmother, Grace, was my grandfather's second wife and they married in their later years. Her maiden name was Burr, one of her relatives being Aaron Burr who killed Alexander Hamilton in the famous duel. For all I know, this button could have belonged to him.

I asked Yvonne if she could tell me anything about my most recent past life. I was surprised by her answer, although I should not have been. She said, "He's a British soldier." Then Yvonne talked as if to herself. "They're in Egypt, what are they doing in Egypt? It's a training camp of some sort." At this point, I asked if he was possibly a sniper. She said, "No, he is more like a spy; he's young, intelligent and very good with things like codes."

Yvonne sat for over half an hour and never opened her eyes. She said, "You have been mourned by many presidents." Something I had read came to mind; it was a telegram of condolence sent to the Gordon family. It read:

"I was greatly shocked and grieved at the report of General Gordon's death. I had the honor to number him among my personal friends and to have entertained him at my house. A more gallant, generous and fearless gentleman and soldier has not been seen by our country."[44] The telegram was signed: Theodore Roosevelt.

Of all the stories of past lives told to me that day, the next one hit me the hardest. Yvonne started with, "You were a Druid, a Druid priest; there was a forest fire." She had no sooner gotten the words "forest fire" out than tears started to fill my eyes. We were still holding hands, so there was no way to wipe them away. The story went on. "The Romans had set the fire to drive the Druids out from a sacred forest that they lived in." She said, "I can see you standing there crying. You know magic but are powerless to stop the fire. You lose many of your family and friends. You make a vow to pay back the enemy; but there aren't any Romans around any more." I said, "There's still fire around; do you know where I work?" She said, "No." I said, "The fire department." Yvonne laughed and said, "Well, maybe that has something to do with it." Our time together was over, but before leaving, I put five or six photos of friends and family on the table in front of her. Yvonne picked up a picture of Anna and started laughing and pointing to it. She said, "This is her, this is the woman from the Atlantis lifetime!" I smiled and said, "Well some things never change." I thought it really strange, the way the Druid story had affected me so emotionally. A couple of days later, I was sitting on the couch watching television, when a picture popped into my head. I went to the closet and dug through a bunch of old photos. I was looking for a black and white Polaroid of an oil painting I had done more than twenty five years before.

When I was stationed in Florida in the 1960s, my mother sent my oil paints to me. Most of my paintings were landscapes, seascapes or still life. However there was one that did not fall into any of these categories. I developed the painting out of my head. I did not know where I got the idea or why I painted it. I did not like it after I finished it, and for some strange reason it bothered me to look at it. I don't know what ultimately happened to the painting; I left it behind hanging on the barracks wall when I shipped out to Orlando Air Force Base in Florida. I knew I had a Polaroid photo of it, but I was unable to find it.

Because of Yvonne, I now believe I know why I painted it and from where the idea sprang. It was a large painting, about 24 inches by 30 inches. The background was just a mass of flames.

Suspended in the middle of the painting was a skull with the mouth wide open as if screaming (I guess you could say it was not a pretty picture). The most amazing thing was what the skull was wearing a helmet—a Roman helmet.

At work a short time later, Gene Maloney brought in a book for me to look at. It was the Lancer Militaria Winter Catalog, which was full of patches and insignias of armed forces from around the world. On a page dedicated to Britain, I came across a pair of wings with a parachute in the center. This emblem had a very thick, dark border around it, almost identical to the one I had drawn from meditation. These were British Paratrooper wings. At the back of the catalog was a section on books. A book titled The Special Air Service had a small write up that told of the book's contents. It's a story of "The world's most elite special unit." A concise history of the SAS starting from "Egypt in 1941." I flashed back to my visit with Yvonne and another puzzle piece fell into place. THE SAS TRAINED IN EGYPT!

I like having at least three different sources for validation or verification on things dealing with past lives. I had received many impressions from the Fusilier's lifetime; Yvonne had also picked up on it. The third verification came from psychic Reverend Michelle Wojcik. I posed the same question to Michelle that I had to Yvonne. "Can you tell me about the most recent past life?" Keep in mind that Michelle had no prior knowledge of my Fusilier. Michelle sat quietly with her eyes closed. She said, "I see brown all around. You are dressed in brown." Then she said, "There are all different colors." As she said this, she moved her right hand back and forth across her blouse just below her left shoulder. I asked, "Are you talking about ribbons on a uniform?" She said, "Yes, he's a soldier, a British soldier." My third confirmation on the Samurai was to come from an extraordinary source and in a most astonishing way.

The place was a Border's bookstore in Stamford, Connecticut. My wife and I went to the store to wait for a friend. Anna roamed the cookbook section while I hovered around the history books. A man and woman with a young boy of around five or six

talked near by. It seemed that the man wanted the woman to keep
the boy occupied so he could browse in leisure. The lady found
a big book on airplanes and placed it on the floor for the boy to
view. They sat on the floor turning pages while the lad made airplane sounds. I watched the boy as he sat crossed-legged on the
carpet. He was a cute little guy. Suddenly he snapped his head
up from the book. He was about five feet away and facing me.
He was looking at me as if he were seeing through me. Silently
he sat; his face set with an expression of deep thought. A few
moments passed and then he spoke, one word, clearly, "Samurai." The woman asked him, "What did you say?" "Samurai," he
replied with the same unblinking, thoughtful look.

A tingling sensation scampered up my spine. He had pronounced the word correctly, which I found odd for a child of
his age. The woman asked, "Where do you see that?" He said
"Nowhere. What is it?" The woman told him, "It's a sword." I
could not hold myself back; I piped in and explained to them
that a Samurai was a person and that they carried swords.

They returned to the airplane book. I looked around and
could not see anything in the boy's line of vision that pertained
to a Samurai; even if it had been spelled out in big block letters,
I don't believe he could have read or pronounced it. The boy sat
making gun noises while looking at the airplane books. I asked if
they would like to hear a story. They said yes. I told them about
finding the piece of cannonball at Spotsylvania. In a book I was
holding there was a map of the Spotsylvania Battlefield, and I
showed it to them.

I explained about the fierce fighting that took place there and
the many lives that were lost. The boy's face grew sad. I wanted
to show him the flip side of the story. I hope when it comes to
things like war, he will look at it from more than one angle. They
thanked me and returned to their book. As I stood there gazing
at this small child, I smiled inwardly, for I knew what had just
happened. When that boy looked up from his book, this young
soul, yet untarnished and unencumbered by life, had been alerted
to another soul nearby. Much like an animal sniffing in the air, he

had honed in on me and picked up something from my past—a past that had been spent on a beautiful island called Japan.

At this time in my writing, I have tapered off on meditating for the purpose of obtaining information on past lives. There are several reasons for this. I would prefer to find hard facts and information of Gordon from books, photographs and assorted libraries. Another reason for the slowdown was that strange things started to happen once I opened myself up to my inner (or higher) self. It can become a case of getting too much of what is asked for. I was starting to have more psychic experiences.

It seems that I would, on occasion, pick up songs from others around me. One morning, in the kitchen at the Fire Headquarters, I stood buttering a bagel. It does not take much brainpower to butter a bagel, so my mind wandered off. Lieutenant Christopher Ackley was a few feet away washing some breakfast dishes. As I worked on my bagel, I was singing. The song was "Santa Claus is Coming to Town," a well-known tune but these unusual factors enter here:

It was the middle of summer.

I was imitating Leon Redbone (who had a very distinct voice and singing style).

I was not fully conscious of what I was doing.

Lieutenant Ackley said, "Do you like that song? I said "What song?" He said, "The one you were just singing, 'Santa Claus is Coming to Town' by Leon Redbone." I looked at him and said, "There is such a song?" He said, "Yeah! I was playing it on my tape player in my truck on the way to work this morning!" I hadn't been aware of this song until that morning. I found this strange but didn't give it much more thought until I had similar experiences.

On a trip to Vermont, Anna and I stopped at the King Arthur Flour Company store in Norwich, Vermont. Anna is a bread-baking nut—square, round, big, little, potato, and banana; she loves making them all. It was only natural then, while traveling through Vermont, we stop at one of her favorite suppliers. There were enough baking items there to give the Pillsbury Doughboy an apoplexy. I leaned against the cash register as Anna scooted back and forth, piling things on the counter like a supermarket sweepstakes winner. As I stood there, my brain drifted off and I started humming a song from Pinocchio called, "Got No Strings on Me." I heard someone say, "Thanks a lot." I looked at the girl behind the counter and said, "Excuse me?" She repeated what she had said and then elaborated. "Thanks a lot. I've been trying to get that song out of my head for three days and you stand there humming it." I said, "Well, I must have gotten it from you, so don't blame me."

Probably the strangest incident of this unasked for ability to pick up other's songs was one that transpired between firefighter Lisa Ruot and myself. Lisa is the only female firefighter on the department and is assigned to my platoon. Lisa is a diminutive brunette with a broad smile and an impish twinkle in her eyes. She is affectionately referred to as The Babayaga. She brought this nickname upon herself by using the phrase one-day. When asked what it meant, she explained it's a Russian witch and that they ride on houses instead of broomsticks.

Every once in a while, I would sing an old song called Pony Boy and do it with a Jewish accent, as I travel through Fire Headquarters. On one of these occasions, Lisa stopped me and asked, "How come whenever I'm thinking of my Grandfather you sing that song?" I asked, "Did he like that song?" She said, "Yes, he would sing it to me when I was a little girl." I asked her if he was Jewish and deceased. The reply was "Yes" to both. I asked her if she liked him, and she said she adored him. I said, "Well, I guess he's still around you." I walked away, leaving Lisa to muse.

These occurrences proved to me that I was receiving these songs externally. There could be no other explanation. The songs are not top forty hits. With the imitation of Leon Redbone in one case and a Jewish accent in another, what other conclusion could I come to? My favorite story of the three is the one about Lisa, because at that time I had been allowed to share a *true* love song from the past.

CHAPTER EIGHT

On the Road Again

MY MOTHER HAD RETURNED TO CONNECTICUT to attend the funeral of her sister, Florence. I was glad to see her again, but not under these circumstances. When it came time for her to return home, I made arrangements to drive down and meet my sister, Joy, at Roanoke, Virginia, where I would transfer my mother to her care for the remainder of her trip to Georgia. Whenever possible, I timed my trips South so that I would reach Winchester, Virginia, at the end of the first day of driving. I stop here because I love to watch the sunrises in the Shenandoah Valley. In the predawn darkness of the mornings, I slip off and get a cup of coffee. With coffee in hand, I sit and watch the night gently fade away as the sun comes up over the Blue Ridge Mountains. The light gray fog rises like a large velvet blanket from the bed of the valley. If you sit there for a while at that time of day, it is not hard to imagine the sound of wagon wheels and horse hooves plodding along the old macadamized Valley Pike. If you have the ears for it, you may also hear a faint sound, a sound much like the low rumbling of distant thunder. Strain your ears a little more, and you could possibly pick up the rhythmic footfalls of thousands of men marching to war.

Just south of Winchester, we made a quick stop at the Opequon Church. During the second battle of Kernstown, July 24, 1864, Gordon's troops pushed the Union soldiers back past this church and through the small cemetery. Many of his men had fought on the same ground two years earlier under Thomas "Stonewall" Jackson. The small stone church, with its white steeple, invites picture taking, so I obliged. Confederate General Jubal Early pressed his army northward driving the Union army out of the valley. General Ulysses S. Grant, after taking charge, replaced many of the Union commanders and returned the Sixth and Nineteenth Corps to the valley. All operations in the valley were put under the command of Major General Philip Sheridan. This marked the beginning of the end for the Shenandoah as a travel route north for the Confederates and as a granary for their people.

Traveling a little farther south, Belle Grove came into view. Belle Grove is a beautiful mansion that was used as General Sheridan's headquarters before and after the battle of Cedar Creek. The area around the house was the scene of some of the heaviest fighting. The battle of Cedar Creek was one of the biggest turnabouts in military history.

The Confederates had come to a point where a decision had to be made either to attack Sheridan or leave the valley. General Early sent General Gordon, Major Jed Hotchkiss, Brigadier General Clement Evans and Major Robert Hunter to Signal Knob, a signal station on top of Massanutten Mountain. From 2,000 feet above Cedar Creek, they had an excellent view of Sheridan's army. Breastworks, cannon positions and even the color of the piping on the soldier's uniforms could be clearly seen (the color of piping is an indication of what type of unit, infantry, artillery or cavalry the men belong to). Hotchkiss made a map, and he and Gordon formed a plan of attack that they would present to General Early.

The plan consisted of night marches to get into position for an early morning attack by four converging columns. Hotchkiss and Gordon scouted a path that would take them around the base of Massanutten Mountain. This route would bring Gordon's men to a point where the assault could be launched on Sheridan's weakly protected eastern flank. The trail, at some points, would have to be traversed in single file, but they felt it could be done. Early approved the plan, and on the night of October

18, 1864, the men started for their positions of attack. All non-essential items would be left behind to avoid making any noise that might alert the enemy. Surprise was a key ingredient of the plan. The officers synchronized their watches and made ready for the attack that would start at 5:00 am, October 19, 1864. At the appointed hour, the Confederates splashed across the north fork of the Shenandoah River and Cedar Creek. Rising up out of the morning fog, they caught the Federals completely off guard. The fortifications were taken and the Union soldiers were pushed back toward the town of Middletown. Just a month earlier, the Confederates had been chased up the valley after the third battle of Winchester; now it was their turn to push back. Back the Federals went, past Belle Grove and through Middletown. Only a portion of the Sixth Corps held its ground, just north of Middletown. Gordon ordered his men to strike the Sixth Corps in front and both flanks simultaneously. He then called upon Colonel Thomas H. Carter to use all the batteries available and bring them to bear on this stubborn pocket of resistance, while his men made their assault. Carter, after surveying the position of Sheridan's men, made this reply to Gordon, "General, you will need no infantry. With enfilade fire from my batteries, I will destroy that corps in twenty minutes." It was at this time that General Early rode to Gordon and exclaimed, "Well, Gordon, this is glory enough for one day. This is the 19th. Precisely, one month ago today, we were going in the opposite direction." Gordon said, "It is very well so far, General, but we have one more blow to strike, and then there will not be left an organized company of infantry in Sheridan's army."

Gordon explained to General Early the plan that was being put into effect and the likely outcome of the attack. Early said, "No use in that; they will all go directly." Gordon then replied "That is the Sixth Corps, General. It will not go unless we drive it from the field." Early said, "Yes, it will go too, directly." Gordon writes, "My heart went into my boots. Visions of the fatal halt on the first day at Gettysburg, and the whole day's hesitation to permit an assault on Grant's exposed flank on the 6th of May in the Wilderness, rose before me. And so it came to pass that the fatal halting, the hesitation, the spasmodic firing, and the isolated movements in the face of the sullen, slow, and orderly retreat of this superb Federal corps, lost us the great opportunity, and converted the brilliant victory of the morning into disastrous defeat in the evening."[45]

Gordon's planned attack did not take place and what followed was what Gordon called the "fatal halting." Hours passed and with that passage of time, the absent commander, Gen. Sheridan returned. Sheridan had been in Washington for a meeting, and while returning, stopped at Winchester for the night. On the morning of October 19, he rode back toward Belle Grove, only to meet his army retreating along the valley pike. He gave orders to his officers to halt the men and turn them about. He galloped on his now famous ride back towards Cedar Creek. Shouting encouragement to his men, he arrived in time to turn his corps, once more, into the fighting force they had been. A smashing counter attack by Sheridan drove the Confederates back over the ground they had won that morning.

Gone was the ground the Confederates had fought for; gone also were the supplies and artillery they had captured. Worst of all, gone were many irreplaceable southern soldiers, either killed, wounded or captured. Major General Ramseur, mortally wounded, was taken to Belle Grove where Union classmates from West Point sat with him and gave him comfort until the end came. Gordon writes of his own narrow escape.

> In the dim starlight, after crossing the creek, I gathered around me a small force representing nearly every command in Early's army, intending to check, if possible, to enable the shattered and rapidly retreating fragments to escape. The brave fellows responded to my call and formed a line across the pike. The effort was utterly fruitless, however, and resulted only in hair-breadth escapes and unexampled experiences. It has never been settled whether, in escaping from the British dragoons under Tryon, General Israel Putnam rode or rolled or slid down the precipice at Horse Neck in 1779; but whichever method of escape he adopted, I can "go him two better," as the sportsmen say, for I did all three at Cedar Creek, eighty-

five years later, in escaping from American dragoons under Philip Sheridan. At the point where I attempted to make a stand at night, the pike ran immediately on the edge of one of those abrupt and rugged limestone cliffs down which it was supposed not even a rabbit could plunge without breaking his neck; and I proved it to be nearly true. One end of my short line of gray-jackets rested on the pike at this forbidding precipice. I had scarcely gotten my men in position when I discovered that Sheridan's dragoons had crossed the creek higher up, and that I was surrounded by them on three sides, while on the other was this breakneck escarpment. These enterprising horsemen in search of their game had located my little band, and at the sound of the bugle they came in headlong charge. Only one volley from my men and the Federal cavalry were upon them. Realizing that our capture was imminent, I shouted to my men to escape if possible, into the darkness. One minute more and I should have had a Yankee carbine at my head, inviting my surrender. The alternatives were the precipice or Yankee prison. There was no time to debate the question, not a moment. Wheeling my horse to the dismal brink, I drove my spurs into his flanks, and he plunged downward and tumbled headlong in one direction, sending me in another. How I reached the bottom of the abyss I shall never know; for I was rendered temporarily unconscious. Strangely enough, I was only stunned and in no way seriously hurt. My horse too, though bruised, was not disabled. For a moment, I thought he was dead, for he lay motionless and prone at full length. However, he promptly responded to my call and rose to his feet; and although the bare places on his head and hips showed that he had been hurt, he was ready without a groan to bear me again in any direction I might wish to go. The question was, which way to go. I was alone in the dark wooded glen—that is, my faithful horse was the only comrade and friend near enough to aid me.[46]

Gordon worked his way back to Fisher's Hill to meet up with the remnants of the Southern forces; the long day of fighting was over. If the Confederate victory had been sustained, it may have caused a different result at the polls for Lincoln. A loss for Lincoln to one of his past Commanders, George B. McClellan (who was running on a peace platform), would have most likely brought both North and South together for an end to the hostilities and an equitable settlement. This did not occur and Cedar

Creek stands as another case of what might have been.

I found it odd that Gordon should mention General Putnam. A little over twelve miles from my home in Connecticut is Israel Putnam Memorial State Park. This park commemorates the winter encampment of 1778-1779 of Major General Israel Putnam's Continental army troops. I took a ride to the park. At the main entrance stands a statue of Putnam on horseback. The horse is at a severe downward angle, Putnam leaning backward with left arm raised, as if shaking his fist in defiance at his pursuers. The metal tablet on the base reads:

ISRAEL PUTNAM

Senior Major General in the Continental army when at Greenwich, Connecticut, in February of 1779, made good a dramatic mounted escape from pursuing British Dragoons down the perilous 100 Stone steps carved into the precipice at Horse Neck.

I have visited what is left of the "100 Steps" in Greenwich, Connecticut. The majority of them were covered over by the construction of Rt. #1. They are not much to look at now, but at the time of Putnam's ride they must have been a daunting obstacle.

Continuing our drive south, we stopped at New Market, for a visit to the New Market Battlefield Museum. The museum is located on part of the old battlefield. This museum houses the best collection of military artifacts I have ever seen. It covers items dating from the Revolutionary War through Operation Desert Storm. Further south, we stopped at Lexington, Virginia, home of Washington and Lee College. General Lee became president of the school after the war and the small chapel on campus is his final resting-place. Inside the chapel is a life-size recumbent statue of Gen. Lee created by Edward Valentine, a noted Richmond sculptor. Lee is portrayed in full uniform at rest on a cot in his headquarters tent. In each corner of the room hangs a Confederate battleflag that had been returned to the South long after its surrender at Appomattox Courthouse. Downstairs under this statue are the burial vaults and Gen. Lee's studies. Just outside the chapel are buried the remains of the General's famous horse "Traveler."

Upon meeting up with my sister Joy at Roanoke, Virginia, we checked into our hotel rooms. While unpacking, Joy reached into her suitcase and handed me something with the comment, "Happy Birthday." Looking down at the object, now in my right hand, it took me a moment to realize what it was. Metal, green with age and an engraved pattern covering the surface. The watchback! She had stopped on the way up and bought the watchback from the man who had found it. I got my magnifying glass and checked the inside and sure enough there were the two letters, J.G. I also checked and found the manufacturer's markings. I thought over why J.G. would be stamped into the watchback when most watches are engraved on the front inside cover. Then it hit me. When watch repairmen work on watches, they need to remove the back to get at the inner-workings. It made sense that in that era, when many pocket-watches were in fashion, the repairmen would need some system of identification for all the loose watchbacks lying around. Why not mark the back with the owner's initials? The main body of a watch could be easily tagged, but not so with the back. By checking the initials in an errant watchback, it could be simply matched with the owner's name on the tag affixed to the watch. I cleaned the watchback ever so slightly and placed it in my suitcase.

Before their return South and my return North, we all paid a visit to Appomattox Court House. I separated from them in order to be alone. Once again, I stood at the surrender triangle near the Peers House. My thoughts drifted back to that day in April 1865. It was an ending, but at the same time a beginning— a new nation that would stand as a model to others. I strolled back through the village to the other side of the town, up a gradual rise to the top of a small hill. Under the shade of some trees was a small cemetery, in it, the graves of eighteen Confederates and one Union soldier. The small gray stones showed signs of age. Weather-beaten, with cracks marring their surface, they stood as a monument to the last battle of the Army of Northern Virginia.

Did these men, now interred here, know that they would be some of the last to die for their cause?

It was to this area that General Lee sent Colonel Charles S. Venable to find General Gordon and ascertain from him what progress was being made on this front. Gordon's reply to Col. Venable was, "Tell General Lee that my command has been fought to a frazzle, and unless Longstreet can unite in the movement, or prevent these forces from coming upon my rear, I cannot long go forward."[47] General Lee, upon receiving this message is reported to have said, "There is nothing left me but to go and see General Grant, and I had rather die a thousand deaths." For The Army of Northern Virginia, the end had come; their struggle was over.

Back in the village, I caught up with my family members. We went to the second floor of the courthouse to take in the slide show that I had missed on my first visit to Appomattox. It was an emotionally moving presentation and I had all I could do to remain through the entire program. Sometimes, I am hit with what amounts to a combination of pride and sorrow for the men of both armies. In my case, it is literally heartfelt.

We all walked to the parking lot, and after hugs and kisses all around, we headed in opposite directions.

I backtracked over Lee's retreat route and shortly found myself standing in front of the Hillman House overlooking Sayler's Creek. On April 6, 1865, Union battle lines were formed around this house and artillery was set up in the yard to fire upon the retreating Confederates under General Ewell. A fierce battle ensued and when it was over, General Lee had lost a large portion of his already depleted army. Hillman House was used as hospital to aid the many wounded and remains today much as it was during the battle.

I have been told by a member of a rescue company in nearby Farmville, that mysterious lights have been seen inside Hillman House. These occurrences happen late at night, after the house has been locked up for the day. To add to the mystery, the house has never had electricity added. The same young man told me that more than once the rescue squad has responded to cars running off the road in the area of Hillman House, the drivers blaming the accident on a Confederate soldier standing in the middle of the road.

I drove off to find Double Bridge. I passed the Lockett House, pausing only long enough to take a picture, then continued down the hill to Double Bridge. The crossing gets its name from the fact that it is at this point that Sayler's Creek and Little Sayler's Creek merge. The wagon train that Gordon's men had been protecting bogged down in this swampy area. Gordon's men formed near the Lockett House to fight back the approaching Union army. After twice repulsing attacks, the men were forced to abandon the wagons and scatter across Sayler's Creek. Driving on, I passed a sign for High Bridge. There were two bridges used by the Confederates to cross the Appomattox River at this point. One a tall railroad trestle, the other a small wagon bridge. Failure to completely destroy these two structures after crossing allowed Federal troops to forge the river and attack Lee's army from the rear. As I headed to my next destination, Spotsylvania Court House, I thought about all the back roads I had covered along Lee's retreat route. Some of these roads are yet unpaved. It is hard to imagine walking, let alone fighting, all the way from Richmond and Petersburg. This woeful trek stands as a reminder of the fortitude and courage displayed by the southern soldiers.

As I entered Spotsylvania Court House Battlefield the sun was edging down over the western horizon. I parked my car in the center of the Mule Shoe near the remains of the McCool House. As I grabbed my camera and exited the car, two deer popped up out of the tall grass nearby. My back was to the West, and as we gazed at each other, the setting sun illuminated their forms. The deer stood in the spot from which they had arisen, ears twitching, big brown eyes casting a questioning look in my direction. We remained motionless, time slowed, and what seemed like an hour was in reality only minutes. The deer, satisfied that I posed no threat, slowly walked off into the woods. I have a special affection for this battlefield. It always seems to know when I'm there and never fails to give me a gift of one sort or another. I had one last shot left in my camera and took a picture of the sunset. I now wish I had taken a picture of the deer, for I found that photos shot directly into the sun do not turn out so well. Seeing the deer reminded me of a most charming story I had read. It was written by John H. Worsham, a Confederate soldier who, at this very spot near the McCool House, had been an eyewitness to the "Lee to the Rear" episode. The story he tells happened a few days after the terrible battle of May 12th and stands in stark contrast to that battle.

> We remained in the rear until the morning of the 15th. We found in the middle of our camp, in the open field, an old hare's bed containing four little ones, the old mammy having run away on our approach! I do not know that I ever saw men more solicitous for the welfare of anything than were those grizzly warriors for those little bunnies. It was raining, and some wanted to make a house over them, others wanted to hold their oilcloths over them, no one was allowed to touch them, one might look as much as one chose, but hands off! When we left it was a sad parting.[48]

I drove to Fredericksburg where I spent the night. I had a leisurely breakfast and passed some time wandering around the area. I stopped at Marye's Heights, Salem Church and The Wilderness. I was waiting for Stars and Bars Military Antiques to open. This was the store I had visited on the earlier trip with my mother. As I entered the store, a familiar face looked up from behind the counter. The woman recognized me because she said "I remember you, you're the one who told me about the cannonball!" She continued, "Now I have a story to tell you!" She proceeded to tell of her walk down a road at a famous battlefield. "All of a sudden, for some unknown reason, I stopped and looked down, and there, right on top of the road was a mini ball." I laughed and said, "See, that mini ball was just laying there waiting for you." We talked a while and this time when I left, the Federal breastplate I couldn't afford on my first visit was now heading north with me. Upon arriving home, the breastplate and watchback took their places in my ever-growing trays of cherished mementos.

CHAPTER NINE

Gettysburg and Beyond

STRANGE AND WONDERFUL THINGS HAPPEN when I travel. I am forever making new discoveries. Gettysburg has been a treasuretrove of information and revelations. I have traveled there many times with family and alone. My oldest daughter, Shannon, attended Dickinson College in Carlisle, Pennsylvania with a desire to become a lawyer. Dickinson College is just thirty miles north of Gettysburg. I came across an interesting bit of history on General Gordon's family.

> After his father's death, Zachariah Herndon Gordon, the father of John B. Gordon worked so his brothers could finish college. Wiley and Charles P. were away studying at Dickinson College at Carlisle, Pennsylvania. Charles P. Gordon became not only a prominent lawyer, but a leader in civic and political affairs of the state of Georgia.[49]

It was sibling weekend at Dickinson College and I said I would bring my other daughter, Samantha, down to stay with her sister. I planned on dropping her off and then driving to Gettysburg to do some more research. Upon arrival at the school, I found that it was my two daughters' plan to have Dad entertain them for the entire weekend. The next morning, the three of us headed south to Gettysburg. We stopped to see the Electric Map program at the Gettysburg Battlefield Visitor Center. The Electric Map gives a presentation of the famous three-day battle by using lights installed in a huge topographical map of the Gettysburg area. During the narration, they told a story about General Gordon asking Lieutenant Colonel H.P. Jones to bring some artillery to bear on an officer on horseback on Barlows Knoll. The officer was 19-year-old Lt. Bayard Wilkeson and his union cannons were wreaking havoc among the Confederates. A cannonball struck Wilkeson killing his horse and almost severing his right leg. The story went on to explain that young Wilkeson completed the amputation with a pocketknife but later died from loss of blood.

Almost in unison, my daughters turned to me and said, "Daaaadd!" What could I say; I just shrugged my shoulders and put on the face of a child with his hand caught in the cookie jar. We visited a wonderful store called The Horse Soldier. It was filled with books, maps, photos and all sorts of Civil War memorabilia. To give myself some time alone, I sent Shannon and Samantha on a mission to find a magazine, an issue of the Civil War Time from May 1985. There was an article on Gordon in this particular issue and I had searched for almost two years, without success in finding it. Thirty seconds later, there was a tap on my shoulder. I turned to see two Cheshire Cat grins and the magazine that I had looked for so long. An old saying came to mind, "The best laid plans of mice and men. "

That evening, we drove east to Wrightsville. This was where Gordon and his men had been stopped from crossing the Susquehanna River by the burning of the bridge. Two markers, one in town and the other at the edge of the river simply stated that this was the farthest east the Army of Northern Virginia ever traveled. After viewing these signposts of history, I was surprised there was no mention of Gordon's men saving the town from flames. It would not be until many years later that I would find a local story of the Confederates arresting the flames in Wrightsville. I found a regional account of the burning of the bridge that day in a booklet printed for the celebration of the Columbia Civil War Centennial (1863-1963):

> Some quarter of an hour passed, and a column of smoke, at first barely detectable, then rapidly growing and traveling downwind made it apparent to all that the bridge was afire. In minutes the group who had entered with their task of destruction appeared, and soon the word passed rapidly through the crowd. They set it on fire.

The link between eastern and western shore was now blocked by a wall of flame which spread rapidly, more rapidly toward the Wrightsville side for a fairly strong northwest wind carried the flames in the direction of that town.

Now the fire increased in intensity and spread toward the Columbia end, sending huge billows of smoke swirling downstream and high in the air, making visibility of the west shore difficult owing to the smoke pall that swept low over the stream. The roar of the flames grew louder as the fire swept eastward, and the town of Columbia mustered the firemen and their engines to guard against spread of the flames to river shore structures and thence to Front Street, and perhaps to the remainder of the town with a resulting general conflagration.

Wrightsville, now occupied by the Confederate forces, did not fare so well. The wind, as previously mentioned, was from the northwest driving the flames diagonally downstream in the direction of the town. Several structures adjacent to river and bridge end took fire almost simultaneously, the flames spreading rapidly. The situation looked very serious from the onset. General Gordon, however, ordered two regiments of his men to form bucket brigades from the river; and with the help of a small hand pumper from the town, the flames were prevented from spreading generally throughout the houses of the small community. This gracious act was long remembered by the citizens, who realized that their town had been spared through the efforts of the enemy at the orders of their Commander.

I started to drive back in the direction of Gettysburg. Shannon piped up and said, "Don't you want to go across the bridge?" From the back seat Samantha added, "Yeah! Don't you want to get to the other side *this time*?" I thought for a very short moment and then said, "Yes, yes I do." Swinging the car around we headed across the river to Columbia on the far side. Driving back across this modern bridge of concrete and steel, I checked the odometer to see just how long it was. Over one mile of bridge spans the river between the two towns. What a sight it must have been in 1863 to see that large wooden bridge become engulfed in flames and disappear into the river. Crossing the river had given me what appeared to be a belated feeling of satisfaction and I relished it as we traveled back to Gettysburg.

For me, the first day of the battle of Gettysburg, July 1, 1863 is very poignant. There are three reasons for this:

First, it is the third and final of my tales of what might have been.

The second reason involves a story of General Gordon's conduct that day.

Lastly, it brings some of my relatives into play.

On that hot July 1, 1863, Lee's Army of Northern Virginia and Meade's Army of the Potomac were engaged in heavyfighting West and North of the little town of Gettysburg. General Early's division arrived on the field of battle on the afternoon of the first. Their arrival was one of those instances ofbeing in the right place at the right time. The right flank of the Union army (11th Corps) was on a knoll overlooking Rock Creek.

Early's men were in a perfect position to execute an attack on the exposed Union flank. At approximately 3:15 P.M., Gordon's Brigade was ordered to launch their attack. The Confederates succeeded in pushing the Union troops back through the town and up onto Culp's Hill and Cemetery Ridge. This is where they remained. The successful route of the Union troops was not followed up. The army of the Potomac retained the high ground and the rest was literally history. There have been many theories attaching blame to many different people. Had the momentum of the first days' battle been pushed up to and over Cemetery Ridge, the outcome may have been disastrous for the Union. This event, or should we say lack of action, has been debated, studied and dissected for more than a century. Most likely it will continue ad infinitum.

In command on the small knoll that now bears his name, was Union Brigadier General Francis Channing Barlow. It was Barlow's men who bore the brunt of Gordon's brigade attack. The Gordon/Barlow story of Gettysburg is one of the most endearing stories to come out of the War Between the States. Through one of those quirks of fate, I stumbled onto a book. The title: *Blood Is Thicker Than Water: A Few Days Among Our Southern Brethren*. The book was written in 1886 by Henry M. Field, DD (Years later Gen. Gordon and Mr. Fields would cointroduce Mrs. Jackson's

book on her late husband, Stonewall Jackson). Mr. Fields, a Presbyterian minister, describes his travels in the South with companions that nowadays would be described as "Movers and Shakers":
Mr. John H. Inman and Mr. Cornelius N. Bliss, both cotton mer-
chants; Mr. J.A. Bostwick one of the founders of the Standard
Oil Company; Mr. H.O. Armour of Armour foods; Mr. Thomas
Rutter and Mr. Harles H. Bosher, both railroad directors with
the Louisville and Nashville Railroad. While in Atlanta, Georgia,
they were treated royally and given a wonderful dinner reception.
Attendees of the dinner included the Mayor of Atlanta, the Governor of Georgia and Henry Grady, Editor of the "Atlanta Constitution" (Grady, at the time, was a good friend of John B Gordon).
During the evening's festivities, the speakers were being most
kind to their northern visitors. Dr. Field seized the opportunity
to convey a story of compassion on the battlefield. He leads into
the story by speaking of General Grant's funeral in New York at
which he represented the Presbyterians. The following is copied
just as Dr. Field wrote it, even the italics are his:

> In the procession of that day rode a Southern officer, of whom
> (ashis home is here in Atlanta) it seems not inappropriate to tell a
> story in harmony with the spirit of the hour. As it has been related
> to me by *both* the actors in the scene described, I can vouch for its
> literal accuracy. I give it as nearly as I can in the very words of that
> gallant soldier of Georgia, General John B. Gordon:
> "It was the first day of Gettysburg. The battle was in progress
> when I came into it with my division, and struck the Federal line
> at an angle, which caused it to break, doubling on itself, so that it
> was driven back in some disorder. As it was retreating, and our line
> advancing, in crossing a field I saw an officer lying on the ground,
> and dismounted to see if I could render him any assistance. Raising
> him up, the blood spurted from him, and I thought that he must be
> mortally wounded. To my inquiry for his name, he answered that
> he was General Barlow of New York. I asked him if I could be of any
> service to him. He said 'No,' and told me to leave him and go and
> do my duty. But on my pressing the offer of assistance, he asked me to
> send word to his wife, who was in the rear of General Meade's army.
> I answered that I would not only send to her, but send *for* her. I called
> for bearers, who were coming on the field to pick up the wounded,

to bring a stretcher. They took him up and carried him back to 'the branch' (the name given at the South to a stream), on which a camp hospital had been improvised; and I sent an aide with a flag of truce to the lines to forward the message to the wife of the wounded and, as I supposed, dying officer. The message reached its destination, although Mrs. Barlow was seventeen miles back from the front, and at two o'clock in the morning word was brought to me that she was at the lines. I sent word to have her immediately passed through, but bade the messenger tell her that her husband was 'desperately wounded.' I had no idea that she would find him alive.

The next morning the battle was resumed, and all that had passed was forgotten in the great struggle. It was nearly two years more to the close of the war. I remained in the army to the last, and was with General Lee when he surrendered at Appomattox. When all was over I returned home to help restore the fortunes of my State, if anything were left to her in the general ruin. Years passed on, and I was chosen United States Senator from Georgia. When in Washington, I was invited one evening to dine at Mr. Clarkson N. Potter's. I did not arrive till the guests were seated. Among the others to whom I was introduced I heard the name of Barlow, but took no notice of it till there was a pause in the conversation, when I turned to the gentleman so designated and said, 'Pray, sir, may I ask if you are a relative of the General Barlow who was killed at Gettysburg?' Imagine my astonishment at the answer: 'I am the man!' 'And you, sir,' he asked in reply—'are you the General Gordon who picked me up on the field?' I could not deny it. At this point he sprang to his feet, and I thought would have leaped over the table. And then he told the story of the scene in which we had met before, at which not only the ladies, but the men round the table, found it difficult to control their emotion."[50]

I recently came into possession of a newspaper article from The New York Times dated July 4, 1888. It was during this time period that the celebration of the 25th anniversary of the Battle of Gettysburg was being held. Generals Gordon and Barlow met once again on that small hill North of Gettysburg. I quote from the article: "The two men met for the second time in 25 years and the meeting was rather affecting. Gen. Barlow was left upon the field on the first day's fight. He was found by Gen. Gordon, who not only saw that he was taken care of, but allowed Mrs.

Barlow to come through the lines to nurse her husband."

At Barlow's Knoll, there is a monument to the 17th Connecticut Volunteer Infantry. This unit was made up of men from around the Fairfield County area of Connecticut (Fairfield County is where I have lived all of my life.) On one side of the large gray stone is a list of names of those killed from this unit. As my eyes scanned down the names, one stood out, Joseph Whitlock. My mind flashed back to a few months earlier; the scene was an old graveyard near the boarder of Ridgefield and Danbury, Connecticut. My uncle, Joseph Knapp, took me to this small family cemetery. Without his help I never could have found it. Stone walls surrounded the graves, an area of approximately 75 feet by 50 feet. Many headstones were missing, while others were half-imbedded in the trunks of mature trees. We were there seeking the grave of my Great-Great-Grandmother, Charity Stacy Whitlock. Information supplied by my greataunt, Auntie Mae, stated that Charity Stacy Whitlock (her Christian name) was a Susquahanock Indian. We could not find her stone, but we came across other Whitlocks. Two stones stood side by side, on the upper most portion of each are the words "CIVIL WAR Co. C 17th CT VOL. INF." One stone bore the name Nephi Whitlock and the other Joseph H. Whitlock. Because of the date of death on Joseph's stone, July 16, 1863, I made mention to my Uncle Joe that he died around the time of the battle of Gettysburg. From the book, *Connecticut Yankees at Gettysburg*, I was able to verify that Joseph Whitlock was mortally wounded July 1, 1863 and was interred in Ridgefield, Connecticut. Nephi Whitlock likewise was wounded that day, but survived. It was Gordon's brigade that came in contact with the 17th CT.

> The fighting now grew fierce as Gordon's troops closed in. At one point a color bearer of the 17th was banging his flagstaff against the flagstaff of one of the Georgia regiments, an episode rare enough to be specifically commented on afterwards.[51]

I marveled to think that it was Gordon's men who killed one of my distant relatives. It is indeed a small world.

Anna and I planned a trip to Washington, D.C. and the surrounding areas. Anna made a phone call to her friend Jane Smith, who lives in Maryland. Anna thought it would be nice to see her old college roommate as we passed through on our way to Washington. Jane invited us to stay with her a while. Anna said, "Oh, Jeff's into Civil War things so we will probably be zipping all over the countryside." Jane said, "Anna, don't you remember what my major in college was?" Anna said, "No." "Political Science," Jane replied and added that the Civil War period had always been one of her passions. Anna said, "Jeff's not into the Civil War the same way you are; he's interested in it for a far different reason." She went on to explain a little about the John Gordon story. Jane said, "Becky (Jane's daughter) reads Tarot cards." Anna said, "Oh, good, if we stay with you, I might as well sit in the corner with my thumb up my butt." We stayed with Jane on the trip and it never became necessary for Anna to assume the uncomfortable position she had described. It was amusing, though, to watch Jane sitting between the two of us, alternating conversations about the Civil War and stories of the good old college days. Jane and her husband, Lee, were kind enough to let us use their house as a base of operations while we visited the surrounding countryside. During one side trip, we went to Thomas Jefferson's home, Monticello. Being a stone's throw away from the Shenandoah Valley, I took Anna over the mountains and into the valley. The weather was not cooperating and heavy rain made the driving difficult. We decided to spend the night at the Days Inn motel in New Market. The motel is built on part of the old New Market battlefield. In the morning, Anna said, "I was worried about you last night. I couldn't tell if you were breathing. I thought some of your old friends came and got you." I laughed and said, "I'm safe; Gordon wasn't at the battle of New Market."

When Anna and I visited Washington D. C., we toured the regular tourist stops, including Arlington Cemetery, the Smithsonian and so on. We scurried past the Wall. I did not care to linger here or read the names of those who had died during the Vietnam conflict, for fear of recognizing some of the names. The Air Force

Hospitals where I was stationed processed many men and women from their tours of duty in Vietnam.

I told Anna before we went to Washington that there was one stop I had to make, the Library of Congress. Standing just inside the entrance to the main building of the library were rows of computers. I fumbled through the instructions and was pleasantly surprised to find what I was looking for with relative ease. I wrote down the floor and room number, and we were off. One elevator ride and a few twisting hallways later, Anna and I found ourselves in the Photographic Section. There are multiple forms to fill out and identification to show before one is allowed entrance to the files. Having done this, I was escorted in, leaving Anna behind in a small fenced-in waiting area. I was given a pair of small, white gloves that are required when handling the photos. I saw an opportunity I could not pass up. Returning to the small waiting area, I called to Anna as I knelt with one knee on the floor, gloves raised doing an Al Jolson impression. Anna just shook her head (she seems to do this a lot, although I can't fathom why).

One of the women that works in the library escorted me to the proper files I sought. She knelt down and pulled out the bottom drawer of the file cabinet. Finding the file on John B. Gordon, she removed one of the pictures. I heard myself say out loud, "Oh my God." The woman looked up at me with a strange look. Most of the photos I had seen of Gordon were when he was in his early thirties or when he was much older in his sixties. This photo showed a Gordon in his late forties or early fifties, close to my own age. The resemblance between the two of us was more than amazing. I took the photo over to where Anna sat reading. I whistled as I held the photo in front of me. Anna looked up at me then the picture. An amazed look came to her face and once more she shook her head.

I returned to the file to search for more photos. Most I had seen before or already had at home. I found some photos of James B. Gordon, John's kinsman, mixed in with his and some of John's in James' file. I pointed this out to the lady who had helped me. She said, "Would you straighten them out, please?" I did, then took a seat to fill out forms for copies of the photos I had selected. I hand carried the forms to the proper office and paid for them. It took a while for processing and more correspondence by phone to get all the photos. It seems one of the negatives had been loaned out for some special purpose and they were having a hard time locating it. Finally, they were all in my possession. As I sat in my living room studying the new photos, I noticed what appeared to be a dark shadowy area over Gordon's left eye. The area seemed to be indented slightly and showed rather well in that first photo I had seen at the Library of Congress. Maybe his scars were showing more with his progression in age. I checked earlier photos and sure enough, there were dark areas over his left eye. If I had not had this strong desire to investigate this strange mark, I probably would have missed something that turned out to be a most remarkable find. On one of the earlier photos of Gordon, this dark mark took on a most unusual shape, roughly a five-pointed star leaning slightly to his right. A visit to the bathroom mirror showed the same shape, in the same place, over my left eye. I believe I may have received mine in junior high school, by running into a bolt sticking out of the wall. (I am not sure exactly where on my forehead it struck me.) There was a dark recess, where a large door that separated the gymnasium into two halves folded, when not in use. I walked through this dark niche instead of using the door from one side to the other. My reward for this action was running into a bolt in the dark.

A teacher saw me as I emerged and sent me straight to the nurse, though I professed not to be injured. My head injury, bleeding badly, as they do, soon turned me into something from a bad nightmare. The school nurse took one look at me and started to turn white. She cleaned my face and both our complexions returned to normal. But where had Gordon received his wound? I remembered reading something written by Jed Hotchkiss, the mapmaker for General Stonewall Jackson and later General Jubal Early. I went to my bookshelf and removed the book. Hotchkiss, in a letter to his wife, Sara, described seeing Gordon wounded in a skirmish in Virginia. "General Gordon was struck by a glancing ball, in the forehead, and bled profusely, but was not much hurt. He did not get off his horse or stop to have his wound dressed, but pressed on after the enemy, all sprinkled with blood."[52]

Now a total of three areas on Gordon's face and mine matched, the small star over the left eye, the area of the bullet entry wound under the left eye, and the jagged line from the right ear across the right cheek. I needed no more proof of my relationship to Gordon, but I continued to be amazed by it when it appeared. Most skeptics would probably chalk all these things up to coincidence or, worse yet, fraud. To coincidence, I say let them sit down with a calculator and figure out the mathematical odds of these occurrences. To fraud, I reply thank you, for giving me enough credit and foreknowledge to mark up my face in adolescence and preadolescence in such a way as to mimic those of someone long dead. Better yet, they may say I doctored the photos. Well, they are welcome to visit the National Archives or the Library of Congress and view the photos for themselves. I have witnessed the security at both of these establishments firsthand and have seen measures used to maintain their collections. They are especially protective of their glass plate negatives for, if broken, they are irreplaceable. Stiff penalties and harsh fines await anyone tampering with items in their charge.

Once while passing through Gettysburg with my mother, I purchased a book titled, *Women of Gettysburg,* and a poster-sized picture of John Gordon. When we stopped for the night, I stood the picture of Gordon upright on the dresser, leaning it against the wall. In this enlarged photo it was easy to see the deep dent under Gordon's left eye. I said, "Some dimple, huh?" nodding in the direction of the photo. My mother confirmed my assessment of the damage and added how amazing it was that he survived such a horrendous wound. I settled down with my new book. It contained a short story on Mrs. Gordon's life. Though Fanny Gordon had not been at Gettysburg, the book was payingtribute to the women of the day. I turned the pages to the storyof Fanny. At the top of the page it read, "Frances Haralson Gordon." It stopped me cold. This was the first time I had seen her referred to as Frances.

I sat looking down at the back of my left hand and what I saw there transported me back to my Junior High School days. I was around age 13 and in the midst of a silent crush on a classmate. She was one of the sweetest people I have ever met; helpful, kind, never saying a bad word about anyone. Her manner and dress seemed to be that of an earlier era. Being young and not concerned with such things as disfigurement or infections, I found myself scratching the back of my hand with the end of a paper clip. A large letter appeared, the first letter of her name. The raised welt became darker and darker until blood flowed. As time passed, a scab formed followed by a scar. My mother asked me, at the time, why I had done that to my hand. I replied, "I don't know." At the time I did not know why; it had just happened. Now, more than thirty-five years later, maybe I have found the answer. The scarring has faded, but remnants still linger. She never knew how I felt about her, but I remember. All I have to do is look at the remainder of the scar that formed the letter F, for her name was Frances.

A short way into the story on Mrs. Gordon it tells of Fanny referring to John's facial wound as his "Yankee dimple." I laughed, recalling how a short time before opening the book, I had used the word dimple in describing Gordon's wound.

One section of the book tells of a collision between two trains, one carrying John and Fanny Gordon. Both were unhurt. Fanny attended to the wounded while General Gordon supervised the removal of the debris to rescue the injured and remove the dead. Being a shift commander of Fire/Rescue units, I know all too well the aftermath of pain and suffering from high speed crashes.

The story continues, telling of Mrs. Gordon's ministering to wounded troops and of her near capture at the third Battle of Winchester. The end of the story gives a brief summary of her life with John. They were married for just short of fifty years. The author included a quote from Holland's Magazine, February 1938, that seems out of place with the rest of the story and would be of little interest to the reader. Speaking about General Gordon, Mrs. Gordon says, "Every Spring he planted capejasmine. Every winter they died." This quote seemed to have been placed there just for me. When Anna and I moved into our new home to begin our life together, having hardly any furnishings, the rooms were rather sparse and barren. On an outing one day Anna spied a small plant on a shelf and called me over to see it. The plant was about five inches tall and seemed lost among the other larger plants in the nursery. We decided to give it a home. Over the years the plant has grown and now stands almost six feet tall. It is still in a pot, although one much larger than the original. Every spring we carry the plant outside, then return it to the indoor as the cool winds of winter approach. Sometimes when it blooms, Anna will pick a few of the delicate white blossoms and drop them over my shoulder onto the table next to me as I work. The wonderful fragrance drifts up to greet my nose. I do so love the smell of Jasmine.

CHAPTER TEN

Synchronicity Plus

ON ONE FORAY DOWN SOUTH, I ran across a string of what one might call synchronistic happenings. The first happened when, instead of taking my normal route through Tennessee, I swung east across the Blue Ridge Mountains and into North Carolina. Shortly after crossing the North Carolina border into South Carolina, I saw signs for Kings Mountain. I said to my mother, "I wonder if that's the same Kings Mountain I read about." I pulled the car over to the side of the road and went to the trunk. Checking one of my books on John Gordon, I came across a story on ancestors of Gordon's fighting at King Mountain during the Revolutionary War. The battle was fought on October 7, 1780. Of particular note that day was the hand-to-hand combat between an English officer and Charles Gordon, Jr.

> Making "a quick, bold movement into the midst of the enemy," he seized the officer by his queue and began dragging him down the mountain, when the Englishman drew his pistol and shot his attacker in the left arm. Seizing his sword, young Gordon killed the officer outright.[53]

The location in the book was the same, so we made a slight detour and drove to Kings Mountain. It was early in the morning and the park was not yet open. Spotting a park employee, I went to talk to him. He said they would not be open for another 40 minutes, but we could go ahead and walk around.

Since time was not a luxury this day, we quickly followed the path around the battle site and after a short visit to the gift shop; we were back on the road to Georgia again.

We stopped at the University of Georgia in Athens. At the library, I perused a collection of papers donated by the Gordon family. I could have spent a year there, but I pried myself away after placing an order for copies of some of the documents. One in particular was worth the trip. A love letter to Fanny from John. It was written during one of those rare periods when Fanny Gordon was not with him as he traveled with the Army of Northern Virginia. John was lonely and missed his wife very much. The letter was a long declaration of his love for her and his sons. After reading so many stories about John Gordon the General, Senator and Governor, it was refreshing to see John Gordon the husband. On the last page of the letter at the bottom in the left hand corner, two words in large script stood out, "Big Kiss."

My next stop was the Main Library in Atlanta. In the research section I talked to a lady at the desk. I told her I wanted a copy of a boyhood sketch Gordon had done for Youth Companion Magazine. She could find nothing in her file. I told her that in a book I had read, it stated that this library had the only copy. As we talked, three or four other reference employees gathered nearby. The lady I was talking to told me that the library had been renovated in the early part of the 20th century and what I sought was probably lost. I informed her that the book I referred to was written in 1955. In a flash all of the reference people disappeared like knights-errant in search of the grail. Ten minutes went by, then twenty, then thirty. Forty minutes later, they all returned as quickly as they had departed. The girl I had spoken to originally stood before me with a big grin and an outstretched hand. "Here it is," she said, "If you had come here yesterday, you would have been out of luck. We found it in a room that had been locked for eons and we just got the key for the room this morning." I made copies and started off on the final leg of our journey to Lafayette. My run of luck, if you care to think of it as luck, was not over yet, not by a long shot.

Early in the afternoon, we arrived in Lafayette. I had unpacked what few things I had and went for a walk. I planned to stay one day and then return to Connecticut. While walking in the back yard, my nephew Justin came walking up the driveway, on his way home from school. When he saw me, he yelled, "Hey, Uncle Jeff, have I got the deal of the century for you!" Justin could be a pint-sized con man at times, so I waited for the followup. There was none. I had judged him too quickly. What came out of his mouth next stopped me dead in my tracks. He said, "My class is going on a tour of the Marsh House and Gordon Hall tomorrow. Do you want to go with us?" Bright and early the next morning, I found myself standing in the seventh grade classroom of Mrs. Davis. Justin asked his teacher for permission for me to attend the tour. I told Mrs. Davis I was writing a book and that one of the main characters was John Gordon. I explained that I had many photos with me and would be glad to answer any questions if I could. She said they would be happy to have me come along, but they were not leaving on the tour for about an hour. I told her I would meet them at Gordon Hall.

I drove to Gordon Hall and waited outside. In a short while, a man appeared. He was from the Chamber of Commerce and was there to unlock the building. He unlocked the door and then asked me if I would take charge of the building, because he had to leave. "Sure!" I said. On my first visit I had to settle on peeking in the windows, now I was "In charge" of the building. What a turnabout. I walked inside and looked around. The main room appeared to have a fresh coat of light blue paint. Over the fireplace hung an oil painting of Gen. Gordon. I found a table on which to lay out my collection of photos for the children to view. I walked back outside, where I met a pretty lady from the Woman's Club. She was the one who was giving the tour of Gordon Hall. Now I had been relieved of command; my time of being "In charge" had been short-lived. A little while later, we could see in the distance the entire 7th grade class from Lafayette Middle School marching down Main Street like good little soldiers. The class was quite large, so the teachers divided it into groups. I went with the first group to Marsh House. The Marsh House is owned

by Mr. and Mrs. Clement. Mrs. Clement was our tour guide on
the trip through their beautiful home. In one room she pointed
out a picture of John Gordon and made reference to the fact that
he boarded there while attending school at Gordon Hall.

In the main hallway, I noticed a cannonball mounted on a
plaque. It was sitting on top of a table that was shoved back
under the staircase. I walked over and took a closer look. On the
wooden base there was a brass plate stating that this was a Union
cannonball that had been fired into Petersburg, Virginia, during
the siege. Mr. Clement stood nearby and I matter-of-factly said,
"My great-grandfather, Lewis Knapp, was with the 1st Connecticut Heavy Artillery at Petersburg and may have fired this very
cannonball into the city." There was a deafening silence followed
by a less than enthusiastic two-word reply from Mr. Clement
when he said, "Oh really." I hurried to catch up with the tour
group; safety in numbers I figured.

On the second floor, Mrs. Clement pointed out a pane of
glass in the hall window that still retains a bullet-hole from one
of the battles fought around the house. Many bullets are still
embedded in the exterior of this battle-scarred home. As I moved
down the hall, to an area just outside one of the bedrooms, just
at the bottom of the attic stairs, a strange feeling ran through me.
It was much like the sensations you feel when you sneeze, but
without the sneeze. I wondered if this had been the very room
shared by John and his brother Chapman? I hung back, as the
group descended the staircase to the first floor. I attempted to
linger a moment, but only a moment, keeping in mind that I was
no longer a renter.

The house tour completed, we returned outside and crossed
the lawn to the old schoolhouse. It did not take long to complete our excursion through Gordon Hall. The building consists
mainly of two rooms, an open floor plan with one room over
the other. I watched the children file past the table covered with
Gordon photos and occasionally answered questions about John
and Fanny.

It was now noon and the class sat on the grass eating lunch.

They were scattered about around the gnarled base of a large and very old oak tree. The tree's leafy arms covered a span of sixty feet or more with the schoolchildren beneath intertwined with the shade and sunlight. It truly was an ideal scene for a painter. One of the teachers approached me, to ask if I would talk to the children about General Gordon after they finished their lunches. I asked, "How long would you like me to speak?" She said, "About fifteen minutes." I said, " I can do that." Just then my nephew Justin, who had been listening to the conversation, interrupted with, "Uncle Jeff are you going to tell them about reincar..." I quickly placed my hand over the child's mouth before he could finish the word reincarnation. I said, "I will tell them what I feel they should know, Justin." After all the food had been devoured, I was introduced to the children. I began by telling them about John Gordon's early life with his family on Taylor's Ridge, just outside Lafayette. I spoke about the men from the Raccoon Mountains going off to war and the many battles they fought. They were intrigued by the story of Gordon's five wounds received at Antietam and Mrs. Gordon nursing him back to health. So the young ladies would not feel left out of all the action stories, I told them about Fanny Gordon's near capture at the 3rd Battle of Winchester. When I finished, there was a question and answer period before it became time for them to return to school. Later that day when Justin came home from school, I explained why I had hushed him when I was speaking to the teacher at Gordon Hall. I said, "It was not the proper forum in which to discuss reincarnation." I also reminded him that we were in the "Bible Belt" and that it would not be too pleasant to see his Uncle Jeff hanging from a tree with flammable liquids all over him.

On my return trip home, I planned my route so I would pass through Lynchburg, Virginia. Driving along one of this city's streets, I spotted a sign out of the corner of my eye. It was a large sign attached to an archway connecting two, long red brick walls. Fort Early, the sign read. Parking the car, I grabbed my camera and walked over to the old fort. It was late in the day and the building in the enclosure was closed.

After the Battle of Cold Harbor, Early and his men were being sent to the Shenandoah Valley via Lynchburg. Upon reaching Lynchburg, they found the Union forces under General David Hunter were no more than two miles away. General Hunter was known as Black Dave, because of his liberal use of the torch in the Shenandoah Valley. Private homes, mills, barns and even The Virginia Military Institute in Lexington were set ablaze by Hunter and his men. Fort Early remains as a symbol of the Battle of Lynchburg. Early was not only successful in his defense of the city, but chased Hunter and his men over the mountains and away from the Shenandoah Valley. After taking a few pictures of the fort, I continued my journey in the direction of Petersburg, Virginia. I had not intended to stop there, but just as so many other times on this trip, Mr. Destiny would step in. In Tankersley's book on Gordon, there is a chapter called "Retreat from Petersburg." In this section, he mentions the home of James Pinckney as being the house where Fanny Gordon and the newborn John B. Gordon Jr. were left, when the Confederate Army pulled out. A note at the bottom of the page states, "The house is still standing and located at 17 South Market Street."[54] The book had been written in 1955. I wondered if there was a possibility of the house still being there forty years later? I decided to find out.

I had never been in the city of Petersburg proper, nor had I any maps. I figured I would drive into the City and ask someone for directions. On the interstate, a sign appeared "Petersburg next 5 exits." I randomly picked an exit. At the bottom of the exit ramp something told me to turn left. It was now around 10:30 PM, the streets were dark and almost devoid of life. I figured I was on the right track, because the road I was on appeared to be the dividing line for the northern and southern roads. Driving along, I checked each street sign as it came into view. Suddenly, my brain said **TURN BACK;** so I did. I turned left and left again, in an attempt to backtrack, but at the next stop sign, my journey ended. I sat staring at the street sign that stood before me. The three words written on it reverberated in my head: **South Market**

Street. Driving along, I checked the houses for numbers. The last two houses on the odd numbered side had no numbers on them that I could see. I parked my car and walked down the street to see if I could find the numbers on the last two houses. The house nearest the corner was of preCivil War construction and beautifully maintained. A large wrought iron fence and gate separated it from the sidewalk. There was an air of familiarity about it, but I found myself standing and staring at a parking lot to the left of this house. The parking lot was for a large commercial building on the corner of South Market Street. I walked back up the street to a fire station a block away. Two firefighters were sitting in the dispatch room. I walked in and said, "Could you guys help a brother firefighter?" They said, "Sure, what do you need?" I told them I was trying to find #17 South Market Street, but could not find the numbers on the last house. Neither one of them knew offhand where #17 was. They got out a street directory and looked for it, but there was no #17 listed. The younger of the two men got up and said, "Let's go see if we can find it." We left the firehouse, and as we passed the window to the firefighters' dayroom he yelled inside, "I'll be right back, I'm going down the street." The firefighter explained that over the years the numbering system had changed. We stood once more in front of the house with the wrought iron gate, but still could not see a number anywhere on the house. It was now past 11 o'clock at night and my hopes were fading fast. Something that I had always known was shortly to be reinforced; all firemen are a little crazy. The firefighter said, "I'll find out the number for you." Before I could stop him, he was through the gate and bounding up the large stone steps to the front porch. He rang the doorbell and knocked on the door. A dog started barking inside the previously quiet home. The young man on the porch turned around so the occupant of the house could see the words Petersburg Fire Dept printed on the back of his shirt. The door opened slightly and he talked to the woman inside, all the while pointing to me standing on the sidewalk. The two of them walked down to where I stood. The lady informed me the house was #29. I told her why I sought #17. She said that she had some old papers on the house and knew some general had stayed there, but she was not sure which general it had been. I thanked her and left one of my cards with her, just in case she found mention of General Gordon in her paperwork. The firefighter cheerfully invited the woman to bring her dog to the firehouse and have his picture taken on one of the fire engines (turns out that the dog was a Dalmatian). I talked with the young man for a while and thanked him for all his assistance. Returning to my car, I was on my way home once more. At home, I made a phone call to Mr. Chris M. Calkins, author of many books on the Civil War and a historian at Petersburg Battlefield. He confirmed my fears; the parking lot on South Market Street was indeed the location where #17 previously stood. Mr. Calkins was kind enough to send me a picture of the house taken from an old Petersburg High School yearbook. The yearbook had been dedicated to Petersburg's Civil War history. Contemplating my second journey to Lafayette Georgia and the return trip home, I continue to be amazed at all that took place: King's Mountain, the key episode at the Atlanta Library, touring Gordon Hall and Marsh House. Most remarkable of all was the trip to South Market Street in Petersburg. The wonders never cease. In the dark of night in a strange city of forty-five square miles, I picked one of five exits (the correct one) and drove to the street I was looking for. How had I managed such a feat? If I did not receive any help from without, that only leaves one other possibility—guidance from within.

CHAPTER ELEVEN

Thoughts and Presentiments

IN SEPTEMBER OF 1996 I treated myself to an early birthday present. I drove to Fredericksburg, Virginia, for a two-day walking tour of the Wilderness Battlefield. The tour guides for the event were Professor Gary Gallagher of Pennsylvania State University and Robert K. Krick of Fredericksburg, who is a leading authority on the Army of Northern Virginia. The first morning of the tour found us on the west end of the Wilderness Battlefield in the high winds and heavy rains of hurricane Fran. The two buses we traveled in would stop at predetermined points of interest and undauntedly, we would disembark and traipse through the rain-drenched woodlands. One stop took us to the area of Gordon's flank attack of May 6th, 1864. It felt strange to hear two highly respected historians banter back and forth about General Gordon on the very spot of one of the high points of his military career. The group emerged from the woods into a large open area known as Saunders Field. We attempted to seek cover under a three-sided shelter near the roadway. The shelter was just short of sufficient size to contain the huddled mass of time travelers. Just outside the enclosure stood Mr. Krick, attempting to shield his papers from the incessant rain. He related stories of what had transpired in Saunder's Field during the two-day battle. As the wind gained in intensity, Mr. Krick's voice escalated in volume. In a short time, he was to the point of shouting. He lead into one story by saying, "All of you are probably familiar with General George Patton's idiosyncrasy or insanity, depending on how you look at it, regarding his belief in reincarnation." My ears perked up. What followed was a story from the book, *The Pattons*, and the setting was the very field in which we stood. The story goes like this: General Patton was touring the Wilderness Battlefield along with his wife and two children. With them this day was a German military attaché, General Friedrich Von Boetticher.

Von Boetticher was a Civil War buff. Patton described the troop deployment, and the sway of the battle back and forth across Saunder's Field. He placed his two children as Confederate units and his wife (being a Yankee) as the Union line. Patton stood on a nearby rise where he declared General Jubal Early had directed the battle. Von Boetticher disagreed with Patton and a loud argument followed. An old man that had been with a tour group overheard the conversation and approached the two men. "The other gentleman is right," he told Von Boetticher. "General Early was on that rise. I was at this battle as a boy." George was pleased. He'd had a feeling he'd been there before; now it was confirmed. "Of course Early stood there," he declared in triumph. "I saw it myself!"[55] I had to chuckle as we boarded the bus.

I am fortunate in that my job schedule affords me the time to travel. Retracing the battles of the Army of Northern Virginia has taken me to many places where history has left its mark— places with mysterious names like the White Oak swamp, Massanutten Mountain or Opequon Church. I have crossed the Rappahannock, Monocacy, Rapidan and Susquehanna rivers; I have traveled over beautiful mountains such as the Blue Ridge and into enchanting valleys like the Shenandoah. These places stood as midwives to the birth of our nation, a birth wracked with pain and suffering. Who was right and who was wrong is still in dispute. Many continue to argue the cause of it all. I feel that if these blessed grounds were given voice, they would all say the same thing. The message would be short: never again the bloodshed or sorrow: learn, grow and move on. The past is filled with lessons from which we should learn. To discount these events, we run the hazard of repetition. I have reached out and touched history, and it has touched me back, both as a spectator and as a participant. I feel as if an unseen hand has come out of the past and guided me, much like a chess piece being moved from square to square. We all need to stop for a moment and listen to the world around us, and in us. Don't just listen with your ears, but use your heart as well. Open your mind and bring all your senses into play. With a little practice and patience you may be rewarded by the gifts that come your way. You may find something; a something that has been talked about, denied, debated and ignored by many peoples for countless years. That something is a soul, your soul. After you have found it, keep in mind what Thomas Jefferson said: "The care of every man's soul belongs to himself." Another brilliant man, Plato, was right on the money centuries ago. Plato's contention was that the soul exists in its own right, that it not only survives the body, but preexists it as well. Moreover, Plato declared that the soul, not the body, forms the real or true person.

No one can make you believe in the soul's existence; it comes with a Knowing. Pause for a moment and contemplate what the world would be like if reincarnation were proven to be a fact of life. How would we then treat others? When dealing with family, friends or acquaintances, we would need to ask ourselves some questions like: Who are these souls? What is their relationship to me? Am I to learn something from them, or am I to be the Teacher? The possibilities are endless. We all live in the same house and that house grows smaller every day. This planet has become the "Global Village." No longer does it take the written word to tell of events on the other side of the earth. With the flick of a switch, we can sit and watch as events unfold. Every country affects all the others with their finances, pollution problems and their petty hostilities. Now more than ever everyone needs to change his or her way of thinking: no more **I**, but **US**— no more **THEM**, but **WE**. We leave our mark on ourselves and those around us; so let us strive to use a gentle touch.

I long for a return to old values and virtues. Things like honor, courage and moral fortitude. I am not speaking of a soldier's life, for in my ideal world there would be no need of soldiers. The most heroic battles are not fought on the battlefield, but in everyday life. We are here to learn through experience and to put those experiences to work for us. Many times our greatest strides forward come after we muddle our way through some of life's difficulties. There are no free rides. For many years, I thought it ironic that we go through life gathering information, and when we are able to understand much of what these life lessons have taught us, we die and the knowledge is lost. I see now this is not the case. The experiences of this lifetime have brought me to the conclusion that we are both the archer and the target, the deceased and the heir. People worry about the legacy we are leaving our children and grandchildren. What kind of world should we leave them as their inheritance? It should be a world that we would enjoy living in, for it might just come to pass. The purpose of my writing this book was to get people to think, to start them on a path of self-discovery and assist them in finding their true identity. Hopefully they will notice in others not just their differences, but their sameness, and maybe some day their oneness.

Strange things continue to happen to me in the month of September. On my last birthday (49th), I sat reading in my back yard. Anna joined me and pointed out a lone monarch butterfly sitting in the grass, about six feet from where I sat. I held out my left hand, palm up, and continued reading. The butterfly flew straight to me and perched on my open hand. This beautiful creature stayed there for about five minutes, slowly moving its brightly colored wings up and down. I found this visitation much more pleasant than the trip to the hospital on my 30th birthday.

Parallels also continue to appear. In Tankersley's book, he mentions Congressman Elihu Washburne attending the formal surrender formalities at Appomattox Court House on April 12, 1865. After the surrender, many Confederates soldiers stood around rather dejected. A crowd gathered around General Gordon to bid him farewell. In a short time, what started out as a small group grew to several thousand. Gordon mounted his horse and addressed the throng that now included Federal soldiers, along with Congressman Washburne. Tankersley writes, "In conclusion, he advised them to go home in peace, to obey the laws, and to rebuild and work for the future of a reunited nation."[56] The Congressman personally congratulated Gordon on his speech and the spirit of reconciliation it expressed. In May of 1996, I gave a short speech during a memorial service for four fallen brother firefighters who died in the line of duty in 1946. The service was held in a local church with a reception afterward in the church courtyard. A gentleman sought me out to tell me how much he liked my speech and to request a written copy. I mailed a copy to his office and received a letter in return. The last two lines read: "As I told you before, your statement was right on target, and particularly moving and inspiring." The letter was signed Christopher Shays, Member of Congress, 4th District Connecticut.

Recently, I reread a chapter in General Gordon's *Reminiscences of the Civil War*, a chapter devoted to stories of "presentiments." These tales of prophetic foresight or premonitions were not uncommon during the Civil War. Gordon heard many such stories from other officers both North and South. Gordon witnessed a number for himself. He tells one about his friend, Colonel Tennant Lomax. Approaching Gordon just before riding into battle, Lomax stopped and extended his hand to Gordon saying, "Give me your hand, Gordon, and let me bid you good-by. I am going to be killed in this battle. I shall be dead in a half an hour." Gordon writes,

> "I endeavored to remove this impression from his mind, but nothing I could say changed or appeared to modify it in any degree. I was grieved to have him go into the fight with such a burden upon him, but there was no tremor in his voice, no hesitation in his words, no doubt on his mind. The genial smile that made his face so attractive was still upon it, but he insisted that he would be dead in half an hour, and that it was 'all right.' The half-hour had scarcely passed when the fatal bullet had numbered him with the dead."[57]

Gordon tells of his younger brother Augustus Gordon,

"A youth of scarcely twenty-one years, he was in command of the Sixth Regiment of Alabama. Before going into the fight in the Wilderness, he quietly said: 'My hour has come.' I joked and chided him. I told him that he must not permit such impressions to affect or take hold upon his imagination. He quickly and firmly replied: 'You need not doubt me. I will be at my post. But this is our last meeting.' Riding at the head of his regiment, with his sword above him, the fire of battle in his eyes and words of cheer for his men on his lips, the fatal grape-shot plunged through his manly heart, and the noble youth slept his last sleep in that woeful Wilderness."[58]

Finishing up the chapter Gordon ponders:

It would require a volume simply to record without comment the hundreds of such presentiments in both the Union and Confederate armies during the war. The few here noted will suffice, however, to raise the inquiry as to what they meant.... They were perceptions. There was about them no element of speculation. Their conspicuous characteristic was certainty. The knowledge seemed so firmly fixed that no argument as to possible mistake, no persuasion, could shake it. Where did that knowledge come from? It seems to me there can be but one answer, and that answer is another argument for immortality. It was the whispering of the Infinite beyond us to the Infinite within us—a whispering inaudible to the natural ear, but louder than the roar of battle to the spirit that heard it.[59]

Reading this, I sat nodding my head in affirmation. From my present vantage point, I could look back and say, "Yes John, you were right"—we are immortal, timeless, ageless spirits. All that I have seen, heard and felt confirmed it. Sometime in the future, would I find myself once again reading books that I had written under different names, answering questions then posed? I smiled as I closed the book and laid it aside.

I sat looking at the pictures and memorabilia gathered from my many trips through the South, names flashed before me, Antietam, Petersburg, Spotsylvania. Places with peculiar names like: The Mule Shoe and Bloody Lane. My gaze came to rest on a tiny picture at the bottom center of one of the wooden frames.

It's a photo of a cold gray stone, a tombstone with letters and numbers carved into it nearly a century ago. "John B. Gordon" it reads. My eyes moved to the second date under John's name, the date of his death, January 9, 1904. As I looked at this date two words came to mind: **Not Yet,** followed closely by two more, **Not Ever**.

Author at gravesite of John B. Gordon

General John B. Gordon Monument at Capitol, Atlanta, Georgia

Photo first viewed by author in magazine
(Valentine Richmond History Center)

Old broadside from author's collection

John B. Gordon and Frances (Fanny) Haralson Gordon

Photo from front Page of Connecticut Post, *June 17, 1994*

*Author (in white) at work during a structure fire
caused by a propane gas explosion*

Wilkeson's guns at Barlow's Knoll

General Gordon raising up General Barlow on the battle-field
from *Blood Is Thicker Than Water* by Henry M. Field (1886)

Wrightsville, Pennsylvania, bridge razed by Union soldiers to prevent Gordon's troops from crossing

Graves of Whitlocks wounded at Barlow's Knoll on July 1, 1863 (Joeseph mortally)

Photo by Michael Warner

BRADY,   WASHINGTON, D. C.

Brady cabinet photo of Gordon from author's collection

Photo by Michael Warner

*Gordon family plot,
Oakland Cemetery, Georgia*

*Gordon Hall,
Lafayette, Georgia*

John B. Gordon   Jeffrey J. Keene

Sutherland House, General Gordon's home at Kirkwood, near Atlanta

Gordon statue on the capitol grounds, Atlanta, Georgia

PART II

CHAPTER TWELVE

A Return to the South

I STARTED WRITING MY BOOK (although I was not aware of it at the time) in long-hand in 1992. Since the completion of the first portion of the book, many things have happened. My girls have finished college. Shannon graduated from Dickinson College and continued on to graduate from Boston College Law School. Samantha received her degree in business at Keene State in Keene, New Hampshire (I used to kid Samantha about her choice of Keene State by saying, "I guess if you get drunk you will always remember the name of the town you live in and the school you attend"). Anna quit her job and went back to school at the Culinary Institute of America in Hyde Park, New York and I have gained weight.

In July of 1998 I sat in front of a new computer in my office at work, a "babe in the woods" of the electronic age. I decided to try a search on the Internet. With my usual two-fingered style, I typed in the word REINCARNATION and came up with 49,000 hits. Because I was writing a book, I picked a website that mentioned a book on reincarnation. The story at this website was not very interesting. Before leaving that site I spotted a reference to another site dealing with a documentary on reincarnation. One click of the mouse and I was there: "IN ANOTHER LIFE: How Americans Approach Reincarnation" read the title. The website talked about a documentary-inprogress and "exploring current attitudes towards reincarnation in the United States." Two things struck me in the first paragraph. One was the mention of interviews with people "who have had direct and verifiable experiences relating to reincarnation." The other was the location of the production company, Atlanta, Georgia. I caught myself thinking out loud, "Boy are they in a great place for a Gordon story." Anyone caring to contribute to this project was asked to contact Steve Sakellarios at Gold Thread Video Productions. On July 4th, 1998, I called and left a message on Steve's phone giving him the "Readers Digest" version of my story and asking him for his mailing address so I might send him some information. Even though it was a holiday (and a Saturday), two hours later I received a return phone call. Steve was very enthusiastic about my story and I sent him the first few chapters of my book along with some newspaper clippings. A week later I received a letter from Steve saying he was definitely interested in including my story in his documentary. He made the suggestion in his letter that he fly to Connecticut to film an interview with me. I think I surprised Steve when I called him and offered to fly down to Georgia for the interview. This would give me a chance to visit Gordon's grave once again and afford Steve a better photographic backdrop for the interviews.

On August 4, 1998 Anna and I flew to Atlanta, Georgia. I called Steve to set up the schedule for the next four days. The following morning I drove to Steve's office. It was nice to finally put a face to the voice on the phone. We used Steve's car to drive to Oakland Cemetery and parked a short distance from Gen. Gordon's grave. I walked over to the gravesite while Steve unloaded his video equipment from the car. It looked like nature was going to supply us with perfect weather for filming. Steve checked out the location and he then placed me in a squatting position just downhill and slightly to the left of Gordon's headstone. Steve wanted to film me with Gordon's grave visible over my left shoulder. Steve made a few adjustments to the camera, did a sound check, and we were ready to film. I did a reprise of my experience at Antietam, the Halloween party, and some of the

discoveries that followed. Things were moving along fine until
one of the groundskeepers started up a leaf blower. Steve stopped
filming and went over to the man. They talked for a while, then
the man kindly moved off to a distant part of the cemetery. Steve
returned and we started the whole process all over again. When
Steve was satisfied with the end product, we moved to the site of
the Gordon family plot. Steve filmed as we walked and I retold
the story of my mother and I finding the family plot on our
first visit to this cemetery. With filming completed, we walked
back towards the car. I noticed some women moving among the
graves picking up sticks and other debris. I approached a woman
standing in the roadway not that far from Gordon's grave. She
appeared to be the leader of this group of feminine caretakers. I
said, "Hello, are you ladies members of the United Daughters of
the Confederacy?" My assumption was correct and I asked if they
were the ones responsible for the cleanliness of General Gordon's
grave. The woman said, "Why, yes; he was a fine gentleman." I
thanked her for the fine job they were doing. She said, "We're
glad to do it." As I turned to walk away, a curious look came over
her face. Afterward, I wondered what this woman would have
thought had she known that she had been talking to an Oakland
Cemetery resident.

Steve had arranged two separate psychic readings for me. The
first was with numerologist Michael Ferniany. We met Michael
at his condominium. After introductions, I was shown to a couch
while Michael sat down in a chair nearby. Steve started filming
from across the room. For the second time in two days Steve's
filming was interrupted, this time by a noisy pet bird. Michael
got up, covered his bird, and once again there was quiet. Michael
had been given only my name, birth date, and where I was born.
Themes of authority, leadership, and responsibility came up
repeatedly. Most of the reading appeared to have been about my
present life. I could see Steve was becoming a little "down in the
mouth." I know he was hoping for some mention of the American Civil War, Georgia, or any hint of a past life as a military figure. As the session was coming to a close, I asked Michael about

past lives and their effects on my present life. He reaffirmed the leadership theme and followed it by saying, "You have had great responsibility; in past lifetimes, you were like a general." With the mention of the word "General," I could see a big, wide, grin appear on Steve's face.

The reading Michael did for me that night was very much on an intellectual level. The next reading was strictly on a more emotional level, like a punch to the heart.

The second appointment Steve arranged was with clairvoyant Candace Zellner. Once again the only information given was my name and birthday. Steve wrote about my session with Candice on his website and I will quote his observations.

> In Candace's reading, the first thing out of her mouth after her opening prayer, was to describe images of Jeff as a soldier, including a general or an officer with great responsibility ... but most of this appeared not to relate to John Gordon, but to Jeff's most recent past life as a British special forces officer. Jeff has had two other psychics (also without any pre-knowledge) describe this latter lifetime, and he wrote about it in the manuscript of his book, which I had already read. So, as she was giving this material, I could see that it closely paralleled his manuscript.[60]

I sat in a chair next to Candace. With her eyes closed, Candace asked out loud to see my last three lifetimes. There was a pause and then she said, "Immediately Jeff, let me tell you something; I see you on a battlefield, in a war, and I'm trying to see what war it is. This is in another country. You're either in France or Germany, and boy, do I feel it's France. You are in charge here leading this group of men." Candace continued, "You carry such a sense of responsibility for these men in this lifetime that I would think that it would be overwhelming to you and that you would still carry that trait more than normal in this lifetime." During the reading Candace mentioned, "Black men speaking French." She said, " I kept feeling something French. I don't understand this, I want to say French black men, it's the weirdest thing." All this would fit in well with the fusilier's lifetime. In North Africa,

especially in the French Algiers area, you would have no problem
finding black men speaking French. A little later on Candace got
right to the heart of the matter, literally. She said, "You're so
concerned about these men it just puts a lot of pressure on you.
You know what, Jeff? This is so interesting. You're not fearing
the battle; oh, this is going to make me cry." I said, " I know
what you are going to say." Candace continued and what followed took both of us on an emotional sled ride, downhill fast.
She said, "You're fearing the loss. You're leading these men into
battle and you're just praying, 'Dear God, dear God, don't let
anything happen to these men'; you don't care about the gunfire,
you don't care about the hand grenades, you don't care about the
bombs, you don't care about any of it. All you care about is the
connection and responsibility you have for these men. I see you
going forward with this burden on you. I can't see what happens
after that, I don't know what happens. It's just like it lifted; it's
just like all that pain just lifted. There was such pain and grief
and so much responsibility you carried." By this time both our
faces were quite wet. She saw the soldier surviving this battle and
being decorated for his actions.

One of the highlights of my trip to Georgia was meeting Steve
Smith. Steve Sakellarios had been doing his research on reincarnation and wanted to contact Patricia Hayes (author of The Gate-
keepers), at Delphi University. A young man named Steve Smith
had answered his repeated phone calls. After a few unsuccessful
attempts to reach Ms. Hayes, the two Steve's started conversing,
and in their conversation my case was mentioned. When Steve
Smith heard that I believed I had been Confederate General John
B. Gordon, his immediate response was, "Oh, Gordon was my
great-great uncle!" It was arranged for Steve Smith and I to meet
at the Atlanta Capitol building. Steve Sakellarios introduced us
and told us not to pay any attention to him, that he would just be
a "fly on the wall." Steve filmed us getting to know one another
in front of Gordon's equestrian statue on the northwest corner
of the Capital grounds. Later he filmed us under a painting of
Governor John Gordon that hangs inside the Capitol building. At

first, Steve Smith seemed a little standoffish; but, after our two-hour talk, he appeared to be convinced of my sincerity. We had fun trading family stories and sharing the information we both had gathered, he from family, I from my life (and past life) experiences. I asked Steve what he thought when he heard my story of reincarnation involving Gen. Gordon. Steve said, "It was a first for me, I almost dropped the phone and my teeth dropped out." I asked, "Do you think it was a coincidence that Steve Sakellarios called you?" His reply was, "No, it was supposed to happen, there's a reason for it." He asked what my experiences had taught me. I told him about the deep soul-searching and that it has been a wondrous journey with few dull moments. I told him, "I've learned that the earth is a schoolroom, sometimes we are the students, while at other times, the teacher. I've found that the "*meaning of life*" is the *experiencing of life* itself. I got a warm feeling inside when Steve Smith said to me, "I consider this a unique honor to know of my relatives and to get to meet you in your search and discovery."

The three of us moved across the street to the First Presbyterian Church; the same church where John B. Gordon's funeral had been held in 1904. As we walked into the old sanctuary, Steve Sakellarios asked me if I felt anything. I said, "Yes, just before we walked in here my heart started beating like a bass drum." It had first started when we entered the church by way of a newer addition, one that had been added long after Gordon's death. We entered the vestibule from the left side. As I stood in the center of the foyer, looking down the steps that led to the street, my heart started beating faster. The beating built in intensity until it felt as though I was being punched in the chest, but from the inside. This pounding stayed with me during our tour of the church and continued until we were back out on the street. We wandered back across the street to the grounds of the Capitol building. Steve Smith told me he had never read General Gordon's book. Before we parted, I took down his address and later sent him a copy of Reminiscences of the Civil War. I inscribed the book, "To Steve Smith, from your Uncle?" I hope he gets a chuckle every time he reads it.

I received no monetary compensation for the filming for the documentary *In Another Life*; just a promise from Steve Sakellarios that he would feature my story on his web site. Steve kept his promise and a short time later, not only my story, but also pictures and film clips became a permanent fixture on his web site. Steve was planning a trip to Philadelphia to interview Carol Bowman, author of *Children's Past Lives* and *Returned from Heaven.* These two books deal with the past lives of children and relatives reincarnated within the same family. After hearing of his plans, I suggested he hold off on his trip until September, 1998 when I would be at Sharpsburg, Maryland for a two-day walking tour of Antietam battlefield. This would allow him to "kill two birds with one stone," interview Carol Bowman and film some footage of me at the Sunken Road. Some strange things happened during Steve's trip, but I will let him tell it in his own words:

Steve Sakellarios wrote the following. It was taken from the update section (dated 9/13/98) on his **In Another Life** web site (www.ial.goldthread.com):

> Carolyn and Steve Bowman were very gracious, down-to-earth hosts. Steve and I talked website construction, and Carol was patient with the technical set up and handled the interview expertly. Afterwards I was invited to a late breakfast with her son Chase, now in high school (it was Chase, as a young boy, who started it all with his memory of being a black Civil War soldier killed on the battlefield), and some of his friends.
>
> Then I drove to Sharpsburg to meet with Jeff Keene at Antietam Battlefield Park. While there, I had two fascinating coincidences (although Jeff insists there is no such thing as a "coincidence").
>
> Having taped Carol Bowman just the day before talking about children recalling their past lives, I was in the dimly lit Antietam Battlefield museum trying to capture a shot of a sword handle, when I heard a little boy behind me on the stairs leading to the room exclaim, "I know that man!" He was referring to a photo of John A. Thompkins, about 24 feet in front of him (I paced it off later). His mother and father didn't take it seriously. But as he came running up to the photo next to me, I asked him, "Who is it?" He answered, "It's John." Then I asked him, trying to keep the ques-

tion vague and nonleading, "What did he do?" The boy answered, "He killed the bad people." This was all he had to say about it, but he had been very definite about these two statements. His mother told me that at age 5, he doesn't read yet, or at best he only reads very simple words. His father simply shook his head and said quietly, "He wouldn't have been able to read that."

Before going on this trip, my mother had told me I had an ancestor, Fidello Biddle, who had fought at Antietam. I happened to be talking about it with Jeff in the parking lot. Now, Jeff was with a Civil War group. Two members of the tour were walking by, a younger man and older one, and when I said "Fidello Biddle," they stopped frozen in their tracks and stared at me! To make a long story short, they were my relatives—Joe Biddle Sr. and Joe Biddle Jr.; Joe Sr. is my mom's cousin—his parents (as my mom told me afterward when I called her) were her favorite aunt and uncle whom she often visited as a child.

Just think of the odds that I would happen to speak Fidello Biddle's name out loud at exactly the moment when these two men were within earshot. Given that I didn't interact much with the tour, it's unlikely that I would have seen the name tags and made the connection otherwise, and they certainly wouldn't have known who I was.[61]*

I kidded with Steve about his experiences. I said, "Here you are in Maryland, a long way from Georgia, you mentioned a Civil War ancestor's name in the middle of a parking lot, and the only two people within range of hearing are relatives of yours. You interview Carol Bowman, who deals with children's past lives and then you run into a little five-year-old boy who, in a past life, had been friends with a Union Lt. Col. whose picture you just happened to be standing next to. Coincidence, right?"

Having my story on Steve's web site began to pay off in ways I had not expected. I thought the exposure might help to get my book published. On August 9th, 1999, Steve Sakellarios emailed me saying, " A representative of Arts and Entertainment has contacted me asking for contacts for a segment they are doing on reincarnation." Steve said they were interested in getting in touch

---

*   It was later discovered that Fidello Biddle became ill and did not actually participate in the Battle of Antietam.

with me, but he did not want to give them my e-mail address without my permission. I gave Steve the okay to give them my telephone number and e-mail address. The very same day I received an e-mail from Actuality Productions with information regarding the documentary. The e-mail stated: We are making a two-hour A&E special which will take a balanced, academic look at the concepts and beliefs regarding the afterlife. It is still in the development process, but right now we are planning to explore near-death experiences (positive and negative), after-death communications/dreams, reincarnation, ghosts, mediums, etc. What followed was an impressive list of doctors and professors from all around the United States. After many rounds of correspondence and signing release forms, a date was set for filming my segment of the program. The filming was done on September first and second of 1999. They filmed an interview at my home, and then the crew followed me to work at the firehouse during one of my night shifts. They did some filming in my office, on the apparatus floor, and even interviewed some of the firefighters. I knew ahead of time that they would be speaking to some of the people I worked with. I did not know what questions they would be asked; the only thing I could tell them beforehand was to answer honestly. With the filming completed, the crew disappeared, leaving me to wonder what the finished product would look like. The production company continued to e-mail me with many questions such as, "Are you aware of any famous people who believed in reincarnation?" My reply follows:

Maybe you should put me on the payroll? In the book *Reincarnation the Second Chance*,[62] there are many famous people mentioned as professing a belief in or leaning toward the theory of reincarnation. I list a few: Spinoza, Voltaire, Ben Franklin, Beethoven, Kant, Goethe, George Santayana, William Blake, William Wordsworth, Napoleon, Schopenhauer, Shelley, Balzac, Victor Hugo, Ralph Waldo Emerson, John Greenleaf Whittier, Poe, Wagner, Thoreau, Gustav Flaubert, Leo Tolstoy, Gustav Mahler, Rudolph Steiner, Henry Ford, H. G. Wells, Kipling, William Butler Yeats, Jack London, James Joyce, Henry Miller, Salvador Dali....

In another book, *Reincarnation, the Phoenix Fire Mystery*, some of the same people show up plus others like, John Milton, Henry More, Frederick the Great, Sir Walter Scott, George Sand (reborn as Taylor Caldwell), Walt Whitman, Elizabeth and Robert Browning, Louisa May (and her father Bronson) Alcott, Emily Dickinson.... Seems I am in pretty good company.

I leave you with this: *"Love is a thing to be learned, through centuries of patient effort."* —D. H. Lawrence

The documentary "Beyond Death" aired for the first time on April 30th, 2000. I was pleasantly surprised by how well the program had been done. My segment followed Carol Bowman's on children's past lives. They used a good bit of footage that had been filmed by Steve Sakellarios at Oakland Cemetery in Georgia and the Sunken Road in Sharpsburg, Maryland. Along with the narration and my interview they used some file footage of a palm reader at a Halloween party. I worked at the firehouse the night of April 30th and the guys got a kick out of seeing their fire station and apparatus on TV. I was also pleasantly surprised at the interviews with two of the firefighters that I had worked with for over 20 years. Firefighter Denis Duffy said, "At first we kidded about it saying, Oh here comes General Gordon and stuff like that." He finished by saying, "Then it started to be believable." Lt. Gene Maloney, when asked what he thought of my story said, "The way he is, his actions, his words, the way he treats people, in a way it's out of another time. That's what adds to the plausibility of his story."

I much admire the work Carol Bowman has done over the years in the field of reincarnation. Of the two books she has written, the one I enjoyed the most was *Return from Heaven: Beloved Relatives Reincarnated within Your Family.* The reason for this is that she delves into the intricate workings of reincarnation. Every case that she presents gives us insight into some of the reasons why we return time and time again. Carol and I have much in common. We both are referred to in Steve Sakellerios's website, "In Another Life." Carol's story was the segment just before mine on the A&E documentary, "Beyond Death." Last, and most importantly, is that we are attempting (and I hope succeeding) to bring the realization of reincarnation to the masses. Though in Carol's work she focuses on cases involving children, adults are also drawn into the dance of life.

In Carol's first book, *Children's Past Lives*, she showed us signposts to use as a guide when a child is attempting to communicate to us events from a past life. I will list them for you.

- Matter-of-fact Tone
- Consistency of Detail
- Knowledge beyond Experience
- Memory of Death
- Behavior and Phobias
- The Age Window [usually between the ages of 2 and 7]

The last one, The Age Window, is what you could call the closing of act one. It is when the veil or curtain between here and the other side thickens, and the child's thoughts and memories begin to reside more here, in the present. I've seen, and heard, of that veil being pierced, many times. Remember the little boy in the bookstore who blurted out "Samurai"? What about Steve's encounter in the battlefield museum with a young man who recognized the picture of his friend the Colonel? These episodes were spontaneous, but they can be brought to the surface by a little stealth and cunning. I offer to you the following with the suggestion that you try it for yourself. Be advised though; use the technique sparingly and at the appropriate time. If your timing is off, wait for another time. If your timing is right, you may be very surprised at the outcome. The old saying is true, "Out of the mouths of babes ofttimes come gems."

One day, as I sat by myself watching television, one of Anna's granddaughters came in from outside. At the time she was approaching the ripe old age of 5. She had been sent inside to fetch her shoes. Finding her shoes, she picked them up and ran outside. As happens often these days, there was nothing much on television worth watching. I decided to go out and get some fresh air. I came across the aforementioned child attempting to put on her shoes. She was not having much success. It seems that there is a phenomenon common among children; they pull their shoes off without untying them and then strain to shove their feet back into them. She asked me for help in putting on her shoes. I said, "Do you know how to tie your shoes"? She said she did not, so I told her to sit on the stairs and I would tie them for her. I took the opportunity to try something. I untied the shoes, knelt down in front of her and pushed her feet into them one at a time. While I did so, I said, "Did you know how to tie your shoes when you used to be big"? She stared off into the distance. I was delighted to discover just how far she was seeing. She said, "Yes, they were white shoes" and then leaned over and pointed to an area on her leg about three or four inches above one ankle. She said, "They were different, they came up to here." She continued by explaining how the shoes were fastened from the bottom all away up to the top. As she spoke, I had no trouble at all envisioning a young lady from the Victorian era struggling with a buttonhook while putting on her high-top shoes. She paused for a moment, and once more stared off into space. Suddenly the little girl before me returned. Abruptly, and a bit gruffly, she said, "I don't want to talk about it any more." The spell had been broken. Off she ran like a modern-day Alice hot on the trail of the white rabbit.

While on the subject of children, I watched a story on the television program, *Sightings*, about an amazing young man; his name is Doron Blake. As a newborn, Doron could mark time to classical music with his hands. By age 2, he was using a computer. By kindergarten, he was reading *Hamlet* and learning algebra. At age 6, his IQ measured over 180. (The test was unfinished because Doron was "bored with it.") Also, at age six, Doron typed out the original draft of his book about a dinosaur named George.63 At ten he edited and put the book on computer. This delightful children's story was published in March of 1994. Doron qualified for a Los Angeles school for the gifted and followed that up by winning a full scholarship to Phillips Exeter in New Hampshire, one of the nation's best high schools. Doron is a product of the Repository for Germinal Choice, an institution founded in Southern California in 1980 and better remembered

as the "Genius Sperm Bank." Mr. Blake's father was known only
as Batch 28 to his mother, Afton. As the first boy born of this
Sperm Bank, he has appeared on numerous television shows such
as *48 Hours, Inside Edition, Hard Copy, Donahue, The Other Side*
and the previously mentioned *Sightings*.

What I found most remarkable about this boy were his tales
of reincarnation. At three years old, he said to his mother, "Do
you remembered the time you and I lived in California? We lived
in huts made of wood, but that time I was your wife." He remembers two lifetimes in Afghanistan, a lifetime in Egypt as a healer,
and being in William Shakespeare's actors' guild. Doron does
not put a lot of stock in genes. He believes much of his knowledge and intellect springs from these past life experiences. He
expressed a desire to some day write a book that will explore the
connection between intelligence and reincarnation.

Arts & Entertainment's "Beyond Death" had some wonderful
aftereffects. A man from Canada contacted me. When he saw me
on the television set, he kept telling his daughter, "I know that
man, I know that man." He was so unnerved by seeing me in the
program and hearing the retelling of the Battle of the Sunken
Road that he paced the floor most of the night. He felt impelled
to get in touch with me. He called the Westport Fire Department and spoke to a secretary. The secretaries are not allowed to
give out employees' home phone numbers, so she took his phone
number and told him I would get the message that he wanted
to speak to me. I wrote down the number and then placed the
long distance call to Canada. The man on the other end of the
phone thanked me for calling him back and proceeded to tell
me a most amazing story. He believes he had been a 16-year-old
Confederate soldier, one of Gordon's men that had been killed at
the Sunken Road. He has had many memories come to him in
dreams. He said at that time Gen. Gordon called him "Sonny"
and that he would often send the young man on errands. Then
he even gave me what he thought was the proper name of this
soldier, John Allen Cutler. The gentleman spoke with an unusual
rhythm to his speech. I asked if he was a native, meaning a native

of Canada. He said, "Yes" and started talking about the Man-
itoba area of Canada. As he talked, it dawned on me from the
way he was speaking and the subject matter he was covering that
he was a Native American. He paused long enough for me to
ask him if he was Inuit.[64] The Inuit people are big believers in
reincarnation. I have read many stories about Inuit men telling
their families, just before dying, that they would be reborn into
their own families as a grandson or great-grandson. When the
newborns arrived, sure enough, they bore birthmarks or scars
that corresponded to wounds that the dear departed had suffered
during his lifetime. It turns out the man on the phone was half
Cree Indian. We talked for quite a while. He had never been to
the Antietam Battlefield and did not have much information on
the battle. I sent him a few website addresses on the battle and a
copy of Gordon's *Reminiscences of the Civil War*. After doing a little
research in the roster for the Sixth Alabama Regiment, I came
across a close name match. The name was Cutner (CUTNER—
Private, Company?, 6th Alabama Infantry Regiment. Adjutant).
No first name, but with the mention of the job title "Adjutant"
a little more credence was added to the find. There is no doubt
that during the Civil War adjutants ran errands. Could this man
in Canada have been a one-time member of the Sixth Alabama
Regiment, indeed, possibly one of Gordon's "Raccoon Roughs"?
With no way of proving or disproving his story, I was left to ponder the question; had I spoken to "One of the Boys"? I hope so.

In early May of 2000, I checked my mailbox at work to find
an envelope postmarked Memphis, Tenn. I found it strange that
it had reached me at all. Under my name was simply "Assistant
Chief, Fire Department, Westport, CT. No street address or ZIP
code. I read the enclosed letter. It was from a woman who had
been born in Little Rock, Arkansas, and raised in Germantown,
Tennessee. She had watched "Beyond Death" and caught the segment about my experiences with reincarnation. She wanted to
give me a little history concerning General John Gordon. The
information contained within gave me her family's lineage back
to her grandmother's mother whom, she stated, was a daughter of

John B. Gordon. She finished with; "Do any of these names ring a bell? Maybe in your family background there's a connection. I would appreciate hearing from you." (Small aside: some people believe there is the possibility of some type of genetic memory.) The last page of the letter bore a telephone number and e-mail address. At the first opportunity I phoned and explained that from all the research that I had done, I could not find any connection through my family tree to General Gordon's. I said, "From what you wrote in your letter it would appear that you are one of John Gordon's great great-granddaughters. Do you know which one of his daughters was your great-grandmother?" She was not sure of her name, but knew she had passed away when her grandmother was three months old. From this information I could tell there was only one answer to my question. Her great-grandmother had to have been Carolyn Gordon. I knew this because Gordon only had two daughters that survived to marriage age. His daughter Francis Gordon was still alive long after the birth of this woman's maternal grandmother. We talked for a while, but before hanging up she surprised me by asking for my home mailing address. A short time later I received a letter from her. She opened with, "Dear, (How do I address you 'Grandfather')." This tickled me somewhat coming from a woman nearing the 80-year mark. She had enclosed a picture of her grandmother, John Gordon's granddaughter. The picture was approximately 3 by 5, black and white; with a woman standing next to a large flowerpot. She appeared to be around 40 years old. There seemed to be a sadness about her. After reading further on in the letter, I learned what may have brought about this unhappy facade. At the age of 13, she and the boy next door ran away from home and married. All this was done in an attempt to get away from her stepmother who had been very unkind to her. The letter also revealed that John Gordon had been mentioned twice in the original *Gone with the Wind*, a fact that I was not aware of. I did not know it at the time, but this little tidbit would come in handy a little farther down the road, when I would meet the author of the book. The letter closed with "Always glad to hear from you. Love, Bettye." There was a P.S. "Sure hope you can read this." She had added this little note because she is legally blind and thinks her writing is not too legible. Little does she know that her handwriting is better than mine. I make it a point to use large type in my correspondence to her. I have enjoyed my phone conversations with Bettye. Though 25 years her junior, I guess it's okay for me to call her by her first name, after all, she calls me grandfather.

One night at work the dispatcher paged me saying I had a long distance call. I took the call in my office. The woman on the other end of the line introduced herself. I told her that her name sounded familiar to me. She told me she had seen the A&E program "Beyond Death" and that her family are descendants of John B. Gordon. She was calling from Chickamauga, Georgia. She said it was not too far from Lafayette. She got a kick out of it when I told her, "My mother and sister live in Lafayette." I told her how I had visited the area, while doing research. I mentioned a few places like Gordon Hall, Gordon Springs and Taylor's Ridge. She said, "You do know about things down here!" She said, "My father has a store out near Taylor's Ridge. Then it struck me why her name sounded familiar. I had driven by her father's store and remembered seeing the name. I told her about doing research at the Cherokee library in Lafayette. She said, "I have a cousin that works at that library." I said, "A girl in the Georgia Room by the name of Dannette would always help me." She yelled, "That's her! That's my cousin." We talked for quite a while and when we'd finished, she invited me to visit the next time I was in Georgia saying, "Stop by sometime, we'll treat you like family."

Another man from Canada wrote me a seven-page letter. I will paraphrase it for you here:

Dear Mr. Keene,
My name is Bradley Gordon Paul Langton. I am 41 years old and reside in a suburb of Vancouver, British Columbia. I'm writing to you in regards to the program on A&E Sunday July 30th, 2000. It has taken me a great deal of thought whether I should write you or not. As I watched the program about you and General John Gor-

don I became very overwhelmed with what I was watching. Though
your face I did not recognize, I surely did recognize General John

B. Gordon's face. It was like an old friend who I would see occasionally in my dreams or thoughts, but I felt as though I did know
this person, perhaps in another life. I must first explain the events
that lead me to write you in the first place.

All my life, mostly from about age 2 to 15 years old, I felt very
out of place living in British Columbia. I yearned for and was very
drawn to the South; Southern music, Southern food, anything to
do with the Southern culture. I was very drawn to the Civil War.
Being a teen and confused anyway, I just enjoyed my own little
world without understanding the why of it. As a teen in school, I
never liked Canadian history or politics; I am still not interested
even today. I've been told that I am different in my way of life
and views on politics and other issues. There have been times in
my life when I just knew I had been in the American Civil War. As
long as I could remember I would get very angry with anyone who
put down Southern people, the Confederate flag or their culture. I
would voice my opinion to them, which was usually in the form of
very colorful metaphors. I've always gotten very teary-eyed when it
comes to the Civil War. The first time I cried was when I was very
young watching The Good the Bad and the Ugly. There was one
scene of a Confederate prisoner of war camp where a Federal soldier
told some Confederate musicians to "Play." The tune was very sad
and I still remember it to this day. The first time Gettysburg was
playing at the picture show I went to see it. My emotions ran circles
inside my head. I was saddened beyond belief, joyous, and at the
same time, proud inside my heart. I tried to suppress my feelings,
but always needed an answer as to why I felt this way.

My mom phoned me very excited but cautious about what she
was about to tell me. My mom had just had an experience. Over
the years, I have come to understand that she is a receiver of information. This information comes from a "Higher Power" if you will.
Mom knew my passion for southern culture and the Civil War. She
said, "Brad you better sit down" and then began to describe the
chain of events and information she had received. She said she had
been told that I had been a young boy named John Paul Verdun,
born in 1850. She was not sure where, but thought it may have
been Missouri. She said, "He was a 14 or 15-year-old Confederate
soldier killed somewhere between Dec. 1864 and April 1865." I
could not believe what I was hearing. I do not go to church, but I
do have some faith. I was unsure if I believed in reincarnation or

not. My mother said that John Verdun had been killed by a sword or bayonet that went through his back and into his heart. There is a mole [or birthmark] on my back and on occasion I get a sharp pain through that area. After a while the pain goes away.

One night I was channel surfing and this program came on A&E called "Beyond Death." I changed the channel, but something inside me said to go back. I was blown away by this show and phoned my mom the next day to tell her about you and General Gordon. Today mom phoned and said she had more information.

She [mom] told me that she asked if John Verdun knew General John Gordon and the answer was "Yes." She also said, "Gordon wanted the boy to go home, but John Verdun refused and wanted to keep fighting." According to mom's notes, General Gordon was like a father figure and tried to watch out for the boy as best he could. General Gordon gave something to John Verdun, a piece of cloth, perhaps colors to put around his neck. After John Verdun was killed, General Gordon was very upset that the young boy had not gone home.

This is the only information I have, it has lessened my yearning for answers, but I have a need to find out more. I feel that there may be some kind of mention in General Gordon's memoirs of a young boy. In my heart, I know, because the feelings have grown stronger each day. Aside from my mom, and you, I have told no one else of my story. I am very exhausted from all this excitement. I hope you enjoy my experiences, though yours are quite different from mine. Some would think that we are kooks, crackpots, but some would understand. I personally don't care what anyone thinks of me. I know I am of sound mind. Having some answers to the "whys" has been a great feeling to my soul and I'm sure I will find more answers some day. I would like to thank you for listening to my story and I enjoyed your program on A&E. Feel free to contact me if you wish by letter or phone. I understand that this is a lot of beans to swallow, but I know what I feel inside and it will forever be with me.

As I read the letter, a picture came to mind. The same picture that so haunted me that I felt it necessary to write about it earlier in this book. It was the photo of a young boy, approximately 14 years old, lying dead in the bottom of a trench at Petersburg, Virginia. I called Bradley on the phone and during our conversation I mentioned this photo to him. I told him I would do some research to see if I could find out exactly where in Petersburg the photo had been taken. After doing so I would send him a copy of the photo. After posing the question of the photo to Robert E. L. Krick of Petersburg, Virginia, I received my answer in the form of a letter a short time later. The results follow:

> Dear Jeff,
> Regarding the forlorn dead Confederate, I am surprised to have found that the evidence is fairly clear about the troops defending that stretch of line on April 2, 1865. Bryan Grimes's emaciated division of the Second Corps ran right through there, fresh from its participation at Fort Stedman the week before. One source places the 53rd North Carolina actually inside Fort Mahone, but other accounts that seem to be more reliable have the 3rd Alabama Infantry as the unit driven out of the fort. Of course everything around Fort Mahone was a network of dirt embankments, and it is possible that the photograph was taken at some adjacent site. There was a series of more than twenty similar shots ("death studies") taken on April 3, 1865, by T. C. Roche. The original caption for the one that you are interested in is as follows:
>
> "This view was taken in the trenches of the rebel Fort Mahone, called by the soldiers 'Fort Damnation,' the morning after the storming of Petersburgh, Va., April 2d, 1865. It shows a boy about 14 years, who must have been asleep when the attack was made, as he is but partially dressed; he was killed as he came out from a bomb proof; he has on the rebel grey uniform."
>
> The site of Fort Mahone today is on the west side of the Jerusalem Plank Road; about over where the enormously tall Pennsylvania Monument is, just west of the marker for Colonel Gowan of the 48th Pennsylvania. It is developed beyond recognition, as you doubtless know.

After receiving the photo, Bradley called me on the phone. He was astounded by the similarity between the boy in the picture and himself at that age. His mother, after seeing the photo, was so unnerved that he said, "She cried for two days." In a subsequent letter from Bradley I was to discover another synchronistic event in his life. He wrote, did you know my birthday is April. 9, 1959? To most, this date would not mean much, but to anyone with a slight interest in the Civil War it rings a very big bell. Apr. 9, 1865 was the day that General Robert E. Lee surrendered the Army of Northern Virginia to General Ulysses S. Grant.

The song that Bradley had mentioned from the movie *The Good, the Bad and the Ugly* had affected me in the same way. I first saw the movie in early '70s long before the start of my reincarnation adventures. I ran right out to buy the record (33.1/3 RPM) of the soundtrack.[65] The song that Bradley talked about is titled "Story of a Soldier." I found the song so haunting that I would play it over and over again. I even said to my first wife, Bridget, "I'd like to have that song played at my funeral." When long-playing records fell from vogue I went out and purchased a copy of the same album in compact disc.

Next to come along was an old "comrade-in-arms." The postmark this time was Virginia, a little closer to my home and to my heart. The letter read:

Dear Mr. Keene,

Last night I watched "Beyond Death" on A&E and heard your particular story. "At last," I thought, "someone has had the same experience as I have had!" My story began in October 1993. Until then, I'd never had any special interest in the Civil War despite the fact that I was living in an area where much of it took place and in an antebellum home. The confluence of three things changed all that: I saw the movie *Gettysburg*, read the book that it is based on called *The Killer Angels*, and lastly was having my house painted by a young man who was a keen Civil War enthusiast. It was at his suggestion that I read the book when I told him I had seen the film. Suddenly, almost overnight, I became a raging fanatic about the war. I subscribed to all the magazines, took books from the library, joined the Civil War Roundtable in my area. At this point in [it was May 1994], I went to my first re-enactment in Orange, VA. They were doing the battle of the "Mule Shoe" which was part of the Spotsylvania campaign in 1864. And I was very deeply moved by the sight of the tents, cannons, horses, men in uniform, and ladies in hoop skirts. I began to wonder if perhaps I might have lived through those times, but, in truth, I could not remember anything like that. This reenactment was held on May 8th, but the actual battle of the "Mule Shoe" took place on May 12th. I was sitting at home on the 11th of May, 1994, thinking about the reenactment and also the fact that on May 11th, 1864, J. E. B. Stuart had been mortally wounded at Yellow Tavern—a direct result of the Spotsylvania campaign. The word "Nemesis" came into my head, much like the words "Not yet" came into yours. I found myself thinking of how Phil Sheridan had certainly been Stuart's nemesis on May 11th, and then I realized that a man named Sheridan had also been my nemesis in my life. In the next instant, I found myself remembering the movie *Gettysburg* and of how Robert E. Lee felt disappointed and let down by Stuart. I then thought of the Lee in my life who, although very fond of me, could not get over his anger at my divorce [for reasons that are irrelevant here]. Lee and Sheridan in both lifetimes I thought to myself. But it was the 11th of May when these thoughts came to me. At first, I thought they might be coincidence, but as time went on I realize that so much in my life paralleled his; my lifelong devotion to horses, my love of Irish music of the sort played during the war, my fascination with West Point [I love books set there such as *Dress Gray*], and a number of other things too numerous to mention. As time went on, I began to keep a journal and I could identify people in my life as people from his. I wrote an 80-page account of all of it and it was crystal clear that my life was indeed an echo of his life including certain physical characteristics, although perhaps not as pronounced as your cheek. I've traveled to many battlefields with tour groups and it is amazing how often the subject of reincarnation will come up. Most people confess that they do not know what to believe, but you, I, and others like us do know. Jeb Stuart is always with me as John B. Gordon is with you. They want us to be aware of them and of their lives. That is why they chose to make us aware of their presence. I would love to hear from you on the subject but, life goes on, and you're a busy man. I told my three sons about my story and I think two of them believe me and one does not. I suppose it is like that for all of us experiencing this.

There was a phone number at the bottom of the letter. I called, and to make a long story short, made arrangements to meet up with her at an upcoming Civil War tour. I spent two enjoyable days touring Virginia battlefields with this woman who claimed to have once been Confederate General J. E. B. Stuart. She was charming and sincere, had a great sense of humor and walked with the swaggering gait common to one who was "born to the saddle." We shared some old stories and some new ones. I learned that she had spent a good part of her life working for the U.S. Government and that her job had taken her to many different countries. When she told me the name of the agency, I just looked at her and said, "Still doing reconnaissance, huh?" The weekend came to a close all too soon. I hugged my new old friend and kissed her on the cheek. It was not a goodbye; it reminded me more of the old cavalry parting phrase "Until the next post." As I walked away, a thought popped into my head, "Did I just kiss Jeb Stuart?" Well, at least no beard this time.

CHAPTER THIRTEEN

Many Happy Returns

SO IT WENT, PEOPLE ENTERING my life with stories of having been
with me in past lives. What many of these people had in common
was a strong urge to contact me, to share their stories. Why?
Because they knew I would understand. They could see within
my story their own. They had found a kindred spirit, a kinsman
on this long and sometimes confusing journey called life. Many
of them expressed feelings that I knew well, feelings of lonliness,
wonder, doubt, fear, longing, joy, sorrow, amazement, pain. The
list could go on and on.

Once again I received a call from the chief's secretary. This
time she gave me a phone number for a Dr. Walter Semkiw. She
said he wanted to get in touch with me regarding the "Beyond
Death" program. Dr. Semkiw had been sent a film clip of my
segment from "Beyond Death." I did not recognize the area
code. I dialed the number and Dr. Semkiw answered. The first
thing I asked was, "Where are you located?" He said, "San Francisco, give me your number and I will call you back." I liked him
already; he was picking up the tab for a coast-to-coast call. He
explained the research he was doing into reincarnation and that
someone had sent him a clip of my portion of the A&E documentary. He gave me a little of his background, his education, jobs
he has held and so on. Then he caught me by surprise when he
told me he believed he had been John Adams (second president
of the United States). Now I knew what it was like to be on the
receiving end. I thought this must be the reaction many people
get when I tell them my story. Being open minded, I decided to
listen to the story from this man "bringing coals to Newcastle."
Dr. Semkiw went on to tell me how his story of reincarnation
started:

My story begins in 1984 when I went to a medium who had the
ability to channel one's spiritual guides. I had never gone to a psy-

chic or medium before, but reasoned that for the $50 fee, the experience should be entertaining at the very least. As the guides spoke, the medium's voice and facial expressions changed. At first, with surprising accuracy, the guides discussed my family and professional life. Later on, they told me about a lifetime in Revolutionary America. The guides stated that had I signed my name on parchment and in doing so, helped secure new ideals for humanity. At the end of the session, they told me that in this past era, I was John Adams. The guides told me that if I researched Adams, I would see myself.

Of course, I didn't believe that I was John Adams. I had heard that psychics routinely tell people that they were someone famous, for that is what people want to hear. I largely dismissed the past life information conveyed. Instead, I pursued my medical career, taking a position as medical director of Unocal 76, an oil company whose slogan happens to be "The Spirit of 1776." The years passed until quite unexpectedly, in 1996, I had an extremely strong intuition to study the life of John Adams and to research astrology. 1996, coincidentally, marked the bicentennial of the start of John Adams' presidency.

As I researched Adams and reviewed portraits of his family and friends, I found that I did see myself in John Adams. Personality traits were uncannily similar and there was a physical resemblance.[66]

Physical resemblance is what brought him to seek me out. At the time he was finishing up his book titled, *Return of the Revolutionaries* and wanted to include my story [which he did]. In a three-year span Dr. Semkiw had accumulated more than fifty past-life cases. He saw in these cases some startling similarities. He observed three principles at work.

People look the same from lifetime to lifetime. *Facial architecture,* the shape of the hands and even body postures are remarkably consistent from one lifetime to another.

Personality traits persist. A person's demeanor and habits of thought stay the same. Spiritually, we seem to pick up where we left off before. Indeed, the work that I am doing now is a continuation of the spiritual thought of John Adams.

We come into life in groups, based on shared karma, emotional attachments and joint projects. We come back with friends, loved ones and work associates from before.

I utilize the three criteria cited above to establish past life matches. In the future, I believe there will be a fourth criterion, that of DNA analysis. Since people look the same from lifetime to lifetime, I believe that a correlate or marker in a person's DNA maybe found.[67]

I have no doubts as to most of Dr. Semkiw's findings (I will leave the DNA to the scientist). As to people returning ingroups, retaining their personality traits and physical features, Ican give testament:

First, I shall submit here two short stories, one from the present, the other from long ago. The reason for doing so is to illustrate "personally traits" of the group I am with today as compared to yesteryear. An added bonus is to confirm the old adage, "The more things change, the more they stay the same." Over the years, I have often wondered if the people I work with were with me during those tumultuous times back in the 1860s. Sometimes their action and deeds caused me to ponder. I will relate a conversation that took place one night at fire headquarters. This type of banter is not uncommon during confrontation of a verbal nature. I am a bit of a chocoholic, so one night I brought in two large chocolate bars and put them in the platoon locker. One hour later I returned to the locker to find only one bar remaining. I asked in a loud voice, "Who ate my chocolate bar?" There was quiet in the dayroom. Nearby stood Firefighter Mike Kronick, his head turning to look at everybody else in the room but me. I said, "Mr. Kronick, did you eat my candy bar?" He turned his head to face me and said, "I ate half of it." I said, "Well then, who ate the other half?" Once again he looked around the room at his brother firefighters with a half-pleading look in his eyes. With no help forthcoming he turned back to me and related the saga of the candy bar. He said, "I ate half the bar and then put the other half on top of the kitchen table. The next time I came by the table it was still there, so I ate that half too." What could I do but laugh. Next time (and there will be a next time) I will have to phrase my question differently to get the whole story instead of a half at a time.

Compare this encounter with one written by John Gordon about an incident that took place at Gettysburg, Pennsylvania in 1863.

> Going into camp in an open country and after dark, it was ascertained that there was no wood to be had for even the limited amount of necessary cooking, and I was appealed to by the men for permission to use a few rails from an old-fashioned fence near the camp. I agreed that they might take the top layer of rails, as the fence would still be high enough to answer the farmer's purpose. When morning came the fence had nearly all disappeared, and each man declared that he had taken only the top rail! The authorized(?) destruction of that fence is not difficult to understand! It was a case of adherence to the letter and neglect of the spirit; but there was no alternative except good-naturedly to admit that my men had gotten the better of me that time.[68]

Second, I offer six photos. Three are of men I work with; the remaining three are Civil War generals. The three firefighters have no recollections of any past lives and have not expressed to me, one way or another, their beliefs in reincarnation. They were kind enough to let me use their pictures. Look for yourself at the three side by side comparison, then you decide if they could be the same people photographed more than one hundred years apart. I have come across more than six different photos of Civil War era soldiers that bear a striking resemblance to people I work with today, or have worked with in the recent past. Not only the photos, but also the description of their personalities, then and now, are consistent.

Union Gen. Wesley Merritt   *Firefighters*
                                      Wm. Dingee and Rob Yost

Compare the face, bone structure and the hand on the hip of firefighter Rob Yost (above far right) to that of Gen. Wesley Merritt. The pose of Mr. Yost was not staged. It is a picture that was taken on top of Mt. Washington with firefighter William Dingee (see Wm. Dingee, next page). In real life, the similarities of looks between Gen. Merritt and firefighter Yost is even greater than displayed in the photos above.

Firefighter Wm. Dingee   *Confederate Gen.*
Edward Porter Alexander

Another set of photos above show once again a similarity of bone structure and looks between firefighter William Dingee and Confederate General Edward Porter Alexander. Firefighters are not allowed to wear beards so I used a photo of Mr. Dingee while he was on vacation and enjoying a reprieve from shaving.

Confederate Gen.   *Firefighter Wayne R. Zaleta*
Cadmus Wilcox

The most amazing resemblance of the three is that of fire-fighter Wayne R. Zaleta to Gen. Cadmus Wilcox. You will note a darkened area on Wayne's left cheek that runs from the tip of his mustache up towards his ear. In the photo of Gen. Wilcox the markings in this area is much more apparent. None of the pictures have been retouched.

They say, "We pass this way but once." We do not live the same life twice, that is true, so I guess what they say is correct. All one can hope for is to do the journey in good company. It appears that I'm doing it this time back amongst the best.

I sent Dr. Semkiw information on my story, a copy of my manuscript and photos. A short time later my case was included on his website along with two cases on published authors.

Police Captain Robert Snow, who wrote *Looking for Carroll Beck-with*. This Indianapolis Police Captain in charge of Homicide Division, went to a past life regression on a dare and experienced profound memories of a lifetime as a portrait artist. He remembered 28 specific facts in the regression, including painting a portrait of a hunchback woman. Captain Snow didn't believe in reincarnation and tried to find an alternate explanation for the experience, such as the possibility that he viewed the portrait in a book or museum. After searching for a year, Captain Snow was not able to locate the portrait in books or museum collections. While on vacation in New Orleans, Captain Snow coincidentally ran into the portrait of the hunchback woman in a gallery. From the painting he was able to derive his past life identity and confirm 26 of the 28 facts from the regression. Captain Snow also looks like his past life identity, Carroll Beckwith.

William Barnes, who describes his lifetime as the designer of the Titanic, in "Tommie Andrews, Voyage into History." William Barnes started having spontaneous memories of the Titanic at age four and told his mother his name was Tommie, not William. Later on, he was able to deduce that he designed the Titanic and died on her maiden voyage.

Westport Connecticut Assistant Fire Chief Jeffrey Keene, who wrote "Not Yet"[69] which documents his discovery of a past life as Civil War Confederate General John B. Gordon. Chief Keene had an unexpected profound emotional experience when he visited a portion of Antietam battlefield called Sunken Road. He later was able to derive that he was a Confederate soldier, John B. Gordon, who was almost killed at that very spot. The resemblance between Gordon and Keene is termed "scary" by many who have seen the comparisons.[70]

On the weekend of April 27th, 28th and 29th, 2000, I traveled with Dr. Semkiw to a conference being held in Sturbridge, Massachusetts. The International Association of Regression Research Therapies put on the weekend of lectures and classes. Dr. Semkiw was one of the lecturers that weekend. He presented many case studies of past lives, including his own as John Adams. I was to be Dr. Semkiw's guest during his reincarnation lecture and I acted as sort of a "Show And Tell" when it came time for my story.

Dr. Semkiw had forewarned me that one of the attendees

would be Dianne Seaman, a woman who believes she had been Margaret Mitchell, author of the best-selling book of all-time (after the Bible) *Gone with the Wind*. Dianne had not made this past life story known to the general public, but kept it among close friends and trusted associates. What little I knew of Ms. Mitchell, I did know one thing for sure, her last resting place is in Oakland Cemetery, the same Cemetery as General John Gordon. Conducting a search on the Internet, I found a web site called Find a Grave. Find a Grave is "A resource for finding the final resting places of notable people." You can search by name, location or claim to fame. The page dedicated to Margaret Mitchell contained a short biography and a few photographs.

Margaret Munnerlyn Mitchell
Birth: Nov. 8, 1900
Atlanta
Georgia,
USA
Death: Aug. 16, 1949

Writer, author of *Gone with the Wind*. She began working as a journalist, using the name of Peggy Mitchell for the *Atlanta Journal* as a feature writer. That same year, Mitchell married Berrien Kinnard Upshaw. The marriage lasted only a few months, but the couple was not officially divorced until 1924. In 1925, Mitchell married John Marsh. Ms. Mitchell shocked Atlanta society by keeping her own name, "Margaret Mitchell" for professional purposes. (In private life, she was known as Peggy Marsh.) It took her ten years to write *Gone with The Wind*, then titled *Tomorrow Is Another Day*. She also changed the name of the heroine, a beautiful and manipulative Southern belle, from her original choice of Pansy to the more evocative Scarlett. In addition to its staggering sales, the novel won both the Pulitzer Prize and the National Book Award in 1937. Just one month after the release of the book, the film rights were sold to David O. Selznick for the then highest paid fee ever—$50,000. Mitchell wanted no part in the movie, and had a clause written into her contract absolving her from any more work on the project. The film won eight Academy Awards, including best picture for 1939, arguably one of the greatest years for film. Apart from a lively correspondence, she personally answered a good deal of her millions of fan letters. Mitchell never wrote again. On August 16, 1949, Margaret Mitchell was struck by a taxicab on Atlanta's Peachtree Street while on her way to a movie with her husband. She died five days later at the age of 49. As of 1998, *Gone with the Wind* was the best-selling book of all time, after the Bible, with a total of 23 million copies sold worldwide. In 1996, figures indicated that almost 200 million people had seen the Selznick film version of *Gone with the Wind*; a gala re-release of a remastered version in 1998 undoubtedly pushed those numbers even higher.

Burial: Oakland Cemetery
Atlanta (Fulton County), Georgia, USA[71]

One of the photos showed a coquettish Mitchell somewhere in her early 20s. Her face was posed in a three-quarter view with her eyes casting a glance to one side. I made a copy of the photo and bio to take to Massachusetts. Upon arrival at Sturbridge, Dr. Semkiw and I checked into the Public House Historic Inn. We were just in time to attend a meeting being held in one of the large conference rooms in the Inn. As we sat listening to the speaker, I asked Dr. Semkiw to point out Diane Seaman. In my hand at the time was the picture of Margaret Mitchell I had copied from the Internet. Dianne was pointed out to me, but she sat with her back towards us, so I could not see her face. A moment later she turned to talk to another person at her table. I compared the photo to the person sitting across the room. Dianne's face was in three-quarter view, eyes looking to one side, just as in the photo. I leaned towards Dr. Semkiw and pointed to the photo saying, "That's her, even the same pose." When the meeting was over, Dr. Semkiw and I walked around the room speaking with some of the other people attending the conference. We finally met up with Dianne Seaman. Dr. Semkiw introduced me to her. I said, "We have something in common." She gave me a quizzical look. I handed her a copy of the page from Find-a-Grave adding "Real estate in Oakland Cemetery." Dr. Semkiw explained a little about my past life as General John B. Gordon. Diane had to confess that at the mention of the words "Oakland Cemetery" she got goosebumps. She, too, had experienced first-hand what it is like to stand next to one's own grave. After spending some time together that weekend, Dianne and I developed a friendship and traded addresses. After Dr. Semkiw's lecture and listening to me speak, Dianne decided it was time for her to stand up in front of the assembled group and tell her story of the Margaret Mitchell past life. I enjoyed watching and listening to her story; we even had a little fun with the fact that General Gordon and Ms. Mitchell were "sleeping together." It is nice to have a fellow traveler walking the same road. One can become lonely moving along the highway of self-discovery. Now I had gained another travel companion. In the coming months, Dianne and I would lend support to each other. I e-mailed Dianne copies of rejections of my book that I had received from publishers. She wrote back "If I may pass on some lessons I have learned from rejections... [1] don't take it personally and [2] do not get attached to the fruits of your labors. You have my permission to remind me of these when I am in need of it!!" I found this to be sage advice. One time I came across a quote from an article Margaret Mitchell had written when she was a writer for the Atlanta Journal. Her profile of General Gordon appeared in the Journal's magazine section of November 29,1925 it read in part:

> General John Brown Gordon, the "Bayard of the Confederacy," whose statue now guards the entrance to the State Capitol and after whom Gordon Street in Atlanta was named, was a handsome man, pleasant of smile and possessed of great dignity and bearing. He was magnetic, drawing all hearts and eyes to him and when he spoke, all others were silent to listen. A stranger coming into his presence could not but realize that he stood before agreat man.

Though Mitchell was only a toddler when General Gordon died, she wrote some very kind words about him. I e-mailed a belated thank you to Dianne and received in return an e-mail stating "You're Welcome." Dianne had not been aware of the Gordon article and wrote "... this in part reinforces why, when-ever I think of you, I place you in Georgia and have to force myself to think of you in Connecticut.... That far north in Yan-kee territory!!" Dianne is also in the process of writing her story. She sent me a two-page excerpt that described her first visit to the house where Margaret Mitchell penned her epic novel, *Gone with the Wind*. Though only two typewritten pages in length, it took me a while to read through to the end. Twice I was brought to tears. Many of the things Dianne wrote vividly described feel-ings I had felt at Sunken Road and other places I have passed on my journey into this world of reincarnation. She wrote about her perception of time changing; being hit with many different feel-ings simultaneously. She wrote about bursting into tears, being scared, and questioning her sanity and finally a feeling of total exhaustion. I knew these feelings well; I've been through them myself. I had even written many of the same things down in my book, although not as eloquently as Dianne had expressed them. I reread the two pages one last time and then went outside to sit on the front porch and gather my thoughts. Many emotions had arisen in me from the description of Dianne's encounter with her past life. After a while these were replaced by the warm, peaceful feeling of knowing you are not alone.

I owe Dr. Semkiw a debt of gratitude for many reasons—being included in his book, on his website, and being allowed to travel with him to conferences. He set up radio interviews and recommended me to a literary agent. The first radio show I did was Uri Geller's *Parascience and Beyond*. You may remember Mr. Geller from his mental spoon-bending days back in the 60s and 70s. The next show was a real treat. The good doctor booked us on Jill Lawrence's show, *Jill and Friends*, broadcast by Wisdom Radio. Capt. Snow, Bill Barnes, Dr. Semkiw and I spent a delight-ful two hours discussing our stories with Jill.

Dr. Semkiw was intrigued with my writing style when he read my manuscript. He noticed what he thought were similarities between Gordon's style and my own.

In *Not Yet*, Jeff includes documents that show similarities between his writing style and Gordon's. In his later years, General Gordon wrote a book called *Reminiscences of the Civil War*, which provides material for such analysis. Let us compare two passages, one from Gordon's book, describing the efforts of his men to put out a fire in Wrightsville, Pennsylvania, and one from Keene regarding his fire department's response to an emergency incident. My observation is that the two documents seem to be written in the same 'voice.' Linguistic analysis may allow us to better define common traits between the passages.[72]

A linguist from the University of California, Berkley did an evaluation that uncovered common traits in six areas. What follows are the results of that evaluation:

Writing Sample One: General John B. Gordon (from Reminiscences of the Civil War)

With great energy my men labored to save the bridge. I called on the citizens of Wrightsville for buckets and pails, but none were to be found. There was no lack of buckets and pails a little while later, when the town was on fire ... My men labored as earnestly and bravely to save the town as they did to save the bridge. In the absence of fire-engines or other appliances, the only chance to arrest the progress of the flames was to form my men around the burning district, with the flank resting on the river's edge, and pass rapidly from hand to hand the pails of water. Thus, and thus only, was the advancing, raging fire met, and at a late hour of the night checked and conquered.

Writing Sample Two: Assistant Chief Jeffrey Keene (from a letter to Fire Chief)

With my radio restored, man power and apparatus were brought in and put under the guidance of Acting Lieutenant Christopher Ackley. While setting up a plan of action, Lieutenant Ackley displayed good common sense, knowledge, training and a deep concern for the safety of firefighters under his command. A large amount of gas entered the structure by way of a open window. Though we tried to remove all possible sources of ignition, we were able to remove all but two. The owner informed us that the house contained an oil-fired furnace and a hot water heater. There was no way to shut them off from the inside or outside. Using metering devices, a positive pressure fan and opening and closing windows, the hazard was removed.

Findings of Linguistic Analysis:
Close in average number of words per sentence: Gordon-21, Keene-18

Use of compound sentences: Gordon—"the only chance to arrest the progress of flames was to form my men around the burning district, with the flank resting on the river's edge, and pass rapidly from hand to hand the pails of water." Keene—"While setting up a plan of action, Lieutenant Ackley displayed good common sense, knowledge, training and a deep concern for the safety of firefighters under his command."

Use of preposed clauses in complex sentences: Gordon—"In the absence of fire engines," Keene—"While setting up a plan of action."

Use of existential-there sentence with negation: Gordon—"There was no lack of buckets." Keene—"There was no way to shut them off."

Adverbial clauses at beginning of sentence: Gordon—"With great energy," "In the absence of fire-engines." Keene—"With my radio restored."

Most of text is in active voice except at the end. In both passages, paragraphs end in passive voice, as if the success came about without the intervention of those involved. Excitement is achieved by altering expected word order, separating two parts of the verb. Gordon—"was the advancing, raging fire met, and at a late hour of the night checked and conquered." Keene—"Using metering devices, ... the hazard was removed."

I had never given any thought to the possibility of a correlation between Gordon's writing style and my own. Dr. Semkiw told me that the linguist who did the report stated, "Similarities in writing style definitely did exist, though it is not proof that the authors are the same."[73]

It would be impossible for anyone to compare two handwriting samples and say with absolute certainty that the authors were one and the same person. It would appear though, that the results of the linguistic analysis of these two small samplings gives some credence to Dr. Semkiw's hypothesis of the same "voice."

CHAPTER FOURTEEN

Joy and Sorrow

ON AUG. 11TH, 2001, MY daughter Shannon was married just
north of Newport, Rhode Island. The wedding ceremony was held
in a house built in the 1920s to resemble a French chateau. After
the reception dinner, I walked into the ballroom to find the dance
floor completely empty. I'm not much of a dancer but, I am mostly
Irish, and having consumed a few drinks I decided it was time to
get the party going. I asked the disc jockey to play "What'll I do,"
a song that I often sang to Shannon when she was an infant. Of
the 70,000 songs this man had in his collection that song was not
one he brought with him that night. I asked if he had Tony Ben-
nett's "I Left My Heart in San Francisco." He did and I told him to
put it on next. I found Shannon near the front door and hurriedly
dragged her to the ballroom. We were far from San Francisco but
this song is a very special one. Shannon's great-uncle Marty Man-
ning had won a Grammy for his arrangement and her grandfather
Arthur (Buddy) Brennan was playing the well-known melodious
piano notes. I took the opportunity, while dancing with Shannon,
to pass on some of the things I had learned in my fifty plus years
of life. I said, "You know, no one ever truly dies, not the way most
people think of death. Everyone that you have ever loved or that
has ever loved you still exists. All the things that I have seen, felt,
and experienced tell me this is true. Your grandmother Fran, your
grandfathers, and all the rest are watching here today and sharing
in your happiness." With this the tears started flowing down Shannon's cheeks. Shannon knew what I was saying was the truth. I had
made a similar statement during my interview for A&E's "Beyond
Death" right after being asked the question "What have all your
years of discoveries taught you?" For whatever reason, they chose
not to include my answer in the finished documentary.

Slowly more couples moved onto the dance floor. Next I
sought out my daughter, Samantha. She had jettisoned the high

heels from her bridesmaid's apparel and was now wandering around barefoot. She claimed not to know how to slow dance. She wasn't going to get away that easily. I said, "Stand on my feet like you did when you were a little girl." Samantha placed her feet gently on mine and we started to dance. It must have been a sight, for the photographer took several pictures of us dancing and a few close-ups of her bare feet on top of my tuxedo shoes. The music changed to a faster rock-and-roll beat and I now was forced to adapt my 60s dance steps to a new century's music. I fared pretty well, so much so, I was later given the *nom de soirée*, "Dancing Boy." My reply to that was to ask, "How many people were dancing before I started"? The answer was "None." I then asked, "How many people were dancing after I started dancing?" The answer to this was "Everyone." I rested my case.

Late in the evening I moved outside to get some fresh air. While standing in the courtyard I talked with the police officer that had been hired for the night. Anna appeared at the front door and yelled, "Hey! Why aren't you dancing"? At this, the policeman held out his arms and he and I proceeded to dance around the courtyard. Anna shook her head and said, "No! I meant in here!" It was a beautiful wedding and a fun reception. The phrase "A good time was had by all" comes to mind. In attendance that day was my brother Joel, his wife Cindy and her son Joe. They were up from Jacksonville, Florida and wanted to do some sight-seeing while in the Northeast. I had not seen my little brother in nearly ten years, so we made arrangements to visit New York City on Monday, August 13th. The four of us took the train to Grand Central Station and walked the few blocks to the Empire State Building. On top of the one-time world's tallest building we found that our view was limited because of weather conditions. I pointed out some landmarks: the Statue of Liberty, the Chrysler Building and the

Twin Towers of the World Trade Center. We returned to street level and made our way up Fifth Avenue, all the while Joe laughing at my stupid jokes and Cindy shaking her head (I don't know why, but women seem to do that a lot when they're around me). We stopped at Rockefeller Center and St. Patrick's Cathedral. From the look on Cindy's face I could see St. Patrick's would be the highlight of her trip to New York. It is hard for anyone not to be taken aback by the beauty of this structure, both inside and out. There was a mass in progress and Cindy asked if we had time for her and Joe to take communion. Joel and I stood in the back of the church while the two of them moved down the center aisle to receive communion. They walked back and sat for a while in one of the last pews on the right hand side. Less than two months later, I would sit in the same area, not as a visitor, but as a mourner.

September 11th 2001

On the morning of September 11th, 2001, I, like countless other Americans, stood transfixed in front of the television as the tragic events of the day unfolded. A plane had hit one of the World Trade Center's towers. At first, it appeared to be a freak accident, but as the second plane came into view, it left little doubt as to what was happening. As the first 110-story tower collapsed to the ground, I turned to Anna and said, "The New York fire department just lost a large number of men." I was aware of how they handled fire operations in high-rise buildings. Firefighters are sent to the areas where the building's occupants are in the most danger, staging areas for manpower and equipment are set up on the floors below. Command and Control centers are put into operation on other floors. All this requires a large amount of personnel, even in normal size buildings. I could only imagine the number required for one of the tallest buildings ever built. Then, I watched the second tower come down like a curtain on a bad play. Only smoke, dust and sky were left where these two majestic buildings had once stood. I called the Westport Fire Department and suggested we send some men with Rescue #8, a vehicle that contains rescue tools, cribbing and a generator for lighting. I was put on the list of members volunteering to respond to New York. A call came later that day to be ready to go with only 10 minutes notice. My fire-fighting gear was in my car along with a plastic trash bag containing blue jeans, socks and other hastily assembled bits of clothing that might be needed for a prolonged stay.

Days passed and it became apparent that our department was not sending anyone to New York City. Some members took it upon themselves to go. Like old fire horses that have answered thousands of calls, their feet started moving to the sound of the alarm. It is difficult to rein in people whose physical nature and character is one of action. I know, because it is one of the most difficult aspects of my job. I must keep careful watch over this strange breed of humans, to stop them from going beyond their limits, because at times, they feel limitless. Early one morning they met at the railroad station for the trip to New York. The Westport crew was put to work setting up a warehouse for rescue equipment near the Engine #10 Truck #10 firehouse (this fire station was the closest to the World Trade Center). A one-time delicatessen was transformed into a supply house for rescue saws with metal cutting blades needed to cut through the heavy beams. They helped comprise one of the human chains that formed to clear away debris from the huge piles of rubble. At one point they were called off the piles and asked to stand behind some barrier tape. They soon learned the reason; it was the first visit of President George W. Bush to "Ground Zero." With him that day were Sen. Hillary Clinton, Gov. George Pataki, Mayor Rudolph Giuliani and Fire Commissioner, Thomas Von Essen.74 These dignitaries passed along the line of barrier tape, shaking hands with the rescuers. While President Bush held Westport firefighter Lisa Ruot's hand, he pulled her forward to whisper something in her ear. He said, "When we find the hole the bastards are hiding in, we'll take care of them." The department did not give these members the go-ahead; they went of their own volition. I felt especially proud of them. They had some amazing stories to tell upon their return. It seems the people of New York City

took very good care of them with free train rides, food, and even
rubbed and powdered their feet while they changed their socks
for them. Civilians lined the street to cheer the rescue workers
going to and from the scene. People stopped them on the street
to shake their hands and pat them on the back.

Television coverage continued to show rescue efforts, but as
the days went by it became obvious there was no one left to
rescue. 343 firefighters perished. With the discovery of each firefighter's body came a somber and touching sight. There is a tradition in the fire service that the department takes care of their
own. All the machinery comes to a stop and the rescue workers
form lines. Firefighters are sent in to remove the body of their
fallen brother. They drape the American flag over the departed
and carry him back down off the pile of debris to his final rest.
As they passed the long lines of workers, some would doff their
headgear and bow their heads while others would salute. With
the sorrowful task completed, the men and machines return to
work. This scene was to be repeated many times over the days
and months that followed September 11th.

On the morning of Thursday, October 4, 2001, the uniformed
emergency services formed ranks down the center of Fifth Avenue.
The assemblage covered only a one-block area directly in front of
the beautiful St. Patrick's Cathedral. Not so long ago, a single line-
of-duty death would have brought out block after block of uniform
personnel. Now, thinned by the tragedy of September 11th and
longer shifts, there were too many funerals and not enough people
able to attend. The New York City Fire Department made a plea to
anyone who could do so, to please attend the funerals and memorial
services for their fallen brothers. The fire service personnel were centered at the main door of the church. A short while later everyone
was brought to attention. The coffin carrying one of New York's
Bravest was lifted down from the hose-bed of the fire engine parked
in the roadway. The marking on the truck was that of Rescue Company One. The bagpipers struck up the familiar old hymn "Amazing
Grace," the song that is always reserved for playing when a coffin
enters the church. Though some consider the sound of bagpipes

annoying, for others the quality is almost mystical. Bagpipes hold the unique distinction of once having been classified as an "Instrument of War." For three centuries a Scotsman ran the risk of death just for having pipes in his possession. There are large numbers of men in the fire service with Irish, English or Scottish ancestry. One would be hard pressed to find a dry eye among them when the pipes are playing, especially a song as near and dear to their hearts as "Amazing Grace." As the final strains of the pipes died away, the formation moved from the street up the stairs and into the building.

I sat in St. Patrick's Cathedral attending the funeral of 41 year-old Captain Terence S. Hatton. Capt. Hatton was with Rescue Company 1 of the New York Fire Department. He received 19 commendations during his 21 years on the department, a hero among heroes. At six-foot four and good-looking, he reminded many of the film star, Gary Cooper. He was known for his coolness while under fire, literally. If you watch the films of the World Trade Center taken on Sept. 11th, you can see a light gray colored smoke coming from a portion of the first tower hit. It appears at the lower portion of the massive plume of black smoke. All firefighters know that this is an indication of water being applied to a fire. When you consider that some elevators could not be used and that the men had to walk up all those flights of stairs laden with heavy equipment, it was a remarkable feat. It is believed that it was Capt. Hatton and his men that did just that. They died attempting to hold back the fire in an effort to give others the needed time to escape.

The funeral service was quite lengthy with an impressive listof eulogizers:

Joseph M. Allbaugh, Director of Federal Emergency
    Management Agency
Lieutenant Michael Pena, Rescue Co. No. 1
Timothy Brown, Supervisor of the Office of Emergency
    Management
Kenneth Hatton, Deputy Chief [Retired] (Father of Capt.
Hatton)
Fire Commissioner Thomas Von Essen

Hon. Governor George E. Pataki, New York State Hon.
Mayor Rudolph W. Giuliani, City of New York

When Mayor Giuliani spoke, you could hear the emotional
impact creeping into his voice. This was a personal loss for him.
Captain Hatton's wife, Beth, is one of the Mayor's aides and
Mayor Giuliani presided over their wedding. It was shortly after
September 11th that Beth learned she was pregnant. Capt. Hatton perished along with 10 other members of Rescue 1. They,
along with all the other departed emergency workers, had died
doing the jobs they had trained for and dedicated their lives to.

I'd like to share with you a quote that is framed and hangs on
the wall at the central firehouse in Westport, Connecticut. My
guess is that it hangs in many other firehouses also.

> I have no ambition in this world but one, and that is to be a
> firefighter. The position, in the eyes of some, may appear to be a
> lowly one; but we who know the work which a firefighter has to do
> believe it is a noble calling.
>
> Our proudest moment is to save lives... Under the impulse of
> such thoughts, the nobility of the occupation thrills us and stimu-
> lates us to deeds of daring ... even of supreme sacrifice.
>
> Edward F. Crocker,
> Chief of Department, F.D.N.Y.
> 1899–1911

After the funeral ceremony was completed inside St. Patrick's,
we formed up outside in front. The coffin was carried down the
steps of the cathedral and placed once more atop the fire engine. A
final salute was given and the funeral procession moved off down
Fifth Avenue to the sound of the drums beating out a final tattoo.
Month after month, the mournful sound of pipe and drum would
echo through scores of cities and towns in the tri-state area.

Moving along the streets of New York City I experienced first-
hand some of the things I had only heard about from others. As we
moved south on Fifth Ave., in our dress uniforms, people would
come up and shake our hands and pat us on the back. They would

say things like, "You guys are my hero" and "Thank you for the job that you do." I would say, "Thank you" in absentia for those whose voices had been silenced. The pretty girls smiled, while others just met your eyes with a look of extreme sadness. The city was a kinder, gentler city. Seldom would you hear a car horn, an old New York City trademark. Like a wounded animal the city was suffering in silence. I knew that it would take time, there would be a recovery, maybe not a full healing, but a recovery nonetheless. The rescue workers digging at "Ground Zero" worked on bent knees but their backs were never straighter. Fathers searching for sons, sons for fathers, brothers for brothers. When the pall of smoke and dust lifted, we all stood a little taller. The wound would heal but the scars on our hearts would remain. Our antagonists had no victory, no triumph; they had only caused an awakening.

I felt compelled to return to New York City and go to "Ground Zero," to see firsthand what others could only try to describe. My travel companions were Lieut. Robert Kepchar and firefighter Denis Duffy. We took the train to Grand Central station, then walked west across Manhattan. Our first stop was Rescue Co. No. 1 to pay our respects. I explained to Bob and Denis that we should keep our visit brief. After we exchanged pleasantries and condolences with the men of this elite rescue unit, I turned over the 18 dozen cookies Anna had baked for them. We were offered coffee [a firehouse staple] and then sat around a large oak table talking. Their pain was palpable. Though we tried to stay off the subject of the World Trade Center, it would keep creeping into the conversation. One of the Rescue One members talked about the noise the first tower made as it fell to the ground. He said, "I will never forget that sound." Another one of the members across the table from him just stared at the tabletop and said, "I didn't hear a thing." It is strange how people perceive things differently during times of crisis. Where one hears a horrible din, another perceives only silence. I felt for these men, they had suffered much. Their suffering continued through the actions of well-meaning people. The department was not sending them on their usual number of calls. They were more or less being held in reserve, which allowed them more time to contemplate the events on September 11th. They were being bombarded day and night by well-wishers knocking on their door. When they were called out, it was usually to Ground Zero to aid in the search. On their days off, they would be hit with the added dilemma of having to decide which friend's funeral to attend. In spite of all this, there was something wonderful about these men. They were not victims; at least not "victims" as it is normally defined. They were tools that wanted to be used. They had a strong desire to get back to work. Instead of standing around they wanted to be busy helping others. If the World Trade Center incident was to be repeated, I have no doubt they would all answer the call once again.

The three of us rode to lower Manhattan as far as the cab could take us. After making our way to West Street we headed south along the river. We passed long lines of trucks carrying their huge cargoes of debris to the barges waiting dockside. As we drew closer to "Ground Zero," the devastation grew in magnitude. Trucks watered the highway to keep down the omnipresent gray dust. All along the way, heavyhearted police officers and soldiers stood guard. Almost every intersection and side street had checkpoints. Once pristine skyscrapers now bore the scars of broken windows and blackened façades. Fires continued to burn everywhere underground. Where once stood towering skyscrapers, now there were only voids and smoldering ruins. Dante could not have imagined a more dismal and ravaged landscape. The scene truly defies description because of the enormity of the destruction and the knowledge of the humanity intertwined with the wreckage. Between the three of us we had almost 90 years of accumulated service in fire rescue, but never had we ever seen anything to compare with this. The sights, sounds and smells that assault the viewer strike within them a chord, one that will resonate forever. One other time I have had close to the same feelings. It was while standing on the Arizona Memorial at Pearl Harbor in Hawaii. But that was different, that was past history, this was present. Even standing there it was hard to believe. I did not want to believe it, but, there were just too many empty helmets resting on coffins, or clutched in the hands of sons and daughters for the truth to be denied.

Photo by Lieutenant Robert Kepchar

CHAPTER FIFTEEN

Then, Now and the Future

MANY YEARS AGO, BACK IN 1992, I awoke one morning with a phrase repeating in my head. "What once was, will be again." I was not certain what this ambiguous statement referred to, but I thought it was something concerning the American Civil War. Another Civil War in America? Highly unlikely I thought. I filed the incident away in my memory bank and that was the end of that, I thought. As reporters gave their stories on the tragedy of September 11th, certain comparisons were being made. The attack on the World Trade Center itself by planes was likened to the sneak attack on Pearl Harbor. The raising of a flag by fire-fighters at Ground Zero was compared to the flag raising on Iwo Jima during the World War II. Then I heard one news reporter say that this had been the bloodiest day in our nation's history in the past 140 years. It wasn't too hard for me to do the math. What the reporter had alluded to was the battle of Antietam. The casualty statistics for the battle of Antietam is approximately 23,000 killed, wounded and missing. Though the total number for the World Trade Center attack did not approach this figure, the death toll for September 11th made it the second bloodiest day on America soil.

During the 60th anniversary of the attack on Pearl Harbor reporters asked survivors to give their impressions of what it was like "being there." A person walking in on this conversation without seeing the screen would undoubtedly have thought they were talking about the September 11th attack at the World Trade Center. The Pearl Harbor veterans described "disbelieving" what was unfolding before them. Others said, "It was like I was watching a movie." Watching film footage from September 11th, 2001, especially when the second plane crashed into the second tower, one could easily envision a production from Hollywood. As we know now though, it was all too real.

While standing at Ground Zero, my senses attempted to take in all of my surroundings. Flashes of news footage replayed in my head, scenes of firefighters rushing into the Trade Center buildings, policemen helping the injured and civilians rushing to get away. So many people caught up in a common nightmare. Horrible scenes of death and destruction interspersed with acts of courage and compassion. In my mind's eye I had no trouble placing these individuals at other events in other times. I could see many of them back on the flaming deck of the battleship Arizona or struggling to raise the American flag over Iwo Jima. Then again, I could see still others lying motionless in a little country lane in Sharpsburg, Maryland. It seems I always find myself back among the soldiery. Once I was in gray, the next time khaki, this time blue.

Our history of aggression has moved from conflicts with sticks and stones to guns and planes. It has continued to escalate all the way to up to nuclear weapons that threaten the earth itself. We have now entered a New Age; an age where airliners filled with fuel, trucks containing explosives, even a letter in the mail can be turned against us. No longer is war restricted to faroff battlefields or knights in single combat. The global village has become the global battlefield. Huge armies are no longer needed. A devastating amount of damage can be done by a single person crossing a border from one country to the next or by buying a ticket on a plane whose destination will be determined in-flight. Hopefully, some day, we will come to the understanding that killing is not an acceptable form of communication.

Once Albert Einstein was asked what type of weapons he thought would be used in World War Three. To this question he had no answer but replied that he knew what weapons would be used in World War Four—"*Stones*." With the passage of time my purpose in life has become clearer. One life task being the completion and printing of this book. It has fallen to me, in this lifetime, to bring what I have experienced and learned to as many other people as possible. One author wrote that John B. Gordon had been one of the most important people in the U.S. in the last half of the 19th century. This was not because of his war record but because of his political and social record after the War Between the States. Gordon used his posts as Governor and Senator of Georgia to help rebuild the South during reconstruction. He used his position as Commander-in-Chief of the United Confederate Veterans and his popularity as a lecturer to rebuild the human wreckage of war and reconcile the onetime combatants to a greater sense of brotherhood. This was no small feat, when you consider the amount of damage done in the loss of lives alone (620,000 dead). Gordon's book, *Reminiscences of the Civil War*, and his lecture, "Last Days of the Confederacy," were very well received both in the South and North. In the late 1890s Maj. Gen. Joshua Lawrence Chamberlain, Medal of Honor winner, the same man that had saluted the Army of Northern Virginia at Appomattox Courthouse, proposed a joint lecture tour with John Gordon.[75] Through all the intervening years these two men had remained like-minded when it came to the reunification of a war-torn nation. Their shared venture never materialized, but still, until their deaths, these two distinguished men of war, remained two prominent men of peace.

More and more people will be telling stories similar to mine in the years to come. To what end? They will tell them until we, all of us who occupy this big blue marble floating in space, realize not **who**, but **what** we are. The stories will continue to take root, to grow and branch out until people take the time to sit down with the program and read it from cover to cover. Some people will grasp the "Master Plan" sooner than others will. We all learn at different rates. We learn from our successes as well as our mistakes, or at least we should. How many times do you have to smash your face before you open the door and walk through the opening?

I will tell you some of the things I have learned and maybe

wecan speed up the evolutionary process a bit. I give you free rein.You can agree with what I tell you, disagree, or just shrug your shoulders and say, "I don't know, I will have to give it some thought." Those are pretty much the only three choices you canmake anyway. There is a fourth choice, but that would be to have a closed mind on the subject of reincarnation, and anyone with a closed mind would not be reading this book. So, here wego with what I will call universal truths.

You choose if you will reincarnate or not. We help choose life-times and situations that will give us the best opportunity to learn the lessons needed for our soul's development.

William Shakespeare wrote, "All the world's a stage, and all the men and women in it merely players. They have their exits and their entrances; and one man in his time plays many parts."I wonder if he realized, when he wrote these words, that he wasspeaking the unadulterated truth? Maybe he did, but did he mean until death or could he see past that final curtain? We helpchoreograph our own dance; we have input in writing our own life's script, even to the point as, Shakespeare puts it, of our exitsand entrances (birth/death). From one lifetime to the next, the roles are ever changing, one day a king, the next a jester,sometimes a hero, at other times a villain. Which is the greater part? Everyone loves a hero, but what about the villain? No playwould be complete without a scoundrel. If for no other purpose,they serve to make us look better. But really, protagonists are a necessary part of the learning process. They put things into motion. Many will listen to the tale (and web) they spin and jointhem in their dance. Others will observe from a safe distance andcluck their tongues. While still others will be stirred to action because they understand there is no safe distance. A cancer left unchecked will consume the body. We should not judge any man because we are not able to ascertain the role he plays nor thescript he follows. What is proper, is to judge their acts. Earth canbe compared to a schoolroom; some people are first-timers—I guess you could equate it to being in Kindergarten—while others are going for their master's degrees and have been here many times before.

We come back in groups, people we have spent eons with. Many of the people you are with in this life have been with youbefore. This makes sense. Why start all over with strangers, or should I say, fellow actors that we have never worked with before? Would it not be easier and more enjoyable to progress with other souls we have worked with over many lifetimes? These others could play off us and each other to bring about thepresent script, which may even involve the scripts of former lifetimes. As a matter of fact, we are so involved (or evolved) with many of these other souls that, if you drew their comings and goings in our lives, it would look like vines on a tree.

We learn, here on earth, by gaining knowledge in three different areas. I give them in no particular order.

- *Intellectual Knowledge*: This is gained through schools, reading or observing etc.
- *Physical Knowledge:* We get this by way of experiencing through the body itself.
- *Emotional Knowledge:* This is feeling our feelings, anger, love, sadness, and joy....

I will walk you through the process and give examples of each of the three types of knowledge I have mentioned:

I studied Fire Science at a state technical college before joining the Fire Department. We read books that contain facts; such as, during structure fires ceiling temperatures can reach temperatures above two thousand degrees Fahrenheit. No one would disagree that this is a very hot situation indeed, but we still only have an "**Intellectual Knowledge**" of how hot it can get during a structure fire.

You are wearing all the proper protective gear (helmet, coat, boots, gloves, breathing apparatus...) as you enter a structure under fire conditions. As you advance a hose-line, you are in a stooped position. Your surroundings are getting hotter, so now you go into a crouching posture. The temperature above you is still climbing and your gear is heating up. (Remember that firefighting gear is flame resistant, not fireproof. There is a BIG difference). You are on your knees now and you can feel the heat of the floor through your clothes. Where your skin is exposed (neck, ears and around your wrists where there is a separation between the gloves and coat sleeves), you can really feel it starting to hurt. This would be the good time to stand up with a thermometer and check the ceiling temperature to see by how many degrees the professor had been off. You decide to take his word for it, because now you have the **Physical Knowledge** of how hot it can get inside a burning house.

Now you are lying on the floor and the smoke has dropped down to your level. You literally can no longer see your hand in front of your face. Your heart beats faster. The whole length of your body is heating up both from above and below. Your brain starts conjuring up pictures of a hotdog on a barbecue grill. The facepiece fogs up from the moisture evaporating off your face. It's you and Mr. Hose against a red devil that is growing in strength every second. Mr. Hose does not seem quite up to the task. Now enters old Mother Nature with her "Fight or Flight" syndrome. With heart pounding and ears burning, you turn around and quickly use the hose-line to find your way back to the door you came in. All of a sudden it becomes very bright, even though you still cannot see through the water vapor covering the facepiece, you are remarkably happy to find yourself outside. You scramble down the front steps to the lawn and even though it is eighty-five degrees that day, it feels as if you just crawled into a walk-in freezer. You now have an **Emotional Knowledge** of what it feels like to be inside a structure under fire conditions.

The education process is complete; you have all three legs of what we will call the *tripod of knowledge*. These three elements are essential for a **Complete Knowledge** of any subject.

How we respond to these learning methods will determine if we have learned our lessons and gained a greater mastery over ourselves. During adverse situations our thoughts and actions will display our progression through this process and determine whether we may need to repeat any or all portions of that particular lesson.

We are guided: Guidance is always there in some form, **thoughts** for one. I have found myself at times giving advice to people on many different subjects—life, death and other problems we face on an almost everyday basis. On more than one occasion I've noticed tears in the eyes of the person I have been talking to. Every time this happens, I find myself taken aback a bit when I realize the effect my words have had on them. I also understand that those words came through me, not from me.

Guidance can come at any time, any place. We only need to heed that wee small voice. Driving home from work one morning I heard that small voice in my head saying, "You should get some carrots for the horses." At the time I was driving past some homes that did have horses, but I didn't think the owners would appreciate someone else feeding their animals. I continued driving. Once again the voice said, "You should get some carrots for the horses." I shook the message off again as I applied the brakes for the approaching stop sign ahead. I made a right-hand turn and, there, dead ahead of me, in the middle of the road, stood two riderless horses. A man was attempting to get them off the road, so I stopped to help. The man told me he had found the horses in the roadway and they were not cooperating one bit with his attempts at guiding them to a safer location. Together we were successful in getting them onto the grounds of a nearby estate. Other people were now arriving to lend assistance, a young lady (who I later learned was the wife of one of the firefighters I work with), a policeman and the husband of the horses' owner. Every time the horses were approached, they would take off running willy-nilly wherever they felt like going. The two of them were having a grand time with the new-found freedom. The owner's husband went home and returned with a couple of buckets of oats. Every time he would get near the horses they would run 100 yards or so and then stop and look back as if to say, "We're not falling for the old oats trick." The pony show (pardon the pun) continued for an hour until someone came along with a big bunch of carrots and had no trouble at all getting the horses follow them.

The police blocked the street while the two horses were led the half-mile back to the safety of their barn. As I continued my trek home, I thought about how much time could have been saved if I had just stopped and bought some carrots when the suggestion was first made to me.

KARMA: When Dr. Einstein said, "Man is not capable of knowing the full results of his actions." I do not believe he factored in reincarnation. Reincarnation makes it possible for a man to see the effects of his actions on others through the passage of time. He may even be the recipient of something he himself authored and placed in motion. Some would describe this as karma. Karma is often thought of in the negative sense. So that there is no misunderstanding, we will substitute the word Experience for Karma. We can experience what we perceive as good or bad, but who's to say which is which? We are pretty sure at the time it is happening to us, which is which, but in retrospect we may come away with a broader understanding of what has transpired. You sometimes hear people tell a horrendous personal story, the type of story that would send most of us screaming off into the sunset. When the listener sympathizes with the person, they are sometimes met with the phrase, "It was one of the best things that ever happened to me." They go on to explain how being in a motor vehicle accident placed them in the hospital in a bed right next to a long-lost relative. Or how the physical exam in the hospital disclosed an ailment that, left untreated, may have led to their demise. Many times an aliment or injury will cause a person to be suddenly forced into spending some time with themselves. This could result in "taking stock" or becoming more reflective on how they have conducted life. They may discover what is really important in this life—not material things like big houses and fancy cars. These things are transient. You cannot own anything. Most of the time these items own us during our stay here, what with mortgages and car payments.

To "**Reap what you sow**" can be carried out in many different ways. If you have wronged someone, you may decide to right that wrong in many different ways. You could experience the same misdeed first-hand or as a second party to the action, whereby you watch a loved one suffer the fate you bestowed on another. Retribution does not have to be punitive. Past actions can be met and understood not just by experiencing them in the form of punishment, but by love and understanding. Let's say you were a murderer one lifetime. Now you have returned to experience what you had forced on others. It is very difficult to teach someone a lesson by killing them, so instead of being a murder victim you become a family member of a murder victim to better understand what this type of behavior does to others. You may find yourself working in the prison system dealing with murderers all day long while attempting to help them make something of their lives. You might very well come back as a doctor, policeman or fireman and save lives instead of taking them. The possibilities are boundless.

One of the greatest gifts God gives us is "**Free Will.**" How would we ever learn, if each and every time that something unpleasant crossed our path, we were spared going through it? This goes for anything from falling off a bicycle and skinning our knee, to watching the ones we love leave us when it is time for them to return home. At a very early age we are all cognizant of the fact that bad things happen. In this world there is no shortage of scenes of great sorrow, death and destruction. Many have wondered why these bad things happen. People always ask, "Why did God do this," or "Why did God allow this to happen?" The answer to the first question is God did not do it. We do these things to ourselves or, I should say, we allow these things to happen for our own edification or as lessons to others. The second statement is true: God did allow it to happen. God must allow things to happen in order for us to learn.

Evil is of man and not God. We should always keep in mind what Edmund Burke said, "All that is needed for the forces of evil to succeed is for enough good men to remain silent."

Unlike God, we can interfere with processes here on Earth. We can use our goodness (or Godness) to intervene, to change things for the better. I was recently reminded of the story I'd heard many years ago. In the year 1914 it was not all quiet on the western front. The first four months of World War I had brought about over one million casualties. In some places the enemy trenches were less than 60 yards apart. On Christmas Eve the sound of singing was heard drifting across from the German lines. The German regiments had just received shipments of Christmas trees, which set the mood for the singing of such songs as Silent Night and O'Tannenbaum. Some of the Allied soldiers decided to crawl over to investigate. Halfway across in "no man's land" they discovered German soldiers crawling in the opposite direction. After meeting up with them, a discussion followed, and it was decided that at dawn the next day the opposing armies would exchange Christmas presents. This one event was to lead to other meetings and it became common for the two sides to play football games between the trench lines. When the fighting was ordered to resume it was difficult to get the soldiers to shoot at one another. They often fired into the air over their enemies' heads in the hopes that no one would be hit. Even with the influx of new recruits this impromptu policy remained in effect. This is a true story, it really happened. Just think about it for a while: they gave a war and peace broke out.

I have often thought about what the possible effects would be on mankind if reincarnation were somehow, miraculously, proven beyond any doubt, to be fact. Can you picture millions of people coming to the realization that everyone of us has been many different races during our earthly incarnations? **Our true nature is spirit.** We come from the same place, we return to the same place. We were born from the same energy, from the same source. I will refer to this source as God. You may use whatever term you feel comfortable with. Coming from God makes us part of God, therefore, our lineage from our creator makes us gods [small g]. We are powerful spiritual beings with the ability to create or destroy; it all boils down to our intentions. We are only renting these fleshy vehicles we inhabit; we have no true earthly ancestry. We are human chameleons with the ability to blend into our surrounding. Our camouflage is so perfect that we are able to hide from others of our own kind and at times ourselves. I wonder how people would act when presented with the truth that we are in actuality ageless, timeless beings whose true nature is race-less (or all-races). When faced with the reality that we are truly brothers and sisters [in the literal sense], what would they think? How would they act?

We should all take a lesson from September 11th, 2001. As those survivors, those ashen specters rose up from the remains of that dastardly act, there was a commonality. As they stumbled into the sunlight, there was no race, no yellow, black, white or any other skin tone, just gray. There are miles of film footage and tons of photos showing people helping and caring for one another. This touching display of concern should stand as a model to all of us. It should not take the worst to bring us to our best. Instead of looking at what makes us different, we need to start understanding what makes us the same, those common threads that run through us all.

I have left the best two observations for last. They are simple and need not be delved into at great length: **No one ever dies** (at least not in the way many perceive death here on Earth), and **Love lasts forever.**

My vision for this book was (and is) to get it into the hands of as many people as possible. I believe telling my story is one of my main missions in this life. The world is in an awakening period and I feel strongly the need to poke it in the ribs, so, dear reader, if you have gotten this far, consider yourself poked.

My journey of discovery has been long and extraordinary. It has taken me on forays into the distant past, which led to an introspective analysis of myself and a good look at our world today. I have some hopeful visions for the future, but it all depends on the willingness of everyone to work together. Like Anne Frank, I too believe, in spite of everything, people are really good at heart. I have already begun my excursion toward a better tomorrow, and it all started with someone else's yesterday.

THE CLOAK

What fools we be, that cannot see, the truth that lay
within.

There in the dark, that eternal spark, that makes us kith
and kin.

Push on I say, and find a way, to let the traveler roam.

Given free rein, though he suffer some pain, the pathway
will lead him back home.

Jeffrey J. Keene
(A gift from an in-between time)

Phoenix Rising

*To the 343 Fire Department of New York Firefighters who perished
on September 11, 2001*

(And to all those who worked "The Pile"
who are slowly following them)*

---

*   "The Pile:" term used by rescue workers to describe the 1.8 million tons of debris from the World Trade Center collapse. Many workers would succumb to health issues in the years that followed and that trend continues to this day.

Moments in Time

"All my previous selves have their voices, echoes, promptings, in me. My every mode of action, heat of passion, flicker of thought, is shaded, toned, infinitesimally shaded and toned, by that vast array of other selves that preceded me and went into the making of me."

Jack London, The Star Rover, 1915

IT IS BUT A MOMENT in time, one minute you are awake the next asleep, but sleep is not always restful and dreams not always fantasy.

Much like Jack London's character Darrell Standing in the book *The Star Rover* I have found myself as different people at different times throughout history. A World War II British soldier, an Irish girl, a Confederate general, a Firefighter, a Samurai, Native Americans, Monks and many others. I remember sunsets and sunrises over the mesas of the Southwest, the haunting horns of battle and armor made of steel, leather and wood. Also, there were beautiful gardens at a Franciscan monastery and a peaceful waterfall in Killarney. In all of my lives I have been chased by troubles, demons, ghosts, doubts, questions and fears. Chased that is until I caught them and faced them eyeball to eyeball. You can only run so far until one morning you open the front door only to finally greet yourself. If I have been all these races here on Earth what does that tell me? It tells me we are all race-less. The skin you are in, you chose to put on, much like donning a new suit of clothes.

The year 2020 started off in a strange way. The coronavirus pandemic traveled worldwide causing businesses to close and people to be quarantined in their homes. The United States Government threw ungodly amounts of money at the problem which quickly elevated the national debt to over 26 trillion dollars. As months went by the quarantine was slowly lifted with some restrictions such as face coverings to enter "essential businesses," social distancing (people staying 6 feet away from one another) and no large group gatherings. Millions had lost their jobs and some would not ever be able to return to the former employment due to the closing of the workplace because of the inability to survive the shutdowns. Then, as if things were not bad enough, there were protests, which turned to riots, and looting and arson began. Black Americans started protesting peacefully and had some legitimate grievances to air. As with many such movements they were quickly infiltrated by provocateurs who took advantage of the situation for their own ends. Enter the Marxist and another group with a long past history called ANTIFA (Anti-Fascists) who joined in and once again proved to be anything but Anti-Fascists. In Seattle, Washington within a short period of time they had even taken over a six-block area, which included the expulsion of the local police housed in that Precinct.

These protesters, rioters and malcontents were created mostly by a commandeered mass media and our educational system. Reporters disappeared and were replaced by repeaters spouting the party line and spreading the scripted talking points. They became very adept at taking sparks and turning them into conflagrations. This did not just happen; it was planned and put into effect over many decades by the Globalist. There is a direct correlation with the dramatic drop in the student testing scores and the creation of the Department of Education. Young people who were home-schooled did markedly better in testing than those who were not home-schooled. So, some states banned home-schooling. "No child left behind" did not bring those in need to higher levels but instead seemed to bring better students down to the lowest common denominator. Our youth were propagandized, indoctrinated and trained to hate America.

Out of this sprang a culture of victimhood. Instead of being taught how to be self-sufficient, free thinking, brave or inward-looking, they were taught to be fearful and helpless. The slightest thing could take our young out of their comfort zone. When "triggered" they became more fragile and would literally run to a "safe space" and do other things such as work on coloring books or cuddle with a teddy bear. Not a good way for college students about to go out into the world to act. I only wish I was making all this up, but sadly I'm not. College prices continued to rise until many were left with very large student loans that most likely would follow the student well unto the future or end in a default. Even after the time and expense in securing a degree such as an A.S., B.S., M.A. or even a Ph.D., it gave little hope of getting a JOB. Those that have been taught that the United States of America was spawned from Evil need to reeducate themselves and study history with less of a jaundiced eye. Maybe they would free their minds from imprisonment and soften their hearts that have been hardened by the greatly-flawed educational system. It made no difference if it was a Republican or Democrat running the government, they endeavored to inculcate our youth with a combination of Marxist, Communist and Socialistic indoctrination. A picture was painted of the United States, from its founding as evil, vile and irredeemably racist.

There were many protests around the nation. The tearing down of statues and defacing of monuments deemed offensive by the crowds became commonplace. Anything remotely thought of as having racist overtones became targets, whether real, perceived or even imagined. The main object of their displeasure was anything relating to the American Civil War, Northern or Southern appeared not to be added into the equation. Famous abolitionists and benefactors to the struggle of the Black race suffered the wrath of the masses. Torn down, beheaded or covered in paint— the people seemed to be making an attempt to erase the past. Even the Robert Gould Shaw Massachusetts 54th monument in Boston received a coating of graffiti. One of the greatest sculptors of all times, Augustus Saint-Gaudens, spent fourteen years on the high-relief bronze monument depicting Col. Shaw and his all Black Regiment, a group of men who were among the first African Americans to fight in that war. This regiment was depicted very well in the movie *Glory*. Col. Shaw, a white officer, died at the battle of Fort Wagner, South Carolina, along with more than 70 of his men. Sergeant William H. Carney, though severely injured, saved the regiment's flag from capture. Sergeant Carney became the first African American to be awarded the Congressional Medal of Honor.

The statue of General John B. Gordon that stands on the corner of the capitol building in Atlanta, Georgia, will most likely be removed before all is said and done. Was Gordon a racist, yes, as were many from that time period both North and South. Believe it or not, this is something we had been growing out of as a Nation. Today's youths have been judging from afar. They have moved on from Confederate statues and gone to the likes of George Washington, Ulysses S. Grant, Theodore Roosevelt and even Abraham Lincoln. While we are on the subject of Lincoln, here is a copy of his letter to Horace Greeley in response to a scathing editorial Greeley had written in the New-York Tribune. I have underlined a portion to draw attention, for those unfamiliar with this document, to show Lincoln's thought on saving the Union and slavery's role therein.

Executive Mansion,
Washington, August 22, 1862.

Hon. Horace Greeley:
Dear Sir.

I have just read yours of the 19th. addressed to myself through the New-York Tribune. If there be in it any statements, or assumptions of fact, which I may know to be erroneous, I do not, now and here, controvert them. If there be in it any inferences which I may believe to be falsely drawn, I do not now and here, argue against them. If there be perceptible in it an impatient and dictatorial tone, I waive it in deference to an old friend, whose heart I have always supposed to be right.

As to the policy I "seem to be pursuing" as you say, I have not meant to leave any one in doubt.

I would save the Union. I would save it the shortest way under the Constitution. The sooner the national authority can be restored; the nearer the Union will be "the Union as it was." If there be those who would not save the Union, unless they could at the same time save slavery, I do not agree with them. If there be those who would not save the Union unless they could at the same time destroy slavery, I do not agree with them. My paramount object in this struggle is to save the Union, and is not either to save or to destroy slavery. If I could save the Union without freeing any slave I would do it, and if I could save it by freeing all the slaves I would do it; and if I could save it by freeing some and leaving others alone, I would also do that. What I do about slavery and the colored race, I do because I believe it helps to save the Union; and what I forbear, I forbear because I do not believe it would help to save the Union. I shall do less whenever I shall believe what I am doing hurts the cause, and I shall do more whenever I shall believe doing more will help the cause. I shall try to correct errors when shown to be errors; and I shall adopt new views so fast as they shall appear to be true views.

I have here stated my purpose according to my view of official duty; and I intend no modification of my oft-expressed personal wish that all men everywhere could be free.

Yours,
A. Lincoln. *
(Source: abrahamlincolnonline.org)

When the Union victory at Antietam came along it set the stage for things to happen. The first of which being the Emancipation Proclamation, which took effect January 1, 1863, and freed the slaves in the states (and parts of states) currently engaged in rebellion against the Union. Lincoln did not have the right under the Constitution to free any slaves, as they were considered property. He issued the Emancipation Proclamation under the purview of being Commander in Chief of the armed forces in time

of war. It took the Thirteenth Amendment which was ratified by
the required number of states on December 6, 1865, to free all
persons under servitude. A secondary effect of the Emancipation
Proclamation was that by bringing the slave issue into the war it
would keep England, or other foreign nations, from entering on
the side of the South. I tell you this as an illustration that there
is a progression to things moving forward in histories' timeline.
Effects do not take place overnight. Civil War, an oxymoron, it is
very hard to keep wars civil. The worst thing about the American
Civil War was that it happened in the first place. With hindsight,
we can all agree that perhaps a better approach to the problem(s)
between North and South would have best been settled by nego-
tiation and compromise. In order to develop and advance you
need a history to build on. We learn from both our triumphs and
tragedies with hopefully an outlook to avoiding backsliding.

First statues are removed and as history has shown, real people are next. It is okay to look back and remember the past but
do not dwell there. Those days are gone and should be viewed
as stepping stones to the present and future. They were lessons
hard learned and should remain as guidance for a more advanced
society. I remember the South in the 1950s and stores and bars
with signs saying, "Colored takeout in the rear." There were gas
stations with three restrooms marked, "Men", "Women", and
the third, "Colored." I was stationed at Gunter Air Force Base
for medical training in Montgomery Alabama in 1965. George
Wallace was Governor at the time and the papers featured sad
tales of church bombings. I remember riding downtown once,
and only once, via the Dixie Cab company. Halfway to town the
driver drove up on the sidewalk just missing a black man (and a
telephone pole) and then back down into the street again. The
driver laughed and said, "That will teach that N..... to walk in
the street." Ever after I always used the Yellow Cab Company.
While stationed at Orlando Air Force Base in Florida, one of the
white sergeants I knew married a black WAF and when their
enlistment was completed they planned to return to his home
state of Arkansas. I often wondered how they fared in their new

life together because at that time interracial marriages were illegal in many states, Arkansas being one of them.

Past happenings are not snowflakes of memories to be melted on the griddle of hot tempers. If you call out prominent points in history you should start by leading up to that point and away from it to get the full picture. So, if you are going to point a finger you have an obligation to be ready to use all ten digits. A good rule is you should not take sides unless you know both sides, it is give and take. Stop looking for outside remedies to past problems, the answer does not lay in gifts, tributes or reparations. Americans have always helped others worldwide and would much rather give a hand up than a hand out.

Not the distant past but the more recent past, up to and including the present has brought about radical changes. A great wrong has been done us all in the United States and truly every country on Earth by those wishing to have a "New World Order" and "Global Governance." The bought-and-paid-for mainstream media spout the party lines and buzzwords over and over again in attempt to demoralize, ostracize and victimize people into classes and groups in order to divide and conquer totally. The free flow of people across borders has been to the detriment of most neighboring countries around the World. I am not anti-immigration; my beloved wife Anna came through Ellis Island in 1952 and my life would be incomplete without her. But there is a very simple rule, no border, no country. Immigration works very well when it is planned, orderly and systematic. If a country is overrun with migrants it is not long before all the reasons they fled to the region in the first place disappear right under their feet.

With age my eyes have grown weaker but still I see clearer each day. I think it would bode well for all of us if everyone would just lose the hyphen. Drop the African-American, Hispanic-American and Asian-American for just plain American. This advice goes for all groups that hyphenate their nationality. There is a big difference between your nationality and your genetic/ethnic or racial makeup. I personally have never used a hyphen; I think it would be a bit odd if I did. Let us give it a try:

I am an Irish-German-English-Swiss-Native American-American.

Those are some of the nationalities that I know of, so I guess you could say I'm a crossbreed or a mongrel. That is fine with me because I have always liked mutts better than purebreds anyway. If you want to have some fun, the next time you are filling out a form in the space where it says, "Race", write in "Human." We need to work our way out of being divided by class, race or religion while moving more into a homogenization of humanity. You can keep your identity and personality, your likes and dislikes, all those things that make you, "You." There is a great benefit for us all at this juncture in the United States to become one people; Americans. That benefit is something called Synergism, the whole becoming greater than the sum of its parts.

Years ago, people would light a candle to find their way in the darkness, they did not sit around bemoaning the fact that the sun goes away every evening. So, they started with fire and moved on to improvements such whale oil lamps, ignitable gases and eventually electric lights. Working with what was available and through trial and failure they continued to create, making everyone's life a little better. I guess you could say they put thought into the problem and truly became (pardon the pun) illuminated. Classroom Earth hands us many challenges to learn our lessons. We must strive to graduate, not be left behind, to take up where others left off and build on that foundation. The people from bygone eras were products of their time as are we all. They had to play the hands they were dealt. Those people from the past would find it difficult to function in our society with their mindset and the reverse is true also. You and I chose to come here and take part in the plot now unfolding. How will it all end? I can't tell you but, you should know, if you have been paying attention so far, that we all get out alive.

We can see shades of books written many years ago, books such as George Orwell's 1984, Animal Farm and Ray Bradbury's Fahrenheit 451 all working their way into our 21st century lives. There is no stretch of the imagination to draw parallels to many items mention in these books that had been written as a warning many years ago. We have already seen electronic book burning, pre-crime in the form of "Red Flag Laws", good think, bad speak and micro-aggression. Then there is the ever-present fear of the "cancel culture" where in an instant anyone can become persona non grata. For every problem there is a solution in the form of more and more laws resulting in less and less freedom, privacy or security for the citizenry. It might be wise for all to make themselves familiar with these books, for it seems that what was old is new again. Take heart though, for the past is fixed but the future is all possibilities.

Since I mentioned Mr. Bradbury, I would like to point out Ray Bradbury's short story Chrysalis (written in 1946-1947) from the book titled *The Cat's Pajamas*. The story is a tale is about two young men, one black and one white, on the beach in California each uncomfortable in their own skin. Walter applies lotion to lighten his skin while Bill strives for a dark tan. The ending is amusing while also being poignant. The boys find that they can't change the color of their skin, but they did find a new view of reality.

We are all God's children but I feel some of us could use a good spanking. I often wonder, have these protestors and rioters that we are seeing of late been here on Earth before in different skinsuits? Maybe in the not-so-distant past they were the repressors and now in this life feel they have become repressed. As you can imagine this could cause great inner conflict. But, reading this far means you know some of the working of a little thing called Karma. Much like the Earth itself, we all have our faults. Internal conflict can be pushed to the point of external manifestations. Let us hope that the year 2020 truly is a year of clear vision.

Instead of becoming stronger our country has been degraded over decades and has become more and more vulnerable on many fronts. Look at the infrastructure, utilities, banking, air travel and the internet among other things that bear greatly on our country's safety and function. Many things that are important to everyday function have been reduced to electronic digits and those digits can get turned off by a foreign enemy in the form of

an electromagnetic pulse (EMP) or even a totalitarian government desiring to turn someone into a nonentity. Contemplate
what your life would be like if all of a sudden, your bank card,
credit card or passport stopped working.

Recent storms have demonstrated what things are like with
no electric power, no cell phone, and no internet. Many found
themselves tossed into a modern-day Stone Age. Storm-struck
citizens received a taste of the "Good Old Days." Once there,
many revisited obscure things like doing puzzles, reading physical books and even the nearly-lost art of making conversation.
A few people had been foresighted enough to buy a generator in
case there was need of one. Many had purchased gasoline gen-
erators but when the generator was low on gas they rushed out
the gas station to find, low and behold, that the pumps at the gas
station run on electric power, the same power they did not have
at their homes. Surprising to many is the fact that most large
grocery stores do not have a massive warehouse in the back of
their stores. The truth is most food stores only keep a three-day
supply of food on hand. These food companies (and many other
non-food related companies) rely on the "supply chain" which
involves farms, factories, truckers, ships, stevedores, and the list
goes on and on. A word to the wise: after a week of food stores
being completely out of food do not open your front door if you
see your neighbor coming up your front walk with a salt and pep-
per shaker in each hand.

The technological, scientific and the medical communities
have advanced much more rapidly than we have with our spiritual
advancement. They have used their discoveries to not only turn
their finds into weapons of war to be used against humans, but to
use them against the natural order of things and God's plan for Earth
and its inhabitance. Our immune systems have been weakened with
unhealthy foods, polluted water, unclean air and genetically-modi-
fied crops and animals. I am reminded of the legend of Atlantis and
how they advanced to the point of their own destruction.

It would be prudent for each person to start some crash
courses in self-sufficiency with the aim of becoming masters of

your domain, you do not want to become dependent on Government because, as many people are finding, Government cannot always be depended upon when needed. It also seems that anything brought forth from Washington to supposedly better our lives come at a very high price in taxes, freedoms and even lives.

We are in a time of prodigious change and have been for a while, "Armageddon" if you will. Most of the salient points throughout the long history of Man are being replayed and acted out once again. In the meantime, God sits back and says, "Let us see how this all plays out." Much more entertaining than a flood and I hear God does not have cable yet. Think historically; sit for a while and think of things from the past long gone (or are they?) like the American Civil War, or decadent pre-war Berlin in the 1930s and conjure up words like Crusades, genocide or slavery. Me thinks I see them again. And yes, slavery is still taking place in our World in different forms under many guises.

I feel a great part of my mission(s)—and we all have them—is to get people to think. Sounds simple doesn't it, but in actuality it can be quite challenging. I strive to be a point of light in an occasionally dark World. It is not easy endeavoring to put others on the right path. I know many will not come along willingly and will have to be coaxed along to become enlightened to who and what they are. Here is a statement I would like for you to contemplate:

Consciousness is omnipresent in all points in time and space.

There is only One Awareness even though many are still unaware of it. We are all part of that Awareness, that Singularity, we are truly One.

Now, even though you might not grasp this concept or outright disbelieve it, wouldn't it be wonderful if everyone acted as if it was a proven fact?

Along the Way

I will, I won't, I do, I don't, I wouldn't, I couldn't, I shan't, I can't. Sounds a bit like a Dr. Seuss book, doesn't it? We make decisions each day, every day, some large some small. Do I eat the last cookie in the box, should we pull the life support? One could give you a little weight gain, the other a great loss. I have been traveling this road of discovery involving reincarnation for many years, nearly 30, and have gained and lost many people along the way. Several of them with stories of their own that either enhanced my story or gave me new insight into the working of the World around us, seen and unseen. I would like to share with you some of the comings and goings of the people I have met and perhaps not just in this lifetime.

Jessica Jones/Jewett

Enter Jessica, a diminutive young lady with big heart and talents that seem endless. Jess contacted me with questions on my story of reincarnation while questioning what to do with her own.

Email dated Apr 22, 2006 at 3:11 AM

"Hi Jeff,

I finished reading your book this morning and reading any book that quick is no easy feat for dyslexics like me. I stayed up until 3 a.m. last night reading it. Just when I would find a place to quit for the night, you'd say something else that made me snap up and say "that's right!" Parts of it made me laugh, parts of it made me cry, but all of it was like reading my own journal (minus

242

the traveling). The end is exactly what I have been trying to tell people my entire life.

I have been going back and forth with myself all day, having finished the book, about whether I should tell you my story or not. We knew each other indirectly (at least I haven't found evidence that we physically met), and our connection is the reason I followed your story for this long, but since you seem to get so many stories you didn't ask for, I will let you decide. I'll leave you with my phone number and you can decide if you'd like to talk further or not. Or I can always tell my story by email if you decide that too. I won't be hurt if you don't want to hear another story, trust me.

Here is my number: (414) 431-xxxx and if I don't answer that, I will answer (414) 364-xxxx.

And as always, thank you for your time and thank you for the opportunity to read your story. It has given me more comfort and guidance than I can express."

Jessica and I did talk by phone, emails and in person. She was conflicted on whether or not to go public with her story. I was to learn that she believed that she had been Fanny Chamberlain, wife of Civil War general and Maine governor, Joshua Lawrence Chamberlain. Generals Gordon and Chamberlain were planning to co-lecture but those plans ended with Gordon's passing in 1904.

Jessica once asked me the following question:
"How much do you divulge as John Gordon and how much do you keep to yourself?"

Her question took me back to a speaking engagement I had in the town of Gordon's youth. My reply to Jessica was as follows:

When I spoke to the John B. Gordon Camp (SCV**) I told them they could ask any question they liked but please do not test me as you would Gen. Gordon. I said, "I am not Gen. Gordon, I

---

*   Gen. John B Gordon Camp #599, Sons of Confederate Veterans, LaFayette, GA

believe I had been him in another lifetime but now I am Jeffrey Keene. You could test me on this lifetime and I would most likely fail with the outset of short-term memory failure. I do believe I can answer questions as Gordon would, seeing how he and I share a common history." They were OK with that and asked questions for over two hours. I guess I did all right because they made me an Honorary Member.

   Best, Jeff

Years later on October 20, 2009, Jessica's book hit Amazon, the title simply and to the point: "Unveiled: Fanny Chamberlain Reincarnated." Jessica writes under the nom de plume Jessica Jewett. I was honored that she asked me to write the introduction for her coming-out-of-the-shadows story.

Edain McCoy

   Edain was a wonderful person with a bewitching smile and for a very good reason; she was a very cute blonde witch. Yes, witch. There are many, many, witches walking around in our midst, good witches, not the black hat pointy nosed type portrayed in the media. When people refer to them as Pagans the uninformed equate it with Satanism, which could not be further from the truth. A Pagan simply is a person holding religious beliefs other than those of the main world religions. Today's Pagan, with a capital P, often refers to people who follow Neo-Pagan religions that honor the Earth. Edain was the real McCoy as they say. She really was a descendant of the famous McCoy family of the legendary Hatfield / McCoy feud. The following information was gleaned from an Amazon write-up;

   Edain has written more than twenty books on metaphysical and occult topics since she was first published in 1993. An alumna of the University of Texas with a B.A. in history, she pursued a Master of Fine Arts at Butler University. She is listed in the reference guides Contemporary Authors, Who's Who Among American Women, and Who's Who in America, and her articles have appeared in Fate, Circle, Enlightenments, and similar periodicals. She spent many years as a licensed stockbroker and financial advisor for several international investment firms before making the leap of faith into her first love—writing full time.

Edain passed a short time back, a fact that I was only made aware of by buying a used copy of my own book Someone Else's Yesterday. I buy used copies when I find them at a low price and give them away. One of these copies arrived in the mail and I was surprised to find an inscription inside that I recognized right away. Most of the time I just signed books, "Best Wishes" and that is it, this one read, "To my dear sweet Edain, much love; Jeff." There was a piece of paper inside the book, it was a short tale about Gen. Chamberlain's reaction to Gen. Gordon's death. I had given it to her when we met at the Effigy Shoppe in Monroe CT. I did not think she would have given up the book willingly with the quote still inside. I could tell she had kept the book close because you could smell her perfume emanating from the pages. A short search on the computer confirmed my fears; Edain had succumbed to complications from influenza in early 2019.

Edain contacted me many years ago about her belief that she had been the daughter Gen. Joshua Lawrence Chamberlain, the same General Chamberlain who had accepted the surrender of the Army of Northern Virginia (led off by Gen. John B. Gordon) at Appomattox Court House. We corresponded back and forth and she informed me that she would be doing readings at Effigy in Monroe and would just be in town for a very short time. In order to talk with her I booked an hour with her and arrived at the appointed time. After being introduced to Edain by the owner of the store, we retired to a room set up for such sessions. There was no reading for me that day, instead we sat and talked like two old friends who had not seen each other in decades. We talked mainly about the two old Generals and their families. I mentioned that the Generals had been planning to co-lecture together on the Civil War and the ending they shared at Appomattox C.H. It was not to be. I gave her the paper that told of Gordon writing to his sick friend Gen. Chamberlain and Chamberlain's reaction to Gordon dying.

Quote given to Edain on day we talked:

> "Years passed and the two distinguished soldiers had long been
> fast friends. Gen. Chamberlain was sick, as it seemed to himself and
> others with but small hope of recovery, and (copy cut here) soldier
> he said; "Dear old fellow, can't bear to lose you." Months went by,
> the northern soldier rallied and the southern commander died, and
> when Gen. Chamberlain was told of the death of Gen. Gordon he
> stepped into a stairway, sat down and wept bitterly. The bravest of
> the brave, it could have been said of him as Thackeray said of Col.
> Newcomb: "His heart was like that of a child.""*

It was a pleasure talking to Edain, she was bright, funny and the
time passed all too quickly. We talked for a couple of hours because
she was not booked for the hour after mine. We did run a little into
the next person's appointment time though but the next person
actually wanted to hear about Edain and me. What are the odds of
Edain's book returning to me? I never was very good at math but I
don't think odds had anything to do with it anyway. Maybe there
was a little bit of magic involved, thanks Edain.

While we are on the subject of people dying, I turned 72 on
September 9, 2019, and have found that one of the drawbacks of
getting older is that the longer you live the more people in your
life disappear. My father died at 66 and my older brother at 53.
The first girl I ever truly loved; Susan Hartsig died at 57 after
a long fight with cancer. My lifelong friend John "Bruce" Baker
and I were classmates all through the Westport school system
from Bedford Elementary, Bedford Jr. High to and through Staple
High School. We even joined the Air Force together. Bruce was a
couple inches taller than me and stood around six foot two. He
was built like an oak tree, had a broad smile and big heart. Having retired to Florida he enjoyed the outdoors and golfing. One
day he was bitten by an ant and went into a coma. Two weeks
later he died. But, is death really an end or just a new chapter?

---

*   I cannot remember the source of this bit of information I gave Edain, but
       I did find mention of it taking place in the Custom House in Portland
       Maine the first month of 1904. From the book Fanny and Joshua first
       published in 1999.

Mildred Lockwood Keene Loubet

Aunt Milly was widowed in her mid-30s and was left with my cousins Dave and Betsy. In our youth Dave and I spent a lot of time together even though we lived in different towns. Sleepovers, overnight campouts, double dating and we even ended up marrying sisters. This fact would later cause a bit of confusion to Dave's son, my nephew Judd. One day young Judd said, "Uncle Jeff" and I replied, "I'm your cousin, go ask your father." He disappeared for a short while and upon his return he said, "Cousin Jeff" at which point I cut him short by saying, "I'm your Godfather, go ask your father." I could tell Judd was growing weary of this roundabout game so we finally settled on Uncle Jeff. Now my Aunt Milly did her best to hold Dave and me in check and as I look back now, she did a really good job. I will always be grateful to her for saving me from myself, from what would have been a life-altering mistake. She also made the best peanut butter cookies and sent me some when I was in basic training at Lackland Air Force Base in Texas. I did not get to eat all of them because once the other guys in the barrack smelled homemade cookies the bottom of the box appeared very quickly.

I have always described my Aunt Milly as looking very much like Marilyn Monroe, not the Marilyn Monroe of Hollywood fame but pre-Hollywood days when she was known by her real name, Norma Jeane Mortenson. Back then Marilyn had a clean, wholesome, girl next door look. My Aunt Milly was also just as sweet as she was pretty. When I found myself in the neighborhood I would stop by her house for a visit. She loved animals, horses, cows, and had a special fondness for dogs. Her last dog was adopted; it was very large and had a great dislike for men and would avoid them as much as possible. My Aunt believed the dog had been abused and mistreated by some man or men and from the reactions I saw I think she was correct in her assumption. I stopped by with an autographed copy of my book *Someone Else's Yesterday* for my aunt. We sat in her living room, her on one side of the room and me on the other in a high-sided chair. As I sat there, I could see this big fuzzy mountain of a dog slowly inching its way closer to the right side of my chair, the side furthest from my aunt which made it out of her line of sight. I put my hand down over the side of the chair and readied myself for either a wet sniffing nose or a painful chomp. I will not hold you in suspense; it turned out to be the nose first followed by the head and then the whole body. The dog sat there while I patted her and scratched her behind the ears. My Aunt and I continued to talk for five minutes or so when she noticed something was going on. She said, "Jeff, what are you doing?" I said, "Petting the dog." She said, "You're the first man she has ever allowed to touch her." I said, "I have a way with some animals" and I do, I once had a squirrel named Hughey, not a pet squirrel but a wild one. Hughey imprinted on me at a very early age and would sit on the rail of our porch looking through the window until I brought out some nuts or other goodies. Sometimes Hughey would sit on my lap and eat or climb on to my shoulder and we would walk around the yard together. Hughey was followed by Piggy, named after her eating habits. A visitor once asked if we had any cardinals after viewing the bird feeder in the backyard. I said, "Give me a minute" and chopped up some walnuts. I went out the backdoor and whistled for the cardinals while I spread nuts on the railing. A short time later there were more than a dozen cardinals taking turns picking up walnut pieces and flying away with their booty. I even taught my grandson Ryan how to hand feed chickadees from the palm of his hand. I really must have been a Franciscan somewhere along the line.

It is not only animals: I have a way with but people, specifically those in the process of dying or recently passed. Aunt Milly had many health problems in her later years. In July of 2003 my daughters informed me that my aunt was in Norwalk Hospital and not expected to live much longer. I drove to the hospital and went to the nurse's desk on the floor where my aunt's room was. I told the nurse I was a nephew and asked if there were any family in her room as I thought I might run into my cousin Dave. She informed me that there were no visitors but I could go in alone. I entered the room and walked to the left side of the bed.

My aunt was just lying there with her eyes closed while IV bottles and machines were clustered around her. I picked up her right hand and held it in mine. A short time later she opened her eyes and said, "Oh, Jeff." I said, "How are you doing?" and she said, "Not so good." We talked a little and then she said that she was very tired and needed to rest. She closed her eyes and I said "Ok, you rest. I love you Aunt Milly." and placed her hand back down on the bedcovers. I talked with my cousin Dave on the phone after my aunt's passing, which had been only hours after my visit with her. Dave said, "You went over and saw my mother?" I said, "Yes, we had a nice talk but she said she was tired so I did not stay long." Dave said, "What did you talk about?" I said, "You, your sister, just things in general." Dave said, "Jeff, my mother was in a coma for three days and has not spoken to anyone!" I said, "Well, she spoke to me."

Sometimes people speak to us nonverbally or with signs. Case in point this time is one of my uncles.

Albert "Pete" Spadaccino

My Uncle Pete was a barber and on some visits to our house he would bring his "clippers." Of course it was upon my parent's suggestion he do so. One time, back in the Elvis Presley era, I had myself some really nice sideburns and wavy hair. A chair was placed in the backyard and I was to be the first haircut. I told my uncle not to take too much off and sat down. He said, "Ok" and started to work. I swear I saw a little wink from Uncle Pete to my parents. Well, it was all over before I knew it, all electric razor and no scissors. I was now the proud owner of a crewcut. I never really forgave him for the de-Elvis job. Over the years I would get other haircuts from Uncle Pete both sitting in the yard or in his shop in Danbury. None of them were a traumatic as that scalping back in the Fifties. Well, time passes and revenge is a dish best served cold as they say.

I visited my Uncle Pete in the Danbury Hospital along with my Uncle Mickey. Uncle Pete was in a coma and had been for days. We spoke to him but of course he did not reply. Just before leaving I went to his bedside and said, "Hey, Uncle Pete, do you remember that crewcut you gave me back in the fifties? Well, I wish I had my 'Clippers' with me I could fix you real good." As I said this, I was running my fingers through his hair just above his ear on the left side of his head. Have to admit, I was a bit jealous; he did have nice thick hair as many Italian barbers do.

One night shortly after my visit to see Uncle Pete I sat typing at my computer. I was continually interrupted by what I perceived to be a fly or some other insect just above my left ear. Looking around the room there was no sign of anything in the air. I looked in the mirror to see if anything was crawling on my head but saw nothing. This went on for quite a while, up and down, swatting and cursing but to no avail. Always the same spot. Then, just as suddenly as it had started it ceased. I was later to find out my Uncle Pete had died the same day as this strange nocturnal episode. I laughed, over the left ear, the same area I had taunted him while in his unresponsive state. A payback and a goodbye all in one.

Frances Wragge Lake Placid, N.Y.

Frances Wragge was my first wife Bridget's grandmother. Some mornings after a nightshift at the firehouse I would have coffee with Grandma Fran in the apartment I built downstairs for her and my mother-in-law Bette. Grandma Fran was multi-talented. She came from Lake Placid N.Y. Attended Julliard, taught piano and had even been in the Ziegfeld Follies. She made a point of telling me how Flo Ziegfeld was a real taskmaster and drove the girls pretty hard. Grandma Fran had some great stories about horse-drawn sleighs (and even cars sometimes) on the frozen lakes during the cold winter months in upstate New York, and mass deer hunt drives down through the valleys. She was a good cook and fed me like I was a lumberjack. We were close and I still miss our talks and coffee together. The night Grandma Fran died we followed the ambulance to Norwalk Hospital only to find that she had expired on the way. The Emergency Room personal informed us we could go in and see her in one of the small rooms used to accept incoming patients.

I, along with my brother-in-law Mike, asked to go in alone and the family told us to go ahead in. I went in and found Grandma Fran lying on the bed with her eyes wide open. It took me a while to tell her how much she had meant to me, and when I finished, I leaned over and kissed her on the forehead. Upon standing I saw her left eye slowly close and reopen. She winked at me? Or, maybe it was just some muscles twitching. I told no one on this happening. Days later we attended her wake in upstate New York. Now, Bridget's brother Mike and Grandma Fran had a strange relationship; she would sometimes refer to him as her "beloved bastard" but they really did love each other very much. While on the porch of the funeral parlor having a cigarette, I could overhear Mike and his brother Birney talking. Mike was telling him about going in and seeing Grandma Fran at the hospital, leaning over and kissing her, and when he stood up—at this point I interjected, "She winked at you" he said, "You too!" Well, if it had been muscle twitches Grandma Fran had some excellent timing. She was a great old gal.

Anthony J. Esposito

Tony Esposito was my friend for over forty years. He helped me through some really rough times like my divorce from my first wife. I could just not get used to the idea of not living with my two daughters and watching them grow. My daughters Shannon and Samantha and I tried for a few months living the life of a single parent dad with a twist, my estranged wife Bridget had to come over and stay with the girls when I worked nights. Also, another complicating factor was that my mother-in-law lived in the lowest level of the house. She was very helpful getting the kids off the bus, but you can see where this arrangement could become quite wearing on me and confusing to the girls. The only solution I could come up with was for Bridget to come home and

me to leave. I found a two-room basement apartment in Westport and moved out. I lost more than fifty pounds during that
period but I do not recommend divorce as a weight loss regimen.

Now, my friend Tony owned the Tabagerie Limited of Westport, a men's gift and tobacco shop, and that is where we first
met back in 1979. I even started working there part time. This
served a couple purposes; one I was earning a little money and
two it kept me busy and not sitting around my apartment on my
days off from the fire department being haunted by my problems.
For the last ten years of his life Tony gradually went downhill
from cancer, heart problems and emphysema. Tony had been a
member of the Ansonia Rod and Gun Club for many decades.
They have skeet, trap, rifle and pistol ranges. Tony sponsored me
and I became a member just as his illnesses were starting to get
the better of him. We would go shooting together at the pistol
range until Tony's left hand went numb and he found loading the
revolvers and pistols very difficult. I would then do the loading
but after a while even holding and shooting the gun became a
chore for him. I would then pick up Tony and drive him to the
clubhouse just to visit with members while I shot at the range
and drive him home again. Then his visits to the club stopped
altogether.

I continued to go to Club but to save money, I bought a CZ
455 22 caliber rifle to shoot at the range. The bullets for a 22lr
rifle are rather inexpensive and I have always loved shooting
rifles. When finished at the club I would then pick up some coffee and food and drive to Tony's to show him the targets and
watch TV. Now, 22 caliber rifles are close range guns and not
really meant for target past fifty yards. I like to push myself so I
set a goal of cutting a playing card in half edgewise at 100 yards.
The 22 is a low-powered bullet and drops in flight approximately
seven inches from the fifty-yard mark out to one hundred yards.
Shooting from a bench using a bipod, the trajectory to 100 yards
looks something like a low-rise rainbow. With a high powered
rifle-scope, you can actually see the bullet drop into the sight
picture as it hits the target. I made a small device to hold a play-

ing card edgewise on the target board and the first day I set it up, the wind was gusting quite briskly. Twenty-twos are very much affected by wind and can be blown off course by a few inches out at 100 yards. Having shot a few targets and zeroed the 24-power scope, I decided to try my luck with the card. The first shots were a little to one side of the card so I held off to the other side squeezed the trigger and could see the bottom half of the card drop to the ground. I had met my goal so I started to concentrate on ever smaller five shot groups. With practice I was getting five round groups under one inch in size and sometimes under a half inch.

After my daily outings I would show Tony my targets to which he would reply, "You can't do much better than that." But every time he would say this, I would prove him wrong. Tony went into hospice and on the morning of July 1, 2019, I was shooting at the range and on one target I could not quite tell where the bullets were going. I looked with the scope all around the target to see if the wind had carried them off course. Upon retrieving the target, I just saw a couple of small holes. I asked the range master if he thought five bullets went through those holes. He said, "Turn the target over." I did as he asked and it then became obvious that five rounds had indeed gone through those holes. When measured from center to center it measured less than five sixteenth of an inch, the head of a 22lr bullet is three sixteenth of an inch.

When I arrived home my wife Anna and my stepdaughter Katie were talking in the driveway. Katie said, "I'm sorry about your friend." I took this to mean Tony had passed, and he had that very morning. I laughed when I looked at the target in my hand, I knew where Tony was that morning, he was looking through my scope and laughing as he said, "You can't do much better than that." I wrote "Tony Target" on the target and put it up on the wall in my office. A week after Tony's funeral I receive a lovely card in the mail from one of Tony's daughters thanking me for being such a good friend to her father. Inside the card was a mass card with Tony's picture on it. I was hit with a rush of sadness. I went to a back window and stood their looking outside. In a short while something caught my eye. Way up in the sky I could see something floating down to Earth. Back and forth it went, side to side, it finally became apparent it was a small feather. There were no birds around and it came literally out of the blue. It settled gently right in the middle of a large bright yellow leaf on the ground, the only yellow leaf in sight. I went outside and picked up the small feather and if it had not landed on the yellow leaf I most likely would not have been able to find it. I took it as a sign and brought it inside and stuck it into the holes in the "Tony Target."

The power of the soul to communicate after death has always amazed me. Not just human souls but animal souls as well. Sid the cat came along with my second wife Anna as did two step-sons and a stepdaughter. Sid was one of the crankiest cats that ever lived. She cranked when she was hungry and many were the times I would hear Anna and Sid bitching back and forth at each other in the kitchen. When Sid wanted to go outside she would let everyone in the house know by emitting a nerve tingling noise that was somewhere in-between a baby's scream and fingernails on a chalkboard. Sid was a beloved pain in the ass and was not a prizewinner in the looks department either, partially caused from multiple surgeries (one to remove her thyroid which left her dependent on daily medication) and a rough outdoor life. Sid was tough and would drag home dead squirrels larger than herself. We had a tree in the front yard that was around three feet thick and acted as Sid's scratching post. The tree eventually died and the family believes to this day that Sid killed it.

She disappeared in her 19th year of life. Nineteen years for a raggedy, deaf, old outside cat is a pretty ripe old age. Anna would keep going to the door calling Sid because she knew she needed her thyroid meds to live. The days past with no sign of Sid. About four or five days after Sid first went missing, I was standing look-ing out the front door when I spotted Sid running across the yard heading for her favorite scratching post tree. I was just about to yell to Anna that Sid was back when the errant cat vanished into thin air a couple feet short of the tree. I kept the matter to myself.

More days passed, and I walked into the kitchen where I

found Anna crying as she washed some dishes. I asked her what was wrong. She turned around and asked me if she could tell me something and would not think her crazy. It appears on two separate occasions while doing dishes she had looked down and seen Sid sitting quietly on the floor just looking up at her. I told her she was not crazy and explained I had also seen Sid but, seeing how she disappeared before my eyes I had kept it to myself. A week or so later, Anna and I went to Pennsylvania to visit relatives. One night Anna got a cell phone call from our daughter Katie who was checking up on our two remaining indoor cats Jasmine and Pywacket. I could see there was a strange look on Anna's face and when she finished the call I said, "Katie saw Sid didn't she?" Anna confirmed Katie had seen her just sitting on the kitchen floor. Well, at least now Sid has finally learned to be quiet.

I have only had one pet in my life and that was a 14-pound flame point Himalayan cat named Pywacket. Pywacket was named after the cat in the James Stewart Kim Novak movie Bell Book and Candle. Py and I were best buddies and he would sit on my shoulder (until he got to big) and I would tell people he was my parrot. He loved for me to chase him up the two flights of stairs in my condo until he disappeared behind the wall halfway up the second-floor stairs. Then I would wait by the edge of the wall until he came back down the stairs, with my face at the end of the wall between the first open spindles he would come to. He caught on to this after a few times and would sneak down the stairs, jump around the corner and smack me on the nose with his paw. Then, the roles would be reversed and he would chase me. One day, just after chasing Pywacket up the stairs Katie walked up to the second floor where I stood. She said, "What are you doing?" I said, "Be very quiet and go look around the corner of the wall on the stairs through the railing." She slowly walked over to the stairs and followed my instructions to the letter. There was a large white paw on her nose within seconds followed by a loud scream.

One of Py's favorite things to do was to get on the couch next to me, turn around a few times, flick his left paw out and lay down while leaning on my leg. He did not care to be petted and sometimes if you tried to pet him, he would get up and leave. He wanted to be with me but on his terms. I have read, that dogs have masters and cats have staff. I believe it. Py would also do this paw flick, lean on my leg thing when I was lying on the floor or after our nightly routine. At night when I turned the computer off and the shutdown music played, you could count to ten and Pywacket would walk into the room, then he would then follow me upstairs. Once I was settled into bed Py would jump up on the bed and wait for me to scratch the top of his head, his ears and under his chin. Then he would get between my legs at the calves, flick his left paw and lean on my leg. He would only stay there for about twenty minutes and then hop off the bed, walk to the doorway, turn and look back in the room one last time before clomping down the stairs (yes, clomp, I told you he weighed 14 pounds). This went on nightly for years.

Pywacket passed when he was almost 17 years old, many years ago. Well, he is gone but he's not. Just last night I took a book to bed with me and as I laid on my back reading, I felt the covers moving between my lower legs. I could not see anything that would be causing this motion but then suddenly there was a familiar pressure on my left calf. Could this be Py stopping by to say hello? Maybe it was just a muscle spasm I thought, so I moved my left leg around and repositioned it back where it had been but this time, I had my legs a little closer together. Once again, the covers moved followed by the pressure on my left calf. One thing was different this time; I could feel pressure on my right calf also that was very reminiscent of the haunches of a large cat I once knew. I turned the light off and went to sleep.

Death is not the end. Take solace in the fact that these partings are only a temporary proposition. Death is not an ending but more like a returning home after a long road trip. Your body is just your connection to this earthly world. In *Someone Else's Yesterday* I wrote about a message I kept getting over and over, "What once was will be again" We are all going home.

Death is one of the few things in this life that you don't have to practice to be successful at. I am looking forward to dying. I don't want to rush it though. Self-inflicted death brings with it the risk of having to repeat a lifetime under similar conditions as the one you aborted because you have a contract with God, and yourself, to complete your mission and life lessons. Yes, mission, very much reminiscent of a medieval knight-errant on a quest, wandering in search of noble adventures. Ladies don't fret; you are not being left out. There have been many female knights down through history, they may not have held the title "Knight," but some chivalric orders accepted females into their organizations. These women, either in an organization or not, would at times don armor, think Joan of Arc.

Even with reincarnation you are only born once. That once was at the time of your creation when you were born in spirit. Everything after in the Earth realm is just a vignette; or think of it as being similar to a television series, but that series and yourself are not constant but ever changing from different eras, countries, languages, skin colors and even gender. It is like bouncing through time and space making little semicircles on your way to coming back full circle. Reincarnation is not a beginning or end but more of a continuation.

The Other Side, the Spirit Plain of existence is so unimaginably amazing, so far beyond the here and now that with our limited earthly consciousness, our human brain, we cannot even conceive of what questions to ask. We are very powerful spiritual beings. Our True nature is Spirit; you are Spirit in the flesh having a human experience. Let us just say that you have an internal light that causes this external Life. Don't think that your body is YOU, think higher as if you are a puppeteer animating or bringing to life the human body. Or you can think of your body as a vehicle, like a car. There are many different models, color, sizes, shapes and choices of options. But still the body is not the true self. Energy cannot be created or destroyed, just changed. But this energy that we possess had to have a start somewhere, did it not? Long before you were born here, you existed and you will continue to exist after your Earth life is complete.

While we are here, on this Earth, we should be cautious about what we think. There is something faster than the speed of light and that thing is thought. Thoughts travel with us and thoughts are things not confined to our brains; they are both internal and external; they can even transcend time. Time, distance and space are human concepts and measurements. We have a biological ancestry here during Earth incarnations but that is a human condition and once again not the true self. You have a Celestial Lineage and Spiritual DNA that traces all the way back to the Creator, God, primum movens or whatever other names you care to use. A little something about prayers; please keep in mind that all prayers are answered. The answers many times are as simple as yes, no and not at this time. The answer may not be the one you are looking for, but it could be an even better one for you to move you in a new direction. When times get tough remember this: when you are digging yourself into a hole the first thing you need to do is stop digging and figure which way is up and out.

Many people's problems arise from wanting or acquiring possessions. We cannot own any physical things here on Earth. Ask any homeowner they will tell you how much the home owns them, what with all the payments and upkeep. And, you can't take things with you when you depart. There is only one thing you can truly own, yourself, your thoughts, actions and deeds, those you have to live with and not just in this lifetime.

I will ask you a question that you most probably cannot answer, though it may seem like a very simple answer. What is your name, your real name? My grandfather on my father's side last name was Keene but, his family changed their name to Keene from the German name Kuhn. To complicate things even more, my father was adopted but had found his birth parents and his birth father, born in Ireland, had the last name Patten. Now Patten is the Irish version of the American name Patton. This I find amusing seeing how Gen. George Patton had a penchant for stories of his past lives. If you have incarnated into this World many times, say twenty just for argument's sake, and had different names each time, what is your name? We may get an exact one in the future according to Revelation:

Revelation 2:17
New King James Version

"He who has an ear, let him hear what the Spirit says to the churches. To him who overcomes I will give some of the hidden manna to eat. And I will give him a white stone, and on the stone a new name written which no one knows except him who receives it."

I think what we may be using as a name in the meantime is more of frequency generation or vibrations.* That would make it simple for others who have known us in another lifetime to recognize us. Like radio stations say 1010 WINS New York or 960 AM or VHF, UHF… If others care to get a hold of you, all they need do is literally dial up your frequency in order to communicate with you. God and the Angels are at your fingertips and a man's reach need not always exceed his grasp.

In some of our lives here the journey may seem fairly ideal all the way from childhood on and up to old age and death. Other lives could be so full of brutality and woes to the point that you may feel the most you can hope for is a soft place to die. You are going to have what you may think of as failures, but are they really failures? Many people throughout history have considered the low point in their life as what moved them forward the most. With advanced age some would look back to those lean years, those years of struggle, with fond memories. A good suggestion is to treat life as a passer-by, for we truly are transients. "This too shall pass" is a Persian adage that reflects on the temporary nature of the human condition. Have regrets? We turn once more to Persia and one of their great men, a mathematician, astronomer, philosopher, and poet:

_____

* A great paper: International Journal of Social Work and Human Services Practice Horizon Research Publishing, Vol.6. No.3 July, 2018, pp. 75-88
A Study to Explore the Effects of Sound Vibrations on Consciousness By Meera Raghu, Independent Researcher, New Zealand
A PDF can be found at hrpub.org (Author's note)

"The moving finger writes; and, having writ, moves on: nor all thy piety nor wit shall lure it back to cancel half a line, nor all thy tears wash out a word of it."

— Omar Khayyam, Rubáiyát of Omar Khayyam

There are lessons not only to be learned but to be taught. You do not come into the World empty handed but with a very large bag of knowledge to use for your own lifetime in this Earthly realm, and to aid others. Now, once here things can become a bit challenging. I have modified the old "lead a horse to water but you can't make him drink" adage to fit the occasion, *you can lead a person to knowledge but you can't make him think.* This goes for oneself as well as those you come in contact with in your travels. You create your own World in your mind and it can be literally a Heaven or Hell. If you would like to get a head start on others when it comes to what Heaven can be like, just watch the movie *What Dreams May Come*, starring Robin Williams. There are some very simple rules and if you learn them early it may save you some grief later. The Mind is the creator; everything starts as a thought and builds from there. That is why Robin William's wife was in Hell, a Hell of her own making and he took it upon himself to save her from herself. Like attracts like, light attracts light and dark attracts dark. If you want love, you must first give love. If you want friends, you must first be a friend. If you chose darkness, grief, pity or any other sorrowful masters, then these will follow until you decide to end it. Believe it or not one of your harshest critics when you get back to the Other Side is not God, but yourself.

You truly only live once but you put on many suits or mantles here on Earth, and you are off with a new persona to take up the mission for God and yourself. You bring in with you many gifts from other lives, gleaned from all the knowledge you have gained from all of those experiences and between times living in sprit. But just what you need for this lifetime is what we shall refer to as a new brain. If you were to try to function on Earth with all your lifetimes swirling in your head you would most likely end up in the record books as the greatest case of schizophrenia ever recorded. Don't despair; you can have access to all your thoughts on your return back to spirit. We have seen a greater entrance of what are called child prodigies or a wunderkind. These are people who are bringing back with them a greater amount of knowledge from other lifetimes.

I worry about many of today's youth though. You know the ones, sitting hunched over, thumbs moving rapidly across a miniature keyboard, the glare of an electric devices showing in their glowing faces. It brings to mind an *Alice Through the Looking Glass* world. I pray these devices do not become permanent mirrors of the soul. We see celebrities full of pride and vanity, terrible role models being flaunted in every media outlet 24 hours a day. Some are simply famous for being famous. Suicide rates are up alarmingly among our young people. We have kids killing themselves because they were "unfriended" by others they never even met on some social media site. Now you can be in the Earth realm and still not be alive. By that I mean you're here, but you're not if you are not a participant and advancing your life or contributing to society as a whole in a positive way. Too often we have seen what people can do out of hate. In your life try and see what can be done out of love.

Returning to Earth

Why must I leave, why must I go out.
To find my true-self of that I've no doubt.
I will depart; though I prefer to stay here.
To better myself and those I hold dear.
To travel so far, such a great distance to roam.
Just to end at the start; right back at my home.
I will solve some riddles and travel afar.
I will fight many battles, even take on a scar.
Countless travels without many journeys within.
I will climb a tall mountain just to see where I've been.
Will others still know me, will they aid in my quest.
Maybe put me to task or just let me rest.
Shall I kiss the young maidens, will they lead me astray.
Will they want me to leave or beg that I stay.
There is an ember inside me that I really must tend.
Though the container may get broken, I know it will mend.
I will find great love but will also know pain.
No matter which one, there is so much to gain.
There's a fire in my heart that I must keep alight.
So it never goes out and will always glow bright.
I shall play my part and to my role I'll be true.
And I will further my soul, not just for me, but for you.

Jeffrey J. Keene
(A gift from an in-between time)

The Phoenix

(The Phoenix is often referred to as a fire bird, because it dies and is reborn out of fire.)

AM I DOING THE RIGHT thing by telling this story that may arouse feelings deep within others? I am a believer in signs and as I write this a small fire-red dragonfly landed on my writing tablet. In Native American legends, the dragonfly is a symbol of resurrection, and renewal after hardship. I took this as a sign to continue.

I spent 35 years in Fire Service and retired as an Asst. Chief in 2003. The mention of September 11, 2001, stirs deep feelings within me. I watched the drama unfolding on the television and when I saw the first tower crumble I cried, yes big boys do cry. I knew in that moment the Fire Department of New York had lost a large number of firefighters. I feel my words are woefully inadequate in describing what I and others were feeling that day. Some words were swear words, while others were prayer words. September 11th was one of those days that will loom large in the history books.

Many questions remain unanswered about that day, was it preventable, what was the root cause, and can we stop it from happening to anyone again? When we are given answers from the "officials" and "experts" on this event will they ring true in our ears? One thing I do know from decades of research is that history books are some of the greatest fictions ever written. Oh, there are truths in these books but many times they are subjective and skewed by the author's point of view or clouded by which side of the outcome they want to be on. Sometimes it is just a matter of not having the whole picture. I do not claim to have the whole picture on anything. I will convey a story to you, a remarkable story, as best as I can and stay truthful in the telling. It will be a sad story but also an uplifting tale of love, struggle and a rebirth of one who was lost but returned to start anew. An honest to God phoenix story, a new life literally arising from the ashes. It began years after 9/11 and in an unusual place, an online forum dedicated to past lives.

Over the years I have been called upon to help others on a popular past life forum owned and operated by author and reincarnation researcher Carol Bowman and her husband Steve. I attempt to help by giving my thoughts on questions that would fall into the areas where I have a working knowledge; these mainly concerned the fire service and reincarnation. The questions are about what people have encountered in their lives when it comes to a strange happening involving their child (or children), and what appears to be past life information. The Bowmans have helped countless people navigate the bumpy road of past life memories.

Sometimes when answering people's questions on the forum I used **bold lettering** to answer their queries right in the body of their post so as not to restate their questioning. The forum allows people to use screen names or cute monikers to keep their identities private if they so desire. Below we have the first post by Baby_rn who resides in the United States on the West Coast. The posts have been cleaned up a minimum amount for reason of readability and to correct spelling, capitalization, etc. I have taken the liberty of changing some names and removed or obscured some portions of the material covered to protect the privacy of those mentioned. *As a timesaver, I have only given my own and Baby_rn's posts and our private emails, as I have her permission to use her material and need none for mine.* You should get the gist of the topic and conversation of Baby_rn's post even without the other person's post. As you read be mindful of the dates and details. These posts and emails span many years. If you have any doubt on the validity of what I write, all you need do is go to Carol Bowman's Reincarnation Forum and you can look up all the posts (unedited) for yourself starting in 2007 under the heading "9/11 Baby - Baby_rn." After each post it lists the poster and the date they posted their forum entry. You will see my entries as either Stars3 or Jeff.

Baby_rn's first post

I've never written on anything like this before...actually makes me a little nervous but anyway...I've been looking on the internet for someone talking about their child having past life memories from 9/11. My son has been talking about it for almost a year now...he's almost 4...He started out insisting that he doesn't just want to be a firefighter that he is one...he would get up in the morning and put on his fire outfit (his big reward for being potty-trained) and tell me he's going to work. He would take his play axe and pretend to chop down the walls etc. because there was fire behind them. that's how it started and the info just progressed... we were reading a Curious George book about him in the big city and he said very matter of fact...bad men knocked those buildings over, pointing at the twin tower picture. (He has

Braden gave permission to use this photo

also never been exposed to 9/11 scenes...I am also a stay-at-home mom. Then he said planes broke in them and he couldn't help...he also told me there were people jumping because they wouldn't wait for him to get them...He told me he was stuck and was trying to break thru the wall to get the people out because they were calling for them ...He has also gone on extensively about the type of trucks he was in...the color bucket on the truck and how it feels to come down from up high in the bucket...very detailed about firefighting and has stated he's not a firefighter he's fire rescue...we have no firefighters in the family but the details I could go on with forever...he also talks about his friend Mike that is also a firefighter...It has opened my eyes to a whole new reality...my husband still doesn't want to believe it but the details are far too much for a three-year-old to make up...it makes me feel better someone else is experiencing this too

Baby_rn, Sep 30, 2007

I am not really sure who I'm responding too...I think it's Carol...you'll have to excuse me I don't have much time to get on the computer these days so I don't exactly know how this works...thanks for responding to me... I'm pretty confident that what my son has been telling me is from a past life...there's no way he would know all this at his age! Also, the tone of his voice is completely different and he also will laugh a lot if I ask him anything...like why are you asking me this you know I know the answers...I'm very aware not to ask him anything specific because he only tells me what he wants at that time...which is always before bed or after he wakes in the morning...tonight he told me he likes to drive thru red lights with the sirens on when he doesn't actually have to and then he laughs! His info comes in spurts though usually a whole lot at a time then a lull and then more...

He told me that I would really enjoy the Christmas parties at his fire station...everyone always have lots of fun...he said they got a new fire truck because their old one is wrecked... he has said this several times about a new fire truck with a

TV in it and maps and a boat on top...also he has tried to give me directions to his fire station...funny coming from a three-year-old actually...he says you take a left then a right and his station is on the left with another across the street on the right. He told me he trains the new guys coming thru and his friend mike is with the older guys...there is so much in the last year I could go on forever...but there really has been less and less in the past few months... detail wise anyway that maybe he his forgetting already...oh he has said his friend Mike has two or three kids but one is the biggest four-year-old boy he's ever seen...I have written it down somewhat but this is just what I'm thinking of right now...he's a very quiet and kind child to everyone and I just hope this doesn't have some kind of lasting trauma to him... although he seems to not be bothered by talking about it on his own terms...almost seems better after he has talked about it...sorry so long winded

_Baby_rn, Sep 30, 2007_

* I was notified at this point to see if I could lend a hand in deciphering what the young boy was talking about and if it made any sense to me. (Author's note)

Hi Baby_rn,

I had to laugh when I read what you wrote about what your little one said, "He's not a firefighter he's fire rescue...". My guess is that he was in a "Rescue" unit. That is exactly the way they talk. I wrote in my book about some of the members of Rescue 1 (they lost 11 men on 9/11) and have seen them instilling this attitude into their children. It is very hard to get into one of these unit and they are the elite of the FDNY*. They think the FDNY is the best and they know they are the "Best of the Best". You might want to ask if Mike had a nickname because most of the men have them. It may be something strange but that is OK,

---

* FDNY stands for, Fire Department New York. (Author's note added for clarity).

there are some strange ones (Pooh-bear, Mad-dog, Mongo....).
Ask and see what he says.

Best,
Jeff Keene (Asst. Chief F.D. ret.)
Oct 2, 2007

PS: You may want to ask your son if he had a nickname or what
the other guys called him. Also, he is right on the money about
the truck, they have maps, some have small boats and the TV
very well could be a computer terminal.

Jeff

I think you are the one that could help me with all the
technical things he has told me about...he has said that
he's also a scuba diver...he talks about his gear and
air tank...but says he rescues animals?? But it's funny
though...he received flippers and mask as a present
from someone, put them on and automatically walked
backwards in them and fell into the pool backwards...
then said "see this is how you do it", that's an aside
but thought it was funny...This has been info he has
telling me over a year so I'm going to try to pick out the
technical firefighting things and see what you think...
He has said he has a bucket truck and he rides in the
bucket...he showed me with his hand how the bucket
goes up and he said when you come down you don't
just come down you bounce a little at the bottom and
showed me with his hand...he told he has lots of firefighter friends and one drives his bucket. He showed
me with his hands again that there are two levers one
is forward for up and another for down or something
like that...also something about engaging levers to
spray hoses from the bucket...he thinks his bucket has
a three on it? 3 has come up a lot...on his truck... but

he kind of waivers back and forth about the #3...he has said it's on his hat he thinks...could he have been on a ladder truck and rescue? He is also sure his hat is black with yellow stripe. he said he has a picture of a wolf with a moon in his truck and always calls it "his" truck...he rides in the front he said...but he is not chief...this may not make sense but it is what he tells me... he has said several times about an old truck getting wrecked or dying and getting a new truck...he has told me firemen follow the leader up a line in a fire and if falls off the line he uses a bright light and sometimes a camera to find them and makes them say cheese (there is the three-year-old talking)...something about to spray water you push the lever down for off and up for on...when talking about 9/11 (I think) he said people were falling from a building because they wouldn't wait...he was on the floor with his breathing mask on and tried to get out a window but it was too small so he used his ax to break a hole so he could get the people out. To answer someone else's question about if he seems scared about this...no its very matter of fact... just statements...although his has lined up four fire hats in my bedroom so he said we could get to them quicker if we need them... his room of course set up like a fire station everything according to where he says it goes...the funny thing is he said to me one day he needs a real air tank and a real ax for his fire station room because the ones he has are play ones and don't work! Pretty funny! Anyway, let me know what you think?

Baby_rn, Oct 2, 2007

Hi Baby_rn,

I don't have all the answers but will help as much as I can. I think the best way to do this is for me to copy your text and answer the questions in bold lettering. This will save a lot of time. OK, here we go.

I think you are the one that could help me with all the technical things he has told me about...he has said that he's also a scuba diver...he talks about his gear **If he used the word "gear" he is correct as anything you wear on the job is "gear" (See how one small word can mean a lot)** and air tank...**Yes, many of the Rescue company members are SCUBA divers** but, says he rescues animals?? But it's funny though...**NYC is an island and many rescue calls are in the water. And yes, they do animal rescues (be it on land or in water). Have you ever seen a Firefighter do CPR on a cat or dog? I have.** he received flippers and mask as a present from someone, put them on and automatically walked backwards in them and fell into the pool backwards...then said "see this is how you do it" that's an aside but thought it was funny...**Yes, in many cases they roll into the water on their backs. If you want to see the reason for this, put on a face-piece and dive in the pool. One of two things will happen, either the face-piece will be pulled off your face or you might have it pushed into your face (which can be very painful).**

This has been info he has telling me over a year so I'm going to try to pick out the technical firefighting things and see what you think...He has said he has a bucket truck and he rides in the bucket...he showed me with his hand how the bucket goes up and he said when you come down you don't just come down you bounce a little at the bottom and showed me with his hand...**Yes, if the levers are not operated very smoothly there is a bounce** he told he has lots of firefighter friends and one drives his bucket. He showed me with his hands again that there are two levers one is forward for up and another for down or something like that... also something about engaging levers to spray hoses from the bucket... **Yes, there are levers to work the bucket and levers to open the gates to flow water to the hose-lines /ladder-pipes.** He thinks his bucket has a three on it? 3 has come up a lot...on his truck… but, he kind of waivers back and forth about the #3...he has said it's on his hat he thinks...could he have been on a ladder truck and rescue? **He is not wavering, if he was on Rescue #3 there would be a 3 on the rescue vehicle and a "Rescue 3" on his helmet. Likewise, if he had been on a "Ladder Company", a 3 on the truck itself and a "Ladder 3" on the helmet (the names Ladder and Truck are used in different ways in the Fire Service)** He is also sure his hat is black with yellow stripe. **Over the years FDNY fought to keep their turnout gear black. For most, their helmets are black with reflective tape on them so that they can be seen better at night.** he said he has a picture of a wolf with a moon in his truck and always calls it "his" truck...he rides in the front he said... but he is not chief...this may not make sense but it is what he tells me… **Makes perfect sense. Remember the WW2 pilots painting pictures on their planes? Many firefighters do the very same thing to their vehicles. When he says "his" he means "his". I know the feeling well. My guess is that he was, at least, a Lieutenant or Capt. of a company and would assume the passenger seat in the cab.**

he has said several times about an old truck getting wrecked or dying and getting a new truck...he has told me firemen follow the leader up a line in a fire and if falls off the line he uses a bright light and sometimes a camera to find them and makes them say cheese (there is the three-year-old talking) ... **Yes, many times they are in a line and they do have high-powered flashlights. If a man should become separated, they could find him with a thermal-imaging camera (say cheese, I love it. That is just the way I would expect a firefighter to act.)** something about to spray water you push the lever down for off and up for on...when talking about 9/11 (I think) he said people were falling from a building because they wouldn't wait...**No Baby, they were not falling, they were jumping. It was not that they wouldn't wait, they couldn't wait. You tell him that for me. (Sorry, had to take a tissue break)**. he was on the floor with his breathing mask on and tried to get out a window but it was too small so he used his ax to break a hole so he could get the people out.

To answer someone else's question about if he seems scared about this...no its very matter of fact... just statements...although his has lined up four fire hats in my bedroom so he said we could get to them quicker if we need them... his room of course set up like a fire station everything according to where he says it goes... the funny thing is he said to me one day he needs a real air tank and a real ax for his fire station room because the ones he has are play ones and don't work! Pretty funny! Anyway, let me know what you think?

His concern for the people shows me that he is a firefighter deep in his heart and soul. I don't see any way that he could not have been a firefighter seeing his knowledge of all the little nuances of the job. One of the worst things you can do to a firefighter is to make him feel helpless. Many were made to feel that way on 9/11.

Best, Jeff
Oct 2, 2007

Tanquerra

This is where my problem lies...I've been listening and not asking much about this for the past year because he is mine and here now...exactly! I do very much believe in reincarnation and always have...just never had much proof or needed much proof...this is an in my face example...unfortunately from my son which I prefer not to be the example... such is Life I guess. His information was dwindling until I actually started to write on this forum and he started to talk again...and no I've said nothing more or less about the situation...I think he knows more about the big picture then a lot of us...he has said to me "did you know when you die you pick a belly and go back into it?" I'm just an open person and listen to what he has to say and love him to pieces...

Baby_rn, Oct 3, 2007

Charles

No worries! It is truly unbelievable and amazing to me what my son knows and remembers...maybe he came to me because I am so open to this idea who knows...But it definitely is kind of a weird position to be in as a parent...I want to know as much as he can tell me but I also don't want him to talk about it so much that he thinks it's now...does that make sense?

Jeff

Thank you so much for all your input on the firefighting info...I guess he's right "he knows" as he says...maybe tonight I will go thru what I've written down and ask you more...Do you know anything about where the fire stations are located in NYC? He gave me directions from his station to Mike's... coming from a three-year-old it could be just a bunch of lefts and rights but who knows? He picked up his little red whistle this morning and said "this is how I wake the firefighters up if they need to go to a fire... or sleep to long! Then he was laughing...There are a lot of little funny comments like these that make me laugh but are probably true...Also this morning and the last few days he has said he going to or got a "space appointment or apointment" (I can tell what his saying cause in his speech c's are t's etc. like typical three-year-old) anyway after he said that he gets his hose or fire extinguisher to spray at it...Does this make any sense...the words anyway...he is getting very upset that I don't know what it is he's saying...Sorry I could ramble for days...thanks again for your help I appreciate it everyone!

Carol

Thanks for helping me out...I did order your book so I will have a little more clarity on this issue...I think from what I can see now he is very protective of his family...He puts on his fire boots and hat every night before bedtime and comes into my daughters room with his fire flashlight to check my daughter's room for whatever and will say all clear and their both happy and she goes to bed...it's interesting though she won't go to bed until he does it but he will only do it if I'm putting them to bed...he said it doesn't work when dad's in there? Don't know what that means...He picks out his books to read at night and the last few nights he's been getting his firefighter books (which he hasn't in a while) but there is a cartoon picture of a training tower and a skyscraper with a cartoon fire truck with a long ladder...anyway he said he likes the smaller building s not the high one because he's scared it will fall on his head...this is the first time he's ever said anything like that...I told him he is here now and safe with me and he said, "I know" and told me to stop talking and read the book...that is the first time I've ever heard him say anything about feelings associated with firefighting. It is usually factual like what I'd ask Jeff about...He is basically telling me he knows about past lives by telling me when you die you pick a belly to come too...he has also said next time he's a baby he won't be scared to go on our boat (when his was smaller he didn't like to go fast on our boat) ... there are lots of examples like that...does that commonly happen with these children in your research? Thanks!

Baby_rn, Oct 3, 2007

J. Keene's reply to Baby_rn

Wow Baby_rn, you are making my brain work overtime. I haven't had to use it since I left the Dept. (LOL). Here we go with some more thoughts.

Thank you so much for all your input on the firefighting info...I guess he's right "he knows" as he says... maybe tonight I will go thru what I've written down and ask you more...Do you know anything about where the fire stations are located in NYC? He gave me directions from his station to Mike's... **This would be very hard to do. One would first have to know which station to start from and there are so many of them.** Coming from a three-year-old it could be just a bunch of lefts and rights but who knows? He picked up his little red whistle this morning and said "this is how I wake the firefighters up if they need to go to a fire... or sleep to long! Then he was laughing...There are a lot of little funny comments like these that make me laugh but are probably true... **He has me laughing too. He had to have been a Lt. or Capt. They have all kinds of tricks to get the late risers out of bed. Bang on lockers, hitting the bedframes with a baseball bat and even bang pots and pans. This last one was a favorite of a Lt. I once had (I took over his position when he retired). While making a loud clanging with the pots he would yell, "Time for all the little chickens to get up". So, if your son tells you things that make you laugh you can pretty much take it as the truth.** Also, this morning and the last few days he has said he going to or got a "space appointment or pointment"*(I can't tell what his saying cause in his speech C's are T's etc. like typical three-year-old) anyway after he said that he gets his hose or fire extin-

---

* "space appointment or pointment" could mean there was an opening or space for a higher rank and he was appointed to that position. (Author's note)

guisher to spray at it...Does this make any sense... the words anyway...he is getting very upset that I don't know what it is he's saying...**Sorry, don't have a clue on this one.** Sorry I could ramble for days...thanks again for your help I appreciate it everyone!

Thanks for helping me out...I did order your book so I will have a little more clarity on this issue...I think from what I can see now he is very protective of his family... He puts on his fire boots and hat every night before bedtime and comes into my daughters room with his fire flashlight to check my daughter's room for whatever and will say all clear and their both happy and she goes to bed...it's interesting though she won't go to bed until he does it but he will only do it if I'm putting them to bed...**Someone used the word "vigilant", perfect word. There are many Vigilant Hose Company stations across the U.S. Firefighters are caretakers/protectors. Remember my old Lt. calling us "little chickens", that's because he was the mother hen (LOL).** he said it doesn't work when dad's in there? Don't know what that means...**I know the answer to this one, it's simple. In your son's life who is the big boss (or Chief) of the house? Dad is. Now the rule in the Fire Service is; the most senior officer on the scene is in charge.**

So when dad is not around he is in charge, get it? He picks out his books to read at night and the last few nights he has been getting his firefighter books (which he hasn't in a while) but there is a cartoon picture of a training tower and a skyscraper with a cartoon fire truck with a long ladder...anyway he said he likes the smaller building s not the high one because he's scared it will fall on his head...this is the first time he's ever said anything like that...I told him he is here now and safe with me and he said, "I know" and told me to stop talking and read the book...that is the first time

I've ever heard him say anything about feelings associated with firefighting. It is usually factual like what I'd ask Jeff about...**You were privy to something rather rare. Firefighters seldom open themselves on a deep level to others. They learn very early on the job to stifle their feelings. They see many nasty things. Some will cover in some way with "black humor" and the like.**

On the call you don't have time to feel, you just do, get the job done. The moment didn't last long did it and then he told you to, "stop talking and read the book". It was right then that he closed himself down again. He must love you very much to have shared with you in that way no matter the short duration. He is basically telling me he knows about past lives by telling me when you die you pick a belly to come too...he has also said next time he's a baby he won't be scared to go on our boat (when his was smaller he didn't like to go fast on our boat)... **Firefighters are not fearless, but they learn to face fear head on.** there are lots of examples like that...does that commonly happen with these children in your research? Thanks! **Hope all this gives you some helpful insights into the heart and mind of a firefighter, I bet he was one of the best they had.**

Jeff, Oct 4, 2007

Jeff and everyone else

Thanks for all the great input...I'm feeling not so alone in this finally!! I could write a book about the amount of detail he has told me in the last year...and it's all kind of blurring together... Is it possible he could remember more than one past life??? I've got two different storylines going on? Just wondering? I know the firefighter one is real...Anyway Jeff thanks for all the firefighting help...it makes me feel like what I'm listening to makes sense to someone...It's interesting what you said about firefighters just do and don't feel right away (actually gave me chills) ... well, I'm a nurse and I know exactly what that means...I do it all the time too...not that I don't care but you can't feel until it is way over! I get it...never really thought about it in another job though! Very interesting!

More technical info for you to sort thru...he said in the bucket you don't spray the hoses you engage levers... he said when he rescues animals, he scubas off the boat...we swim a lot where we live but it is funny his swimming without flippers is completely different than swimming with flippers! With flippers, he always goes in the pool backwards, cruises fast, rescues his animals and is actually able to dive from swimming position to the bottom of the pool. Take into account he learned to swim 4 months ago...He has lots of animal rescue toys and rescue boats and one of the sets came with ...he calls it a motor (looks like a torpedo with handles to me and is about 4 inches long) he says it is like his real one but this is how you use it...he goes under water and swims really fast with this thing in front of him... (Don't know if that's scuba or rescue related. He has said his friend Mike is on a different truck and he rides with the old guys...He said that he (my son) rides with the young guys and shows them what to do...

Here is where I said he waivers (to clarify) he always says his truck says a 3 or 33 or both...that is why I was wondering if he could have been on a ladder and a rescue truck? Every once in a while, he will say 343 so I don't know what is what...He always uses 3 or 4. Another thing he has said that I thought was funny was one day he was standing in his bed (toddler bed) after he woke up in the morning and said "welcome to my fire truck! Can I give you a tour? We just got this new truck for Christmas...our firehouse is so much fun. I think you'll like it!" I have asked him about names but he always stops talking, looks at me, laughs and says what? never an answer...So I asked about nicknames and told him mine at work so he would understand what a nickname was...he thought this was hysterical and was laughing so hard he got the hiccups and then said, "I don't do names!" He was at the park with my daughter and I and I was pushing them on a toy that was hot on my hands and I said "that's hot' He runs over with his water cup and says" his isn't my job but I like you so I'll do it...He put the cup on my hand and told me to let him know when it felt better...he said it said BBFD or BBD on it?

He still doesn't know his letters so that is what it sounded like...if you ask him what those letters look like he wouldn't know that's why I thought it was interesting that he said it... Sorry again for such a lengthy post... My husband is scared to death of this whole thing so I just don't say anything anymore and there are a lot of people that I think are skeptical so this is the first place I feel ok to vent or talk however you want to look at it.

I was thinking...do you think my son remembers so much more detail because the past life is so recent??? Most of the others seem to be past lives from further back...Just curious!

Baby_rn, Oct 5, 2007

Once again for Baby_rn. *(Maybe I was a poet in a past life)*

More technical info for you to sort thru...he said in the bucket you don't spray the hoses you engage levers...**In years past when they used ladder-trucks the hose was brought up the ladder. Now, with the advent of bucket-trucks there is a pre-piped waterway to the bucket**

and the ladder-pipe (or master-stream) is turned on by turning a wheel or moving a lever. So, you don't stand there in the bucket with a hose-line in your hand (though you can at times) but rather operate the nozzles built into the bucket system.

he said when he rescues animals he scubas off the boat...we swim a lot where we live but its funny his swimming without flippers is completely different than swimming with flippers! With flippers, he always goes in the pool backwards, cruises fast, rescues his animals and is actually able to dive from swimming position to the bottom of the pool. Take into account he learned to swim 4 months ago...He has lots of animal rescue toys and rescue boats and one of the sets came with ...he calls it a motor (looks like a torpedo with handles to me and is about4 inches long) he says its like his real one but this is how you use it...he goes under water and swims really fast with this thing in front of him... (don't know if that's scuba or rescue related. **This devise is just what he says it is, a motor, divers have been using them for many years. It pulls divers through the water at a pretty good speed, which is its main purpose; two get them from point A to point B in the shortest amount of time. In Fire/Rescue time can be a very big enemy.**

He has said his friend Mike is on a different truck and he rides with the old guys...He said that he (my son) rides with the young guys and shows them what to do... **Very insightful, there is something known as "Country-clubbing". Older firefighter are sometimes moved the less active stations in large city (or busy departments) because when you get older you become more brittle and tire easier. I know this for a fact (LOL). When I joined the department in Westport, CT. in 1976 we did around 300 calls a year. When I left in 2003 we were doing nearly 4000. This is done to a lesser extent** with officers because there are fewer positions for them at stations. As I said, your son was most likely a Capt. or Lt. which puts him in a supervising capacity.

Here is where I said he waivers (to clarify) he always says his truck says a 3 or 33 or both...that is why I was wondering if he could have been on a ladder and a rescue truck? Every once in a while, he will say 343 so I don't know what is what...He always uses 3 or 4. **He could be right on all counts. During a firefighters career they will be on many different vehicles, trucks, ladders or rescues all with different numbers. Some vehicles are stationed alone while other stations may have two or more vehicles (such as Engine 43, Truck 3 or Rescue 3 and Truck 33). The station nearest the WTC (so close it was heavily damaged) was known as Ten House. Why, because it held Truck #10 and Engine #10.**

(Later it was pointed out by another forum member that the number 343 was the number of firefighters killed on Sept. 11th. I do not know why I did not catch the importance of this number at the time because ever since 9/11 our department wore an American flag with 343 embroidered on it on our uniforms jackets and I was the person that designed it.) (Author's note)

Another thing he has said that I thought was funny was one day he was standing in his bed (toddler bed) after he woke up in the morning and said "welcome to my fire truck! Can I give you a tour? We just got this new truck for Christmas...our firehouse is so much fun. I think you'll like it!" **LOL, PR and Public Education, a big part of Station life. Giving tours, letting the kids try on boots and helmets or ringing the bells. Sounds like he was good at that too.**

I have asked him about names but he always stops talking, looks at me, laughs and says what? never an answer...So I asked about nicknames and told him mine at work so he would understand what a nickname was...he thought this was hysterical and was laughing so hard he got the hiccups and then said, "I don't do names!" **Once again, if he was an officer he would not "do nicknames". Nicknames are for the "grunts". It would not be very professional for a firefighter to be calling a Fire-officer "pigpen" or "horse butt" in public would it. Would you care to share what your nickname is that cracked him up so bad? Must be a good one.**

He was at the park with my daughter and I and I was pushing them on a toy that was hot on my hands and I said "that's hot' He runs over with his water cup and says, "this isn't my job but I like you so I'll do it...He put the cup on my hand and told me to let him know when it felt better...he said it said BBFD or BBD on it? **(This may be something that EMS uses for burns. Check with a local Ambulance crew, they might know).**

He still doesn't know his letters so that is what it sounded like...if you ask him what those letters look like he wouldn't know that's why I thought it was interesting that he said it... Sorry again for such a lengthy post...My husband is scared to death of this whole thing so I just don't say anything anymore and there are a lot of people that I think are skeptical so this is the first place I feel ok to vent or talk however you want to look at it. **OK Baby_rn, now something for you and your husband. Education can cancel out a lot of fear. Go to my profile and send me an email or message with your name and mailing address so I can send you a copy of my book. You and your husband can read it and then save it for your son when he is older.**

Best, Jeff

PS: Something I just thought of for you to try. Stand behind your son and say, "Hey Cap" and see if he turns

around. **Don't yell but just use a normal speaking voice. You can do the same at another time saying, "Hey Lou" and check his reaction. Lou and Cap are just short for Lieutenant and Captain and if he was an Officer he would have been called by these names many, many times through his career.**

Stars3, Oct 6, 2007 #28

EMAIL TO ME at My Home from Baby_rn

Oct 6, 2007 at 6:24 PM
(This is a message from Baby_rn.)

Jeff

I want to thank you for all your help with the info I've been telling you about my son...You have helped me a great deal because now I know that what he is relaying to me is not stories he has made up...he's creative but not that creative! I didn't realize you had written a book or had remembered a past life experience yourself...just saw it when I was trying to figure out how to send you a message...pretty cool... and thank you I would love a copy of your book! It may take some time to get my husband to read it...he is very logical about EVERYTHING...he's a (removed)! I will give you my name and address, but I would like to keep it private from everyone else...not cause I'm paranoid or anything... it's just for privacy for my son! Thanks for understanding...My other question is if he gives me enough info to figure out who he was (obviously not too difficult because this was so recent) would you think that would be helpful or harmful? I'm very torn about this because I have quite a bit more info than I've written...don't want to bore everyone with it! I'm also afraid if I give too much info someone might figure out who he was and then what? Do they let that family know??? Or what happens? What do you do with the info?

Sorry so many questions but I for some reason feel you are the one to ask...Let me know what you think!! You know, I'm from the east coast too and go back every summer with my kids and my son is at home with himself there...don't know how else to explain it! It is very interesting to see. Anyway, it is beautiful back there especially now! I miss it! Which brings me to my address now:

Address Removed
Thanks again for everything and please keep this private for my son! I appreciate it and all your help!

P.S. My nickname at work is Hotty Totty...he thought it was very funny...

-----Original Message-----
From: Jeffrey Keene
To: xxxxxxxxxx@aol.com
Sat, 6 Oct 2007 6:39 pm

Hi Baby_rn,
    You don't have to thank me I'm glad to help. Yes, I'll keep your Name and address private. I will get a book off to you shortly. I will answer your questions as best I can, using the same method as on the forum. It saves time because I suffer from a form of dyslexia and it takes me a while to get things done properly.

Jeff

I want to thank you for all your help with the info I've been telling you about my son...You have helped me a great deal because now I know that what he is relaying to me is not stories he has made up...he's creative but not that creative! I didn't realize you had written a book or had remembered a past life experience yourself...just saw it when I was trying to figure out how to send you a message...pretty cool... and thank you, I would love a copy of your book! It may take some time to get my husband to read it...he is very logical about EVERYTHING... he's a (removed). **Very logical, good so am I. I wrote the book to show people my story as it unfolded and what the process was that I went through. He's a (removed)! Yes, someone responsible for other people lives. As an Asst. Chief so was I. If you give him the book when you are done, I think he will read it.**

I will give you my name and address but I would like to keep it private from everyone else...not cause I'm paranoid or anything ..it is just for Privacy for my son! Thanks for understanding...My other question is if he gives me enough info to figure out who he was (obviously not to difficult because this was so recent) would you think that would be helpful or harmful? I'm very torn about this because I have quite a bit more info then I've written...don't want to bore everyone with it! I'm also afraid if I give too much info someone might figure out who he was and then what? Do they let that family know??? Or what happens? What do you do with the info?

OK, Baby, take a deep breath and let it all out very slowly. Take baby steps, (or Baby_rn steps, LOL) there is no hurry. Let things unfold and then base your actions on the information placed before you. Things happen for a reason and you will discover that you will be moved along by an unseen hand. People, places and events will happen in the order that things are to be revealed to you. Trust me on this one. I was pushed around like a shopping-cart. Right now you are anonymous and no one even knows your real name. It is not so important "who he was" so much as "what he was" and you know the answer to that. I know you are a mommy but try not to worry so much and let things flow. You will see what happened to me when the book gets there. You love your son and he loves you. Share this time with him. Take

notes and write it all down. Most likely, in a little while, all these old memories will fade away as if it had all been a dream. When he is grown you can give him what you have and let him decide for himself what to do with the information. Sorry so many questions but I for some reason feel you are the one to ask...Let me know what you think!! You know, I'm from the east coast too and go back every summer with my kids and my son is at home with himself there...don't know how else to explain it! It's very interesting to see. Anyway, its beautiful back there especially now! (It was 85 here today) I miss it!

P.S. My nickname at work is Hotty Totty...he thought it was very funny... **Hotty Totty, I love it. Yeah, you cracked him up real good with that one.**

Check out my story at Google videos (*use YouTube). Show it to your husband If the link does not work go to Google (*use YouTube), then click on "video" at the top of the page and then type in "Jeffrey Keene Proof Positive" in the search window, this will call up a 13 min. video. *(This last portion revised 2020 to lead to proper video)*

http://video.google.com/videoplay?do-cid=7566586090414738463&q=reincarnation+evidence&total=23&start=0&num=10&so=0&type=-search&plindex=6   (link no longer works)

All the best, Jeff

-----Original Message-----
From: Jeffrey Keene <jeffreyxx@yahoo.com>
To: xxxxxxxxxx@aol.com
Sun, 7 Oct 2007 11:05 pm

Hi Baby_rn,
    OK, I have some information for you and I hope you are sitting down. I checked the firehouse.com website for men who

died during 9/11. Using the information you gave me I came up with only one "hit" and I think it might be "dead on" (no pun intended) for several reasons. (1) Rescue #3 did not lose a Lt. that day. (2) There was a Lt. lost on Eng. #33 but that was a regular Engine Company. (3) This is the most likely the one; Lt. on Ladder #3. This Ladder #3 was an ESU (Emergency Service Unit*) this is not a rescue unit but is indeed "Fire/Rescue". All the things your son said apply very well to this unit. Irish (what else), smart guy, he was a professor at New Jersey City University. If you would like to see a picture, click on this link. http://cms.firehouse.com/911/detail.jsp?id=290

A story on Ladder #3 "After the fall" can be found at; http://www.cbsnews.com/stories/2002/09/03/60II/ main520684.shtml (not working)

He was found. Nice article; http://cf.newsday.com/911/victim-search.cfm?id=1118 (not working)

Here is a picture of the station. You can see "3 Truck" on the door. The names under the photo are the men they lost on 9/11 http://64.233.169.104/search?q=cache:SRSkqK0N-jhEJ:www.jfischweb.com/blog/photos/ group/24649124%40N00/photo/538689860/New-York-City-Fire-Department---FDNY-Battalion-6---Hook--Ladder-Co-3---Water-Tower-No-2---3-Truck. html+Kevin+Donnelly+Ladder+3+FDNY&hl=en&ct=-clnk&cd=20&gl=us (not working)

Ladder 3 took the biggest hit of any single company in the FDNY; http:// archives.tcm.ie/irishexaminer/2002/09/07/

---

* I was a bit perplexed by the ESU (Emergency Service Unit) designation because this, I thought, was a PDNY (Police) designation. Doing a little research, I found my answer in an online forum at firehouse.com. "FDNY got the in-charge agency designation for ALL building collapses." So, Ladder3 would run on ESU calls where there was a building collapse. (Author's note)

story869539343.asp (not working)

This should keep you busy for a while. Now, if you care to, you can do the Cap/Lou trick using Kevin instead. If this was your Son I was right, he was one of their best.

Much love to you and your family,
Jeff

(Author's note; On Sunday the 7th of October 2007, less than one week after Baby_rn first made contact with me on the forum, we had pretty much determined her son Braden had been Lieutenant Kevin Donnelly of FDNY Ladder Company 3 in a previous life. From this point on, the evidence just kept getting stronger and more evident. KD was indeed a member of a rescue company; from the wantaghfd.com website, "Lt. Kevin Donnelly, was a past member of Wantagh Rescue 2 and Engine 4." Something I find really interesting is that Braden was born in October 2003 which makes it one of the fastest reentries I have ever heard about.)

xxxxxxxxxx@aol.com

To:

jeffreyk7@yahoo.com

Sun, Oct 7, 2007 at 11:40 PM

Jeff

Thank you so much for all your advice...it is wonderful and funny because I think you have the same sense of humor as I do! I connected to your link (or however you say it in computer terms). Anyway, your story is amazing...you even look alike...I never thought you could actually look like the person also...The best thing is that you seem just like me or my husband...very down to earth and trying to find answers! My son is the sweetest child and soul. So, whoever he was must have been wonderful! I have to also say that what you said about a hand guiding me gave me the chills... you know what, my whole life has been that way...its amazing! I'm a very easy-going person and literally go with the flow...its a little more difficult to do that with your own child involved but I've been doing it for the past year and a half and it's been a fun ride...the hand that's guiding me has found you so I'm sorry for you!!! Ha! But you're right! He originally gave me info a little at a time, piece by piece (only 2 and1/2 years old) and it dwindles and picks up really depending on if I'm receptive to it or not if that's possible? But, I wanted to tell you that last night I tried your test sort of... He was in the bath and had all his new rescue "vehicles" (sub, big boat and fire truck) as he calls them...It was his birthday and everyone knows what he likes...firetrucks and rescue vehicles so he got loads of them... (Sorry, girly babble) he said the captain is riding in this seat because he's in charge...so I said "oh is that like you?" he looked at me and said "no". Then I said "oh are you Lou" He stopped and looked at me and said "how did you know?" I just said "I thought so" and he gave me a hug when he got out of the bath and said "that's why I came to you!" He really is amazing...and very intuitive if I dare say......Also, which I don't want to put on the forum...he has said he was "from Ladder co 3 or 33" (said just like that) ... when I looked it up, ladder 33 has the bucket truck... or however you call it... but he also says that he is fire rescue and he thinks he has a three on his hat... so he has been very specific...I'm just not sure what to do with that info... I don't want everyone to know... but I feel the need to tell you... such is the hand that guides... I know I believe in past lives but by talking to you I feel like I can get the technical similarities that I need for my own mind to accept what it is that he is saying... I will continue to post on the forum but I was wondering if it is ok with you that some of the stuff I don't want to share with everyone I could email you? Let me know if it's too much... I completely understand...no problem at all! There is so much I'm trying to digest and sort out right now it may come across as ridiculous so I apologize! Thanks for everything!

Thank you

Baby_rn

xxxxxxxxxx@aol.com

To: jeffreyxx@yahoo.com

Mon, Oct 8, 2007 at 9:44 AM

Jeff

Amazing...I think you may be right because to top it all off he told me yesterday that he is 43...It is all a little surreal... when I looked up Kevin's name on Google I found some wonderful articles about him...Talking about how he loved the water and anything to do with the beach...sounds just like why for whatever reason I wrote to you about my son seeming so comfortable on the east coast because we stay at my mom's beach house and go to the beach every day. Also would explain his uncanny ability to swim like a professional with flippers and goggles at age three!! Wow! We'll see... gotta go my kids are waking up...more for you later... again thank you!!!

xxxxxxx@aol.com

To: jeffreyxx@yahoo.com

Oct 8, 2007 at 2:10 PM

Jeff

I felt compelled to send you my son's favorite picture...it's from his third birthday party at (where else) the fire station... He said "mommy take a picture of me in the truck" After when I printed it out because he wanted it in his room...I noticed what it said on the firetruck window...many things like this have happened...pretty crazy...his name is Braden*. (It is kind of hard to see on this picture it is so small...) if you can't tell it says, *In memory 343 FDNY 9-11-01*

Thanks Baby_rn

-----Original Message-----
From: Jeffrey Keene <jeffreyxx@yahoo.com>
To: xxxxxxxxxx@aol.com
Sent: Tue, 9 Oct 2007 8:41 pm
Subject: Picture
Hi Baby_rn,
Cute little guy. I will be mailing out a book tomorrow. Please let me know when it gets there so I know you received it.
Best, Jeff

xxxxxxxxxx@aol.com

To: jeffreyxx@yahoo.com

Oct 12, 2007 at 11:12 PM

Jeff

Just received your book! Thanks again...I'm going to start reading it tonight...is it ok with you if I keep emailing you? For whatever reason I feel like I need to "vent" or talk to someone who understands that I'm not

---

*   (* I was informed that Baby_rn's husband had a nickname he would use often when Braden was a young child, he called him "KB.")

crazy!!!... The thing that strikes me is that he so ada-
mantly told me he was 43 the other day...even when I
argued with him that he is four...take into account the
child can only count to about 20 if he's lucky! Also, I've
been trying to figure out who this Mike is that he so
often talks about...in one of his books are some Fire
Rescue guys (I think) that are helping people out of
a flood in one of the rafts... Every time he sees this
picture, he says that looks like Mike...These are the
directions that Braden has told me about from "his" fire
station to his friend Mike's: He said, "my fire station is
to the left and down the hill the other station is to the
right..." I would not think anything of this but for the
fact he doesn't know right from left...he said mike has
two kids he thinks maybe three but the four-year-old
is the biggest 4-year-old kid he's ever seen! (Which is
funny because Braden is the size of a 5 or 6-year-old!)
I don't know if this has anything to do with anything but
he keeps bringing it up so I think it may be relevant! So
sorry I'm babbling again! If you have a chance, could
you help me out? If this is too much for you let me
know and I will not bother you, ok? Just let me know!
Thanks for everything!

Very sincerely,

Baby_rn

Baby_rn back to postings on the forum

Thanks for everyone's help...last night my son said why
did the bad men knock those buildings down (referring to
a picture of the twin towers in a Curious George book) I
said, I don't know...he said "but why?" "Didn't they have
families?" Where are they from? "Did the people get hurt?"
Did firefighters get hurt?" That city's a mess...These ques-

tions were shot at me all at once...I don't think he wanted answers he was just saying it...the only question he asked me again was where are they from...so I said I think Iraq... he just said "oh"... then wanted me to finish the story...what do you make of this?

Baby_rn, Oct 8, 2007

See what I know...look at that I'm giving him the wrong info! HA! Thanks for clarifying...if he asks about it again, I'll let him know...he really doesn't seem to show any emotion when he says all of these things...it is almost as if he's trying to figure out how and why it happened? Make any sense? Because the way he asked it was almost like he couldn't understand why these "bad men" did this if they had families...I thought it was interesting that he asked if they had families...not something I would think of if I knew someone intentionally knocked buildings down. I just started to read Carol's book so this may be discussed but I was wondering if in the research with children that remember past lives also know how they came to this life? To clarify...if they say "after you die you pick someone else's belly to go in" or something similar? Is this because his past life is so recent or is it a common occurrence? He asks about this kind of thing a lot...It's funny to me because he has asked me "why did you pick your persons belly" how do you answer that?? So anyway, just wonder if that is common?

Baby_rn, Oct 13, 2007

Vicky

(*Baby_rn to another forum member about their sons saying they picked them for their mother*).

Glad to hear it is just not happening to me!!!Is this also

something that they forget about too? How long did it take for your son to start to move on? Mine tells his friends he has firetrucks and they say "I know we're playing with them and he says, "No I have real ones." My friend is pregnant and Braden said to me the other day "I don't know why she would want to be a baby again because then you have to pick another whole family to go to." Could you tell me a little about your son's past life if you have a chance? I took my son to the fire station today because they had an open house and he was thrilled... they let him spray the hoses and go into a smoke box (something like that he said its called). They thought his dad was a fire fighter because he knew how to open the compartments on the truck and how to work the hoses...pretty funny actually...they said is your daddy a firefighter and he looked at them in all seriousness and said, "no, I am a firefighter" they got a kick out of it... If they only knew...

Baby_rn, Oct 13, 2007

Vicky

Thank you for your son's story...sounds very similar to what's going on with my son as well...Did he remember more than one past life? I think my son does...he says he's a firefighter/animal rescuer... at first, I thought it was one all in the same but I'm beginning to believe there are two different stories going on...he sometimes combines them it seems...I get more specific details about the firefighter though...I think enough to figure out who he is but don't know where I go with it...keep it private maybe? He really doesn't show any emotion about it though...weird really, he just gives me facts and makes a lot of little jokes about it. He said at his fire station someone made popcorn once and burned it and they put it outside and sprayed it with the hoses! He thought this was hilarious! Just little funny things! Anyway, he says he's a scuba diver that rescues animals (as I've said before he's shown me in the pool and I believe that, I can't even do things like that...especially walk on the ground in flippers) pretty funny! But he said he has an aquarium and big tanks...he said his house is in the mountains overlooking the water...he insists he has a tiger shark in the tank and that I need to buy him one for the house...he showed me how he catches poisonous snakes with some kind of stick that catches their head first or something! Got to go more info to come...just wondering if your stories were similar life themes or complete opposite ends of the spectrum? Anyone know if a child remembers more than one past life if they are similar like his are help-ers or rescuers? Just interested to see if this is true?

Baby_rn, Oct 15, 2007

Thanks for replying... I thought it might be common that if they remember one they will remember more...I have a question for you ...once your son let you know who he was in a past life did he then start to have less memories of the past life...I pretty much know who my son was (he will not say his name) but from details he has given me...I'm won-dering if he wants me to figure it out or if it is something that has no bearing on anything? The other problem is that this is so recent a past life this persons family is still mourn-ing their loss...so maybe I don't need the name...I'm not sure where to go from here mostly because this is such a recent event?! Anyone have any ideas? There is still more to explore from what he is saying but I'm not sure if it is better not to know the person's name? I'm kind of at a loss with this one...sorry off the subject a bit but I need some advice...Thanks!

Baby_rn, Oct 16, 2007

Carol

I just started to read your book...very interesting and infor-mative...I did not realize your children remembered past lives also...I just came here to this forum kind of blindly and now I'm so happy I found it! It makes me feel so much bet-ter that this is something happening to lots of kids and not just my son...We'll see what happens if he starts to forget or not...do you think his name is important to know? He had started to give me specific details that is why I stopped posting for a while because I wasn't really sure what to do with the info...It is so recent and that's my problem with the whole thing...also I had asked earlier if there is more than one life remembered do they tend to have similar life themes?

Like rescuer, teacher, warrior etc... Has this ever been researched? I always think of questions like these...guess maybe I should have gone into research... it is interesting to me...sorry off the subject but just wondering if this has ever been investigated? When I go to work my son always says he's going to work too because nurses (I'm a nurse by the way) and firefighters sometimes see each other... and then he tells my husband he doesn't have a "real" job because he's a (removed)... (my husband loves those comments!) but he says cause we help people it's a job... so just wondering if it is somehow ingrained in him to be a helper...just curious...

Baby_rn, Oct 16, 2007

*On Oct 17, 2007 Baby_rn was given some sage advice by the forum owner Carol Bowman on Identifying Baby_rn's son's former identity and possible contact with family members. She was told that she needed to be very sure and have specific details and possibly run thing by the forum members before making any contact with any of his family.

*(Author note, not a forum post)

Baby_rn posted this in reply to the advice given by Carol:

Thanks for the info...he has told me his age, company number and rank...so yes, I have a pretty good idea of who he was...there is some more info from him I'm waiting for to be 100 percent sure...I'm a fairly private person and the people on this forum and my mom are about the only ones that know anything about this...I just wish I knew what to do with it? I can't imagine someone coming to me to say that their child's past live was my son...it might really confuse someone especially if they don't believe in reincarnation...it might confuse and interest where they want to talk to my son and I don't want him somehow damaged by this you know? I guess I'll wait and see...anyone have any pros to this? I keep coming up with cons!!

Another question about birth marks... my son has a small round dark pigmentation on the right side of his neck that has been there very light when he was born and has been getting darker as he gets older...I've heard sometimes these coincide with injuries is that true? Also, kind of weird and may have nothing to do with anything...but when my son was about 16 months old (I think) he all of a sudden couldn't use one of his legs...he would be walking fine and then just fall and drag that leg behind him...it never seemed to hurt but he couldn't walk on it...this happened on and off for about three weeks... I took them to doctors and no one could find anything wrong with it...at the same time he was waking up from his naps screaming and in a panic it seemed but he seemed still asleep...it was like his whole body was tensed up... I found this odd because this child is the most mellow, easy-going child and never screamed about anything unless I was going somewhere without him (like any other child that age).

This could be way far off but do you think that it was something that happened from a past life at that time? I thought of this after I'd read something on the internet about Jeff Keene's experience at age thirty...It was just one of those weird things I remembered vividly because I was so afraid something was terribly wrong with him...it was gone in three weeks and never a problem again...just wondering if you've heard of things like this in children remember past lives?

Baby_rn, Oct 17, 2007

Vicky

That's funny that you say that about your son crying whenever you leave...mine did for quite a while too! He still to this day always wants to know where I am... If he can't see me then he's always calling me, if I'm in the bathroom he's knocking on the door etc. He also tells me he's going to work the same nights (I just went back to work at night occasionally) as I go because firefighters see nurses sometimes...I've been home with my kids for four years and just started back to work. So when I have on my scrubs he literally comes out in his fire outfit and says I'll see you later... Pretty cute actually.

Carol

I think last night might have been the first glimpse of emotion having to do with my son's past life death (if that's how you put it) My husband and son were wrestling and playing in the living room like they always do...my son was hiding his treasure or something like that under a blanket. My husband took the blanket and put it over my sons head and wrapped him up in it and my son absolutely freaked out and started screaming and ran into the other room...keep in mind he was under the blanket for maybe 5 sec... my husband looked at me and said what's that all about because that is unusual behavior for my son (he pretty rough and tumble kid). Anyway, I went into the room and asked him what was wrong and he was still crying and said "it was so heavy on my head and I couldn't get out!" But I said, you're ok, you're out and daddy was just playing. He was so shaken up and the look in his eyes was pure fear...it freaked me out...then suddenly he ran out of the room and started playing with his dad again as if nothing happened... without the blanket of course. I think he might have had a memory about what he had said earlier about the building falling on his head...do you think?

Oh yea I just remembered something he said yesterday... he said, "mommy I'm a really good scuba diver" I said, "I'm sure you are" He said, "No you don't know...I'm REALLY good at it" Then he preceded to tell me how I taught him how to catch sharks and tag them...he said I looked different then and then laughed! I don't know what that means but it was in the same type of tone as I get the firefighting info...

Baby_rn, Oct 19, 2007

Sorry I've been away for a while...holidays are hectic at my house as they are at everyone else's I'm sure...There is still quite a bit of info I'm sorting thru with the things my son has said...but I thought of Carol the other night when my son said he is scared of big fires and going up high. She has been asking if he has voiced any fears...well here they come I guess...He was really concerned that we didn't have a plan to get out of the house if there was a fire and that he couldn't reach the 'real" fire extinguisher in his closet to put out a fire...he said how is he supposed to rescue everyone if he can't get out his own door (he has a slider in his room) and can't get the fire extinguisher...he was really upset about it...so my husband made a 'plan" for him and let him listen to what a smoke alarm sounds like so he would be more comfortable and practiced where to go etc...

Then a few minutes later my husband set off the alarm again and told him "OK pretend this is a real fire what do you do?" (Thinking he will go do what they just practiced) No not quite...He ran and got his real fire hat (a friend gave it to him recently) and began trying to climb on things in his closet to get the real fire extinguisher, then covered his face with his blanket and began yelling to my husband get out and get low...so it was not quite the fire drill we were planning on. I'm just afraid that if he does come across a real fire, he might actually try to fight it...scary. He insists he's an excellent firefighter and the other day was standing with his hat on reciting something that sounded like an oath or something...do firefighters say those?

Anyway, I'm not sure how you help him with a fear of fire when he wants to fight it if it happens? Does that make sense? Thanks to you all for all you help in the past. Its greatly appreciated! I want to ask Kristajohn, if she is still around, if she could tell me a little more about what her son said about her daughter being back with him. When my daughter was sick last month, he kept trying to "fix" her and was very worried because he said he can't do his job without her because she is the Doctor he brings his people too...interesting that she says she wants to be a doctor when she grows up!

Baby_rn, Jan 23, 2008

Thanks everyone for the great advice... Ailish I will give that a try...makes more sense! I think sometimes when your taken off guard in a situation like that it is hard to say or do the right thing initially...I don't anticipate his reaction to things sometimes...

Thank you for the info regarding the oath...I'm not sure what he was saying but the way he was saying it sounded like an oath...if I ask him anything about firefighting things or things he's said most times he laughs or looks at me like I'm crazy...he only talks when he wants to not usually if I ask him things out of the blue...He saw a picture of a firefighter in a scuba outfit and said "that is just like mine and he has two tanks on his back because he is doing a deep water dive"...1. I did not even notice there were two tanks on this man's back because it was a side view2. He showed me the two meters or something like that on the top of the tanks and that is why he knew there were two. Anyone know if that is true...do you need two tanks for a deep-water dive? Makes sense I guess...

Regarding who he was... I'm not sure how far I want to go with it... Thanks for the info. Yes, it sounds similar to what he is describing. But there are some things that are differ-ent that he has said and I've not written... who knows, this is a four-year-old we're talking about... I guess he can't have all the details...but thanks for researching...I just don't know what I would do with the info because this is such a recent tragic death of someone...

In regards to my daughter...she is three and he insists that he needs her to help his people...she on the other hand does not say anything about being a doctor other than she wants to be one...she does love to play up the part of the damsel in distress and is always calling out to my son...help I need to be rescued and out he runs to help her...very funny actually... oh yeah, he has described putting people on "the bed that rolls" and taking them to the ambulance place (exactly how he said it) make of it what you want I guess...

Baby_rn, Jan 25, 2008

Blue flutterby

I'm glad to hear you are or have experienced the same thing...my son is 4 1/2 years old and also started at almost two years old with these stories...I was wondering if your son was wanting to wear fire hats or fire gear always at this young age also? Do you remember if he talked about people jumping? I only ask because it sounds similar to my son and they are about the same age so I'm interested to know what you remember? I know mine has said so much that I forget even after a conversation from that night... Also, I'm wondering how your son reacted to seeing broadcasting from 9/11? Mine has never seen anything...It worries me that when he is old enough to talk about it at school or see it on TV he may flip out...he still to this day asks who did it and why...none of my answers seems to resolve this...he can't fathom people would do this...just curious how your son reacted? Did he ever say names? Sorry so many questions but this sounds so similar to my son's story I'm curious...in regards to another thread about remembering more than one past life...my son does too...he's been talking about being a scuba diver...but not in rescue (that's how he differentiates it) ...

Baby_rn, Apr 23, 2008

Post by Baby_rn:He is still talking about it but not as often... little bits here and there...it's a little different now though... I think because he's a little older...A lot came out as he was playing when he was younger... it is hard to explain...he will start talking about his medals he has won and bits from that life in that serious tone of voice then he'll stop himself and say "I'm just pretending I think" So it is almost as if he realizes that now is now but he's not sure where the other info is coming from (sorry sounds confusing)...he just started again to go into my daughters room every night with his fire hat and flashlight to check before she goes to bed...he hasn't done that in a while either...so it comes and goes... has anyone ever talked about someone actually having habits from a past life? This has happened several times that he will be with his fire hat on and seems to be doing something with his "pretend" tools that he clears his throat several times and says "it's ok I've got work to do here" He told me one day he was repelling from his training tower (he actually has a fire bed with a tent on it and a slide) He tied a rope to the top of his slide and was saying this...anyway he was doing the same thing of clearing his throat...just curious if anyone has heard of a habit or something like that being remembered also. He only does this when he is in that "zone". On another note, he still asks why those bad men knocked the tall buildings down and why didn't they think about the people in there? There is no answer I've ever given him that he is happy with on this one...

About the scuba diving past life...I think its happy memories...he has been talking about this for quite a while too but I thought it was tied into the fire rescue...I don't think so now...he has talked about how he cleans his boat after diving ...also that he like the deep sea dives where you wear a helmet and boots, not flippers, and you are attached to a line that they pull you up on when you're done with your dive...anyone know if this makes sense? He dives backwards into our pool with flippers on and can swim the length of the pool with his flippers like a pro...the other day he was swimming and had his head under water with his one hand next to his head coming out of the water like he was holding something... when he was finished I asked what he was holding and he said his snorkel...and then looked at me like I should have known this...The same day he was diving under and kept coming up with his hands grasping something and I asked what was he doing and he said (very serious again) he's retrieving very rare shark eggs...then two minutes later he was back in four-year-old mode and said I think I'm just pretending though...any way maybe he is just pretending who knows...he's never said anything negative about the scuba diving...he has talked about having large tanks and that his sharks are next to the sea otters and things like that...who knows...

Baby_rn, Apr 24, 2008

Simon-thanks for your thoughtfulness...I think my son seems to be fine thank you...Iris...yes you are right I think...my son was in his zone, as I say it, the other day and I asked him if he did scuba diving with the firefighting or is it something different? He said it is with the firefighting and his gear is in the garage on the side of his truck...he also said he likes to do it for fun...so yes he might have done it as a hobby. He said he has two different trucks...one with ladders and one with 2 boats with his scuba gear...This is the first time he has actually clarified what he is saying...like I said he is older now and can express himself better in general...he said "my turnout gear is black with yellow stripes so you can see me when its dark"

He also told me "I am really big and can break the door with my hand". He just started this again where he's talking about himself as firefighter in first person...Maybe he's got more to tell...Always at the same time as this happens, he starts checking my daughter's room every night with his fire hat and flashlight on...interesting too...he always wants to rescue my daughter when in the pool...he told her to pretend she's sinking and he'll save her (really scary if I wasn't in the pool with them!) But he puts on his scuba mask and swims underwater to her and grabs her like a lifeguard would (only way to describe it) and swims her back to the stairs, saying "don't worry I've got you"

He has not been swimming long (which worries me too) but he uses his flippers and dives to the bottom of the pool and comes up like its nothing...I thought maybe he worked thru these feelings and that is why he stopped talking about it for a while but here it comes again...

Baby_rn, Apr 28, 2008

Thanks Deborah-I appreciate it! It's a lot for me to process and I'm always worried about sounding silly in what it is that I write because sometimes it is unbelievable to me! I have thought about videotaping him but it is hard because I'm always in the pool with him and my daughter...plus, because he is a new swimmer and she just learned a few months ago it is a little dangerous in him "rescuing" her!

He actually does an amazing job but she will just let him "rescue" her and not try to swim...not a great idea! So, I have to be in there with him and always reminding her she needs to swim for him to help her...very odd...anyway that is why there is no videotaping going on... I can't safely yet! But when we get to that point I will...he would love to see himself I'm sure...he told me today that he can teach me how to dive and snorkel if I wanted...I said do you teach people how to? He laughed and said" oh yea I know I can teach you...want me to teach you right now?"

This is where the problem lies with me...do I let him think he can teach me or do I bring him back to "now" and say that I can teach him with a snorkel etc... It's hard for me to know what the right thing is to say when he's in the zone...Don't get me wrong, this zone time is usually a few moments in a day and otherwise he is the typical crazy four-year-old running around and playing with his toys! I tried to ask him something about what he had talked about with firefighting yesterday and he said, "I don't know...I don't want to talk about that page" So he will only talk about these things on his terms!

But as long as I can remember he has always referred to

the past or memories as pages*...don't know if that is some word he picked up when he was younger or what...different though...

Baby_rn, Apr 30, 2008

I can try to video tape him in my daughter's room...I've tried to tape him in his own room one time when he seemed to be standing in his fire outfit reciting some kind of saying or "oath"...but as soon as he saw me he stopped and looked at me and said "cheese" for the camera and was completely out of his "zone"...so I will try it...it's almost now that he's older (sad that I'm saying 4 1/2 is old, not quite!) if he talks about a past life and then I ask him when he's not in that frame of mind he says "I think that's just a story"... it's the same when he was younger and always wore his fire hat around and people would say oh its firefighter (his name) and he would always get upset and say "Don't call me that" So he seems to be trying to forget it.

(*Baby_rn was given free rein to say yes or no on items I had written. While proofreading what I had written about her and her son she made the following comment in this section. *"Important to note: He referred to himself in the third person until he was about 5, Braden did this or that."*) (Author's note)

To address whoever had asked about if he's happy talking about the scuba diving...the more I think about it he is very excited about swimming or anything that has to do with water... he loves it...he even pretends the bath tub is his scuba raft... so these seem to be exciting and happy memories...

The idea of talking about pages...he has been talking about that for as long as I can remember...I used to correct him

---

*   Page or pages very well could be a reference to Braden's Book of Life. Yes, a real "Book of life" with pages, chapters, pictures... (Author's note)

and say you mean last time etc... and he just continues saying "remember on that last page this happened or this happened on another page..." It almost like he remembers things from when he was little as pictures on pages...I'm talking about his life now...kind of confusing I guess...*

Baby_rn, Apr 30, 2008

When I was reading books to my son the last few nights, he keeps insisting that I am a firefighter also...I always laugh and say "no, I'm a nurse". He laughs louder and says "no, you are a firefighter like me! I know it, that is why you know what I'm talking about all the time!"** Has anyone ever heard of something like this? I don't know if he's thinking this way because he feels he can talk to me about his firefighter info or something...I'm very confused by this...but he is insisting!

I've never had any past life memories and the only thing I remember as a child is having terrible nightmares of my house being on fire and being scared to death of fire...and I still am to this day...anyone have any thoughts on this? I'm at a loss here...

Baby_rn, May 29, 2008

Thanks for all your great input...I'm still working on figuring out what he means by this firefighter comment but sometimes it takes time... he only talks about it when HE wants too...

Carol, this weekend is the first time I clearly saw a fear or

---

* Memories can be set off by many things, sight, sounds and even the sense of smell. Believe it or not scent is a big one for kicking in a memory. (Author's note)

** (Braden may have thought of his mother as being a firefighter due to my helping her. He felt she had insight into the life of a firefighter) Author's note phobia expressed by him related to the past life I think...

We were away for the weekend and staying at a hotel and the main part of the hotel was several stories high... maybe 40 or so...on the top it had an American flag...he was obsessed number 1 with the height of the hotel and number 2 the American flag...he said he is scared of those high buildings...I asked what do you mean? He said he's scared of them and that they are not safe and can hurt you and you could fall (this was in his regular kid talk not the zone as I call it).

I asked him if he's scared of the high elevators and he said "no, the high buildings..." Then, he went on to say several times during the weekend that he can't believe someone would go on top of that building and put the American flag up there...He said" That person has to be the bravest person ever to put that flag up there so high!" Luckily, we stayed in the three-story suite part of the building to the side of the taller one but he sat on the balcony and stared and said I really don't like high buildings!

So, he is afraid of heights (I think) and for sure any build-ing that looks to him to be too tall...throughout this conver-sation he said nothing of firefighters or himself as one... just the plain fact that he is scared of tall buildings and the people at the top have to be very brave...I know you were wondering if he showed any emotional issues or phobias related to this and I'm sure this is one...The road we take to get to where we're going is a curvy, steep mountain pass road and he also gets really upset on this road and says it is too dangerous and scary and isn't there another way to go??...It's all coming together now I think...anyone have any ideas about this?

Baby_rn, Jun 5, 2008

Rod

Thank you for all the great insights! Do you have any background with firefighting or in the medical field? From what you write it sounds that you may...He has been talking about "pages" for as long as I can remember...it makes me feel better you have a personal recollection of such things! I also think he has been remembering more than one past life for a while now...the scuba and firefighter I think are related but I still think there is something related to scuba diving and aquariums that keeps coming up separate from the fire/rescue...with your memories did past life memories overlap and get intertwined? He has described his fire/rescue boats and described what he wore but, also has talked about deep sea diving and fixing the sharks then putting them into his aquariums and describes in what tanks different animals are in....To me, the problem is that these thoughts are separate but, they seem to overlap in the fact he always describes rescuing his animals or the people... what are your thoughts on this?

Baby_rn, Jun 21, 2008

Yes...I have gone back and forth on this one...I can't quite figure out if this was a hobby or separate...he is very concerned about "what age" he has to be to do certain things... he asked how old does he have to be to do "real" snorkeling and scuba diving. he will swim around the pool with his mask on and always has his hand by the side of his head like he's holding a snorkel...when I ask what he's doing he says, like I should know, "I'm looking for my sharks, but I need to go a little deeper so I need to get rid of this snorkel and put the heavy gear on..." So I have no idea...but it is simply unbelievable to me how well he swims with flippers and without... he dives with his flippers to get his dive sticks to the bottom of the deep end of the pool... I think it's 7 ft... Maybe this is typical of a four-year-old who knows...I can't do it! He's never had a swim lesson...This could be normal but one is always amazed by your own child!: laugh:

I haven't gotten anywhere with my search for fire stations that were using new equipment before 9/11...anyone have any ideas how to find this out?

Baby_rn, Jun 23, 2008

Thanks for all the interesting comments! I have a question for those of you with children with past life memories like mine...Have they ever asked about God and how this world works...like heaven and how we got here and how God decided who we were etc.? I was raised Catholic but never in my life have I ever thought about what my son has been asking about...we have a dog that passed away and my son has been asking a never-ending amounts of questions about what is going on up in heaven with the dog and God! The weird thing is that I really have never thought or talked about such things...it is as if he has a better understanding about things at age 4 than me and I'm in my thirties! What he talks about actually makes me think...pretty amazing! Just wondering if anyone else with kids with past life memories have a better understanding of the makeup of the world as well?

Baby_rn, Sep 24, 2008

He has said several times about choosing me...but continues to ask why I chose my mom? He has talked about being with me before as well, but that I looked different! He has a very childlike but intelligent practical view of God and heaven...he also has a problem with why God created what he calls "bad" people...he has asked that several times as well. Interesting though he does NOT like to go to church! He complains about Jesus on the cross with blood coming from his hands...I used to go to church all the time when I was young and never noticed or cared I guess. He thinks about the "spiritual" more than I ever did at the age or now for that matter! It's amazing how a child can open your eyes to the "big picture"!

Baby_rn, Sep 26, 2008

I know it has been a long time...but thank you for your info... he is now very concerned with going to heaven...he says he: confused: doesn't want to because he hates the "fast part" of getting there...he says he doesn't want to go back there...if he has to, he will come back in "2 days" or so he says...he has been talking about it a lot lately...he wants to know why I would want to go there...without him...I have no recollections of such things so I'm kind of at a loss for words...any suggestions? Thank you to everyone for your great advice!

Baby_rn, Dec 12, 2008

Its been a while...has anyone revisited the PLM* of their children after you think it has already passed? My son is heading back that way...it has been 2 years and all of a sudden, its resurfacing...any ideas?

Baby_rn, Apr 6, 2009

Baby RN POPS IN AGAIN ON MY HOME EMAIL

xxxxxxxxxx@aol.com

To: jeffreyxx@yahoo.com

Aug 7, 2009 at 1:42 AM

Jeff

I know it's been forever.... Just thought of you tonight. I just

---

*   PLM = Passed Life Memories (Author's note)

wanted you to know I showed Braden a picture of Kevin* a
while ago and he said" where did you get that? That's not
a very good picture..." later saying in the tub one night...this
is for Kevin up in heaven...he loves to be out in the yard and
gardening at age 5...and is ever concerned about safety...
asked him the other day if he remembers telling me about
firefighting stuff when he was younger and he said no what
did I say?

Most interesting.... He is almost six and has started to wear
the fire outfit again which is now very small! We went to visit
our friend who is a firefighter and went to his station at Braden's request because he wants to know "how it all works"
he told our friend. He just kept nodding and saying" I know'
and was thrilled by climbing the ladders onto the building.
We got into the car and he asked "how old do I need to be
to be a firefighter? At least 5? As I told him he needed to be
older he said why? "I already know all this stuff? "

So interestingly enough...he doesn't remember what he
used to tell me but he has circled back to firefighting and
wants to start now!!! He starts kindergarten in the fall and
still talks about scuba diving and calls all my daughters
dolls "Mary"** if asked a name.

Just an update...on Memorial Day this year he decorated
the house himself this year...attached is picture...under is
himself in fire outfit.... this was all his idea...had multiple
flags around our house as well by his request and would
not let anyone change a thing!

Thanks for all the great insights into this and life.... hope all
is well for you!

Baby_rn and Braden

---

*   Speaking of a picture of Lt. Kevin Donnelly (Author's note)
**   Turns out Kevin Donnelly had a sister named Mary and the woman
(longtime companion) KD was living with at the time of his death was also
named Mary. (Author's note)

THAT WAS THE LAST EMAIL TO MY HOME FROM Baby _RN (during this time period)

Baby RN back on the forum again in Sept. 2009

I have still been around...thanks for your interest...there are still things here and there my son talks about firefighting not as much as he used too.........

Baby_rn, Sep 29, 2009

He has been obsessed with George Washington lately... he is in kindergarten so I don't know what is covered in school...but he found a large feather and told me George Washington dips it in paint to write, ... also we were driving down a street lined with American flags... and he asked why they were there and what holiday it was... I said I don't know which I didn't because it was at the end of October, he said, "maybe it is because George Washington died and he came back so everyone has flags out for him..." I asked about what he meant by that and he said" he died but he is here now and everyone loves it". Anyone else have this matter-of-fact info come out of the blue while driving in the car? I'm just going with it but I don't know where this comes from...he is just an "old soul" without any better explanation...right now there are American flags "decorated" all over his fire fighter gear in his room which he refuses to move or change.

Just a little update... We were in New York City recently... my son had never been there (in this life) ... was afraid to bring him but had to because there was a death in the family...anyway we were driving across the George Washington bridge and he says" mom have I been here before? I think I recognize this place...no... no... I do recognize this place...I said, "no you've never been here..." he said "yes I have...

where are the buildings the bad men knocked down?" I said not here anymore...they were knocked down...he said his head hurt... we were there two days and by the afternoon of the second day he kept complaining of a headache (which he has never complained of it ever before) He had to spend the afternoon and night in the hotel with my husband because his head hurt so bad ...he is now six and doesn't talk too much about things anymore but apparently still remembers...interestingly enough when we walked out of the hotel front door and down the NYC street the third door we came to was a NYFD museum store or something like that...he wanted to go in and look around...we spent a while in there but the only thing he wanted was a little firefighter 9/11 pin which he didn't know that is what it said on it...but insisted on putting it on the left side of his shirt...also picked a Irish* firefighter badge...

Baby_rn, Feb 25, 2010

Funny... he got this headache when we were taking a carriage ride around central park (which he also swore I had taken him there before) and got worse as we got to natural history museum...so bad that my husband took him back to hotel...weird though, because when I got back to the hotel with my daughter he was laying in the bed saying he didn't feel good... then within 45 minutes he jumped out of bed and was totally fine like he never felt bad...he was running around the hotel room and insisted on having NY pizza...he ate a bunch but refused to go out to eat...he wanted to have it in the hotel room...kind of bizarre..

The pin and badge he picked out are in his room...he took that pin and some others he had from his great grandpa and had me help him pin them all onto his firefighter outfit

---

* (*Always proud of his Irish heritage, St. Patrick's Day was said to be Kevin's Donnelly's favorite holiday*) (At the time of this posting on the forum Braden is around 7 years old) (Author's note)

on the left side cause that is where he said they go...he stood in the mirror and admired himself (kind of cute)...the 9/11 pin he got in NYC he put on his shirt from the first night we got it and made sure he wore it every day after that when we were in NYC and east coast...he would move it from shirt to shirt every morning...when we got back to west coast he put it on his fire outfit ... its been there since... the Irish firefighter badge he put on his training tower (part of his fire bed) and is obsessed right now with St. Patrick's Day and being Irish...

Baby_rn, Feb 27, 2010

I am half Irish...But he said the other day he is so happy he is Irish...he decorated the house for St. Patrick's Day and said, "Did you know firefighters put these on their fire helmets? (Pointing to a shamrock) ... I have one too...he is counting down the days until St. Patrick's Day which is funny cause we never decorated or did too much on St Patrick's day...

The other day when he was admiring himself in the mirror with his pins on his fire jacket...he said," this looks pretty nice but I wish I had my real ones back..."

With the headache ...I'm not really sure what that was about...I really think he remembered being there (he said so anyway) was overwhelmed or maybe confused...just strange cause he doesn't typically have a headache with no other ailment with it...

Baby_rn, Mar 1, 2010

This may be a little off subject but just wondering if you can make any sense of this...my son has been kind of obsessed lately with heaven and me going there before him. He has been saying he doesn't want me to go before him...yesterday he was sitting on a chair in the office spinning around and singing...I wasn't really paying attention I was with my daughter but when I finally heard what he was repeating..." I'm going to heaven with mommy and that's a promise"... repeated over and over... when I went in there he started laughing and said, "Oh you heard me...I mean it"...not sure why he keeps saying it. He has described to me how he thinks you come back after heaven...but he seems worried I will go to heaven without him...not sure even what to say to this...

Baby_rn, Mar 3, 2010

My son has been asking me at night when he goes to bed, "what do you want me to tell you about tonight?" It's weird ...before all his information used to come out matter-of-factly...now it is like he wants to teach me about what he knows...He got out his little kid pointer purchased at school and began telling me about his fire trucks...he also went on about the structure of the empire state building and said if there was ever a fire in there it would be bad...he said the top part of it would fall to the ground and destroy the houses and buildings around it. The top part is not supported well and is too light to stay up after fire and smoke. He also said there are not enough stairs to rescue the people to get them out. then he stops and says what else do you want to learn...He's six now but the information he describes comes out in very "adult" language and confidence...He has the same books he has had since he was a little having to do with firefighting so he is not picking it up elsewhere... I said to him last night after he "taught" me about other things... how do you know so much about firefighting? He said, "I lived it"

Baby_rn, May 17, 2010

I don't know how to describe it... It went from info that was matter of fact and in the present tense to him now describing it as something he studied or something he can teach me about. He asks," what do I want to learn about" and I say I don't know, and he says, "how about this" and describes in much detail that things no 6-year-old or adult, for that matter, would know about...There isn't an emotion to it still...he just seems determined to teach me what he knows......he even comes to me sometimes at 3 am asking if he can tell me a "story "or how his day went and will go into this info... very detailed and very confident sounding...

Baby_rn, May 19, 2010

Sorry about the last phrase...was posting and texting at the same time...the two got mixed up...so last phrase meant nothing. Yes I guess it could be... that he has resolved one part of it and now he just wants to let me in on everything (facts) that he remembers. He is so confident in what he is saying also...He was telling me about the oxygen tanks firefighters carry and told me how long each tank will last before they are empty...I told him that didn't seem right... he actually insisted and told me to look it up and I did. He was right! When he talks about these things now he always stands up and kind of paces around just like a teacher would...weird actually...

Baby_rn, May 20, 2010

My husband did hear him say in the car that he recognized this place...he just looked shocked...I think my husband knows my son knows information that he shouldn't and he's ok with it now...he believes him but cannot understand or want to the concept of past lives or at least appears that way. Afraid of the whole thing...he said it throws his balance off...I think he's happy that my son is telling me the information and not him! But, there is just so much my son knows about in certain areas that even he can't rationalize out... so he has stopped trying to figure it out and takes it for what it is. He says whatever that may be...my son was talking about different guns the other night and who uses them and types of "ammo" and snipers very specific and my husband heard...we asked a friend who's on SWAT and he said he's right... My husband doesn't have an explanation for it

Baby_rn, May 21, 2010

Thanks for asking and I would love to post a picture but in his best interest I would like to keep him protected... any mother I think would understand this...I think his stories are pretty amazing to me but he only shares them with me which at this point in time makes me think he wants to be private about it. It might not make sense but that is how I see it. I have another picture I could post of his "decorations" in his room but to be honest I have no idea how to do that on this website. If someone can explain a simple way to do this I could give it a try...

Baby_rn, May 22, 2010

It is a very interesting idea you have about leaving it up to the family to contact me...the thing is I'm not sure who he actually was ...I guess I could just write the facts I have... and leave it up to them. There are also many, many catholic firefighters who do not believe in any of this. I don't want to throw other people's worlds off balance like I did with my husband and it is his own child! Just not sure I want to possibly dredge up very raw feelings in these awesome firefighters that have already suffered so much you know? I appreciate your great suggestions but am afraid it might confuse family and friends rather than help... I don't know if I would want to know or not if it was me...any ideas?

Baby_rn, May 30, 2010

Thank you for the insight...It's good to know there are people willing to except this and use it to heal. I couldn't want anything more than to help a grieving family...problem being I'm not 100 percent sure who he was and if I throw the facts out there to this fire station it could possibly match most of the guys there... There have been some very specific things he has said to me which have not been posted but nothing is pointing me to one specific person by name...I'm not sure he wants me to know to be honest...maybe this is where I'm supposed to stop? Don't know! When his information stops, I always think, ok this is it... this is where it ends...then more info comes so I don't know...I have read about James* and it is an amazing story and very similar to my son's dad...but my husband doesn't want to research or ask any questions to get more info from my son because it just rocks his world to be honest. He accepts it but, will not and can't investigate any further for his own reason I guess. My son decorated for Memorial Day for the family today before we woke up and we have American flags all over our house...it was his surprise to us this morning... he said, "This is for everyone who fights to keep us safe... mommys, daddys, grandmas, grandpas, soldiers, snipers, navy, angels and God".

Baby_rn, May 31, 2010

Thanks for your continued interest in my son's story...he is now just turned seven and I'm not sure he remembers what he has told me when he was younger...he knows a lot about fires and skyscraper and escape routes but he says he doesn't know how. So he does remember information but has no idea how. He now draws a lot and there is

---

*   This would be James Leininger, see the book *Soul Survivor: The Reincarnation of a World War II Fighter Pilot* (Author's note)

always a picture of New York City. I ask him why he decided to draw about NYC and he says he knows I like them and that he thinks about it a lot. Interesting thing is there is always the empire state building and another smaller building and always a person in an elevator in the middle of the building... don't know if that really means anything but every picture he draws has those two things with different scenery or cars around them. We also have a friend that is a firefighter that talked to my son the day before 9/11 this year and said there were a lot of brave firefighters that day (no other details)... my son said, "I know and I don't want to talk about it! Just lower your flags for respect!" So he may remember more than he shares now I'm not sure. He has a lot of information in his head about different things like the civil war and weapons and I have no idea where this comes from either...very detailed and when I ask him where he learned it he just says..." I just know it."

Baby_rn, Jan 6, 2011

Carol,

Thank you for all your help and providing a safe place to discuss this...I can't tell you how much I appreciate it! Yes, the drawings are of interest to me too...he has given me at least ten...All contain empire state building and building with person in elevator...floors labeled up to 14 always too...he just always draws them and gives them specifically to me because he knows I like them he says...but he will also stare out the window before he draws things and then will draw "what he just studied" he says after staring into space for a while. Don't understand it but it is always a picture from history...He is now a "typical" seven-year-old except for the comments he has sometimes...interesting too...he gets along with kids much older than him and also looks much bigger and older than kids his age. He just turned seven and is in first grade but is the size of the fourth graders or bigger... and in the context of history knows more than me!

Baby_rn, Jan 7, 2011

Thanks for the interest in my son's story... it has made me see the world in a different light! This may not have to do with past lives but kinda out there comment my son made the other day. I was driving him, my daughter and a friend home from school and they were playing in the back seat. Somehow, my daughter said, "I'm dead" to her friend and pretended to play dead and her friend was pretending to try to help her (just silly kid game) ... my son got upset at my daughter and said "you are not dead .... you don't even know what dead people look like. I do...I have seen a lot of them in my lifetime and it definitely doesn't look like that!... I just turned around and looked at him and he said, "What? I have!" then he changed the subject and the game...Anyone have any thought on this...It was the same kind of serious voice and that is why I noticed it...

Baby_rn, Jan 31, 2011

I guess I didn't put it in the right context...Yes... it does make sense but I think it took me off guard because he has not talked about it for a while and never information like that without a reference to some kind of firefighting fact. I don't know... I guess it came out in a different way than it used too. Sorry...now I read it again, (its sounds kind of silly the way I wrote it) I do know where it came from but it is the first-time he made a comment like that without first starting to talk about something with firefighters...so different for me...

Baby_rn, Feb 8, 2011

This ended Baby_rn's posts on Carol Bowman's forum.

BABY RN and I RECONNECT VIA PRIVATE EMAIL

I had just that one short email from Baby_rn on 8/7/2009 and that was it until 10/20/2019. I emailed her to see if I could still make contact and if so, ask her for permission to use her forum entries for my book. Our first contact had been on Oct 2, 2007, back then Baby_rn had felt it was not a good time to come out with the story of her son due to her concern to protect her son and worry over the effect it might have on Kevin Donnelly's parents and siblings. Now with the passage of time and distance away from 9/11/2001, she feels the story can be told. The old saying, "all in good time" in this case may translate into, "All in God's time." We mourn the Donnelly family's loss but at the same time rejoice in Braden's return, for this young man displays many of the wonderful characteristics that were evident in Kevin Donnelly's character. Braden's mother has described him as being kind, sweet, caring and loving with great concern for others. From what I can see, his insides have manifested on the outside for he is a very handsome young man in his mid-teens now, with an athletic build (6ft., 195lbs.) and great smile that most likely will be melting more than one young lady's heart. Why is he back you may ask? I believe he is back for many reasons. There may be more "Life Lessons" for him to learn or other people to help along the way in his life journey. The foremost reason is by returning he has demonstrated the survival of the soul after physical death, which in turn may bring some comfort and closure to those families affected by the events of 9/11. Personally, as far as I am concerned, he is back so that I could write his story and pass it on to you.

Lieutenant Kevin Donnelly FDNY

After reading the information provided by the forum entries and private emails to me, let us now turn to the story of Lieutenant Kevin Donnelly of the Fire Department of New York. I will try to give a good account of his life and passing from material pulled from many sources. I have known many people in my life who were, by my estimation, exceptional human beings; Kevin Donnelly certainly fits into this category. From an early age on into adulthood Kevin showed an extraordinary capacity for caring about others and their wellbeing. The book *Sons of Valor, Parents of Faith* contains a short story of Kevin's life along with a portrait of his parents, Edward and Cecilia Donnelly* and their coping with the loss of a beloved son. Kevin was also survived by two brothers Edward and Brian, a sister Mary and long-time companion Mary Coughlin.

Obituary

Donnelly – Edward L. of Levittown, NY on June 26, 2017 at the age of 89. Beloved husband of the late Cecilia for 61 years. Devoted and loving father of Edward (Suzanne), Mary C. Martin (late William), Brian (Kari) and honored father of the late FDNY Lt. Kevin, who died heroically on Sept. 11, 2001.)

I have found a large amount of material for my writings in book form, newspapers, FDNY, Memorials and on the internet... I have tried to leave no stone unturned in my quest for information. I am not infallible and may inadvertently pass on misinformation gained in my search. I have done my best to apprise the reader with accurate information.

Kevin W. Donnelly was born July 7, 1958, to an Irish Catholic family in Levittown, Nassau County, New York on Long Island. All of the Donnelly children received parochial educations. Kevin was known as KD to many and as a kid loved to run and swim, two loves that would never leave him. A strong work ethic must have been instilled into Kevin because before even becoming a teenager he started KD's Lawn Service in the Levittown/Wantagh area. As a teenager he got a job as a lifeguard at the town pool.

At Legacy.com I came across a wonderful entry by a woman named Laura. The entry was dated Sept. 15, 2009. It differed from the others in that it appeared to be written by a woman

---

* (Both of Kevin's parents have passed in the years since 9/11.)

who seems to have had a schoolgirl crush on Kevin Donnelly.
Now, I would never make fun of anybody professing deep feelings
for another person. I know from experience the strong nature of
young love as I imagine many of the people reading this do also.
Laura said she knew Kevin from her high school days back when
he was a lifeguard and volunteer firefighter. The high school was
right next to the firehouse (on the border of Wantagh & Levittown) and she would visit him there. She said the other lifeguards
at the Wantagh Pool had a nickname for Kevin, "Hollywood,"
she thinks because of his many admirers and his good looks.
Laura had not been aware that Kevin had joined the FDNY until
years after 9/11. She was walking in Manhattan when she saw his
name on a passing Firetruck. I think she must have come across
the present-day Ladder 3 with a 9/11 tribute board affixed to the
handrail on the rear turntable. It reads:

September 11, 2001
3 Truck
WE WILL NEVER FORGET OUR BROTHERS
B.C. John Williamson FF. Timothy McSweeney
Capt. Patrick Brown   FF. Jeffrey Giordano
Lt. Kevin Donnelly   FF. Steve Olson
FF. John McAvoy   FF. Joseph Ogren
FF. Joseph Maloney   FF. James Coyle
FF. Michael Carroll   FF. Gerard Dewan
B.C John Moran SOC
Box 5-5-8087

Laura had thought herself lucky to not have lost anyone special in her life during that tragic day in 2001 but she found out
that she had been wrong in her assumption. Laura finished up
by saying than Kevin Donnelly would always be in her heart as
he has been since 1975. I believe that statement is as true as
the Sun rises in the East and I will tell you why. In my many
hours searching for information on the internet, I stumbled upon
a photo that struck a familiar chord in me, so much so that I

tracked down the photographer to ask the location where the picture was taken. He informed me he had shot the photo at the *Brooklyn Wall of Remembrance* located on Coney Island. The wall is a monument to the First Responders lost on 9/11 and consists of dark stone tablets with the likeness of those persons laser etched into the stone. The photo I speak of was shot at an angle trailing off to the right, with the only completely legible tablet being that of Lt. Kevin Donnelly. Kevin's portrait is very well done and he looks handsome in his Lieutenant's dress uniform. To the left of his picture is a single rose taped to the stone, to the upper right is a very sweet note for Kevin dated 9/11/12. The note is signed with a single name: Laura.

It is said that Kevin kept a bathing suit and towel in his car at all times and would find any excuse to head for the water. I get the impression that the only thing in the World that could top his love for running and swimming (and people) was the Fire Service. In October of 1976, Kevin joined the Wantagh Fire Department and began filling the vacuum in his heart with everything fire related. In 1979, having just turned 21, Kevin Donnelly was appointed to the New York City Fire Department where he was first assigned to Engine Company 222, located in Brooklyn. Later in his career he would be transferred to Ladder Company 176. He was promoted to the rank of lieutenant in January of 1994 and assigned to Ladder Company 3 in Manhattan. During his years with the FDNY he received four medals for "Acts of Heroism and Bravery." When not working, KD could be found swimming or running (he ran in multiple New York City Marathons) and when not physically active he was pursuing a higher education. Kevin worked his way up to a master's degree from John Jay College and became an adjunct professor at Jersey City University teaching fire science courses.

Lt. Donnelly had been relieved of duty the morning of September 11, 2001 after completing a 24-hour shift. He along with other off-duty Ladder 3 members grabbed their gear and commandeered some taxi cabs to drive to the World Trade Center site. The last audio report from Ladder 3 came from their Captain

Patrick "Paddy" Brown, "This is 3 Truck and were still heading up." These are the last words dispatch heard from Captain Brown at 9:21am from the 35th floor of the North Tower. Lieutenant Donnelly climbed to the sixtieth floor. *He started to make his way down right after the South Tower collapsed. Those reports show that Kevin was able to make it all the way down to the fifteenth floor before stopping to help more people who needed to be rescued. Kevin's last conversation was with a firefighter from Ladder Company 5. "Hey Lou, we've got orders to get out!" Kevin replied, "Go ahead. I'll catch up as soon as I finish helping these women." Lieutenant Kevin Donnelly and eleven 11 other firefighters from Ladder 3 would never make it out."*** There was a memorial service for Kevin on October 6, 2001 in Wantagh, New York. His body was found on March 12, 2002. He was buried in Westbury on March 18, the day after Saint Patrick's Day.

In the search for Braden's friend Mike, I came across three Mikes who may be the one(s) that Braden has spoken of in his talks with his mother. When Braden talked to his mother it was sometimes hard to tell exactly what or who he was referring to. His thoughts might not have been about a single Mike and she was dealing with a very young child. There was most likely more than one Mike in Kevin Donnelly's life just by the sheer fact of how common the name is in the Fire Service. I venture that if you were to walk up to any Fire Station and yell "Mike" through the door you would be surprised how many times you would receive a reply. I discovered three Mikes in KD's life and who knows, there very well may have been more.

The first Mike, Michael Duignan
Michael Duignan, Wantagh, NY.

On Legacy.com, there were over 100 messages left on a memorial site dedicated to Kevin Donnelly. The entry on February 4, 2009 was from Mr. Duignan and told of KD giving him work such as lawn cutting and painting during a lull in the real estate business

---

*   (*O'Donnell, James J. **Son of Valor, Parents of Faith**. WestBow Press, Bloomington IN, 2017. Pages 35-36)

back in 1989. He also vividly remembered KD at Station 2 (in Wantagh) sharing his time and knowledge with the junior men and teaching the volunteers "how the pro's do it." So, I would surmise that Mike Duignan was a volunteer firefighter at that time at Station 2. Kevin Donnelly gave him the nickname "Big Mike," which he still cherishes.

The second Mike, Michael Carroll
Firefighter Michael T. Carroll (Ladder 3)

Michael T. Carroll, 39 yrs. old, firefighter, FDNY, Ladder 3. A 16-year veteran. Mike Carroll fits the bill for Braden's Mike with children, because I had read that two days before the attacks, on Sunday, Sept. 9, 2001, Nancy Carroll took her two kids, Brendan and three-year-old Olivia, down to Ladder 3 for a "family outing." It is said that Mike had a strange practice of breaking the handles off all the coffee cups at the firehouse. Try as they may the other firefighters were never able to break him of this bad habit. Mike Carroll perished along with his brother firefighters at The World Trade Center.

The third Mike, Michael Boyle
Firefighter Michael Boyle (Engine 33)

Firefighter Michael Boyle, 37 yrs. old, FDNY Engine 33. Mike Boyle lost his life on September 11, 2001 at the World Trade Center. Michael might have one day followed in his father James' footsteps as President of the Uniformed Firefighters Association. Like Kevin Donnelly, Mike Boyle was a marathon runner and like Kevin was off duty the morning of 9/11 but still went on the call from which he would not return. Ladder 3 would sometimes run with Engine 33 to calls in Manhattan. I ran across a video of just such a call on YouTube. I believe this may be the Mike that Braden said was a firefighter but worked in another station. Braden gave his mother directions to his friend Mike's station: In a private email to me on Oct 12, 2007 at 11:12 PM Braden's mom wrote, "<u>These are the directions that Braden has told me</u> <u>about from "his" fire station to his friend Mike's: He said, "My</u> <u>fire station is to the left and down the hill the other station is to</u> <u>the right..." I would not think anything of this but for the fact he</u> <u>doesn't know right from left...</u>" The station for Ladder 3 is at 103 E. 13th Street just in from 4th Ave, and Engine 33's station is at 42 Great Jones St. (in line with W. 3rd St.) I was not a math whiz in school but I would say that is ten streets apart for the two stations. Now, if you were standing in the middle of the intersection at 4th Ave and 13th St., looking South or downhill (Approx. 70 ft. elevation at this point but for lower Manhattan that is a respectable hill), ten streets down on the right is Great Jones St. the home of Engine 33. Remember, these directions were given by a three-year- old, so they were simple but they seem to describe the positions of Kevin Donnelly's station in relation to Mike Boyle's station very well.

Kevin Donnelly and the two FDNY Mikes have another thing in common. John Jay College has a 9/11 Memorial Sculpture made up of the N-4 beam from Ground Zero. It is so named for the large N-4 painted on the beam itself. The sculpture consists of the beam protruding from a granite base. The names of 67 of the fallen from John Jay are etched in dark granite base top. The lower section of the base carries the inscription "Dedicated in Memory of Those From the John Jay College Community Who Lost Their Lives on September 11, 2001." You can see the names Kevin W. Donnelly, Michael T. Carroll and Michael Boyle inscribed along with one other I recognized: Patrick J. Brown.

BROWN - Captain Patrick J. FDNY. Age 48, 21-year veteran. Captain of Ladder 3, former Captain of Engine 69, former Lieutenant of Truck 28 and former firefighter of Rescue 2, Rescue 1 and Truck 26. Patrick "Paddy" Brown was well known in the fire service. Mayor Giuliani called him, "A legend in the life of the Fire Department" during a mass for Capt. Brown at St. Patrick's Cathedral. Patrick Brown was a highly decorated member of the

FDNY. He was also a Marine veteran and a recipient of the Silver Star.*

    I feel I must say more about Captain Brown to show the contrast between his early life and upbringing as compared to that of Lt. Donnelly. These two men had quite different backgrounds and life experiences. Kevin Donnelly's youth up to the time of his joining the FDNY seem somewhat ideal, full of love, friendship and happy days. This I believe was the manifestation of the rule you get back what you put out, and in his case appears to be well deserved. Both men had built up their character over many years before entering the fire service. Paddy Brown's road was a rather bumpy one. I watch a movie called *Finding Paddy* which was done by a filmmaker friend of Capt. Brown by the name of Steve McCarthy. *Finding Paddy* was one of the most honest films I have ever seen.

    It is a real human story told warts and all without any sugar coating, gritty and at times disturbing. There was abuse as a youngster, signing up for the Marines at age 17 and serving two tours in Vietnam. Some times, being of Irish heritage brings along with it a battle with the bottle. Wars can also bring wounds unseen and Paddy was not immune. He suffered with nightmares and insomnia. Always the fighter though, he overcame many of his problems with professional help and the love of his friends. Twenty four medals in twenty four years in the department is an outstanding record, but his greatest accomplishment was his victories within himself. Kevin Donnelly and Patrick Brown traveled different roads but ended up at the same destination, same job, same unit and sadly, the same fate. Gratitude is owed to both and to all those who work in service to others.

    I asked Braden's mother if she wanted to say anything to the readers and if she did, to please let me know. I received a reply; she wrote:"Tragedy can yield a beautiful awakening. The soul does live on in whatever way you believe. My son's story is just

---

*   (*The Silver Star Medal is the United States Armed Forces' third-highest personal decoration for valor in combat.)

one of many examples of how life is much bigger than we think. If we listen to our children, really listen, they can teach us more than we can ever fathom!"

So true, as the old saying goes, "Out of the mouths of babes oft times come gems." Those gems can sometimes be more profound and insightful than may be realized by the casual observer. A good practice for all would be to pay attention. Pay attention to the World around you, to other people, and even to yourself.

I have not returned to lower Manhattan since my last visit when it was still a pile of smoking ruins. There are some things in my life that I prefer not to revisit. Oh, I know it bears little resemblance to how it once looked and they have done a wonderful job of transforming the scenery. Still, it is not a happy place but one reserved for reverence and reflection. It is a scar on the face of the city, a reminder of the evil that men do. Can you remember any time in Earth's history without evil, sadly you can't; can you? Did you ever notice that Evil spelled backwards is the word *live*. It is part of life and its existence all depends on how people choose to conduct their lives, and for better or worse we have all been given "Free Will." When it comes to the 9/11 memorial, I choose to view from afar through the looking glass called the Internet and do my visits and investigating virtually. I don't want to see it as it is; I remember it as it was.

The 9/11 Memorial in lower Manhattan covers eight acres with beautiful green grass and many tall trees and plantings. The twin Memorial reflecting pools are said to be the largest man-made waterfalls in North America. Almost 3,000 names of those killed in the attacks of both September 11, 2001, and February 26, 1993, are permanently engraved in the bronze enclosure around the twin pools. Online you can check the location of individual names and I did so with Kevin Donnelly's. I found something remarkable that ties my story told in *Someone Else's Yesterday*, written in 2003, to the present writing of this section, The Phoenix.

I have written about Capt. Brown and earlier about attending Capt. Terry Hatton's funeral, but had not mentioned Chief

Downey. Now I find that all three of their names are adjoining each other on the wall of the South Memorial Pool. This was not a random occurrence. There were "Requested Adjacencies", requested and honored. The 9/11 Memorial and Museum site states these, "requests for adjacent names were made by next-of-kin or affiliation." I can see no direct affiliation between Rescue 1, Ladder 3 and SOC (special operations command), so it would seem that the requests may have come from the next-of-kin. The Chief Downey and Capt. Brown requests were to be next to Capt. Hatton and the Capt. Hatton request was for both Capt. Brown and Chief Downey.

On Saturday 12/15/01, along with other Firefighters from Connecticut, I boarded the Port Jefferson Ferry out of Bridgeport, CT, to attend a memorial service for Raymond Downey Sr., Chief of Special Operations Command. It was held in Deer Park on Long Island. Saints Cyril and Methodius Roman Catholic Church was overflowing and thousands of firefighters lined the street while SWAT Teams lined the roofs of the buildings along Deer Park Avenue. Let's just say I find it amusing and touching that I find all three of their names literally touching.*

Something happened in Braden's life that neither I, nor the people on the forum were ever aware of. There was another trip to New York City and this time it was something more than just recognizing the twin towers on the front cover of a Curious George book: A visit to the 9/11 Memorial Museum which is home to numerous artifacts and displays relevant to September 11th, 2001. One of the largest items placed into the underground museum was so large that it had to be lowered by crane into the hole before construction on the museum could be completed. It was the crushed remains of FDNY Ladder 3 (also known as 3 Truck). Some reports say that a total of 91 FDNY apparatus and vehicles were destroyed, while 130 more were damaged. So what do you think the odds are that it would be Ladder 3 that was

---

*   (The names of the men of Ladder 3, Rescue 1 along with Chief Downey can be found in sections S6 through S10 on the South Memorial Pool wall facing West St.)

picked to go in the museum? The park-like setting belies what lay beneath its well-manicured facade. Approximately seven stories below the Memorial is the Museum of over 100,000 square feet. The Museum is large and cavernous with a 70-foot ceiling and barren concrete walls.

Braden's mom passed on to me what had transpired during their family trip to New York City. She told me that their visit to the 9/11 Memorial took place in December of 2016. She said, "I didn't think Braden remembered anything about his childhood past life memories because he was now 13 years old." It was snowing that day and they decided to walk around the Memorial Pools first reading the names as they walked. She said, "We were all saddened by how many loved ones were lost that terrible day." Their next stop was the subterranean Memorial Museum. Venturing inside Braden's mother noticed that Braden was starting to yawn. She said, "He has a habit of yawning when he gets nervous." Now most people take a yawn as a sign of being tired but in Braden's case it was just the opposite, he was waking up.

One of their stops was at the exhibit entitled "In Memoriam," consisting of 2,977 photos of individuals killed as a result of the terrorist attacks. Now, suddenly, the names they had read outside on the Memorial pool walls had become pictures. They were only there a few minutes when Braden said, "Get me out of here." Quickly moving along they came upon the battered remnants of Ladder 3. Braden's yawning continued and he informed his mother, "I have such a headache" and told her he was ready to go. It appears that the family may have set a record for the fastest museum tour. Once outside Braden's headache disappeared and the yawning stopped. His mother said, "He went right to throwing snowballs at his sister! The only thing he said about the Museum was, "That was a totally claustrophobic place and I don't ever want to go back in there." I do not think the word claustrophobic can be properly applied to describe the immense area where Ladder 3 was placed; nonetheless it was undeniably closing in on him. The passage of time may have dulled Braden's past life memories, but it had not erased them completely.

The headache was understandable; Braden had stood in the absent shadow of the North Tower where he perished in a past life, looking at the wreckage of the vehicle Lt. Donnelly was assigned to, Ladder 3. Good vibrations, bad vibrations, things do linger. Think of the vibrations of events given off throughout time as being recorded, very much like a long-playing vinyl record. The vibrations are recorded into the vinyl as a groove that allows them to be heard by putting a needle of a record player into the groove. Braden was the needle that day and not only walked into one of those grooves but fell into a chasm, a Harmonic Resonance. Much like me in the Sunken Road at Antietam battlefield he had come full circle and met himself, a reintroduction to his past life alter ego, Lieutenant Kevin Donnelly.

In 2021 Braden will turn 18, the age of adulthood. I hope I have done a good job of introducing his story to the masses. Earth years have been catching up with me. I see the clock on the wall, the hour hand licking the face like a cat finishing a meal. I do not know how much longer I have to tell these stories. But it is very important that these stories be told and retold to awaken those still in slumber, those dreamers of faraway places and other lands. Those that hum haunting tunes from a bygone era, or yearn for a woman they can only see in their mind's eye. Once awakened to the fact that not all dreams are fantasy, they can never again return to a state of complete unconsciousness. Doors open, people enter your life while others leave, but all is a learning experience, a life experience and the meaning of life is the journey. It appears that both Braden and I have been battered and bruised in our past lives. Indeed, in all our lives but, we have also loved and been loved and in fact will continue in that mode for eternity. Who knows, maybe in this lifetime Braden will pick up where I leave off and keep the stories alive and if not this life, maybe the next one.

Notes

[1] Gallagher, 1987, p. 59.

[2] *Who's Who*, 1903–1905, p. 424.

[3] Gordon, 1903, pp. 87–91.

[4] Gordon, 1903, p. 91.

[5] Bailey, 1984, pp. 96, 107.

[6] Eckert, 1989, p. 50.

[7] Gordon, 1903, p. 92.

[8] Gordon, 1903, p. 102.

[9] Gordon, 1903, pp. 74–75.

[10] Lee, 1915, pp. 94–95.

[11] Gordon, 1903, pp. 147–48.

[12] Gordon, 1903, pp. 321–22.

[13] Eckert, 1989, p. 7.

[14] Eckert, 1989, p. 8.

[15] Gordon, 1903, p. 309.

[16] Gordon, 1903, p. 312.

[17] Worsham, 1912, p. 212.

[18] *The War of the Rebellion: A Compilation of the Official Records of the Union and Confederate Armies*, p. 1035. Here on known as Official Records.

[19] *Official Records*, p. 1035.

[20] *The New American Desk Encyclopedia*.

[21] Gordon, 1903, pp. 322–23.

[22] Gordon, 1903, p. 102.

[23] Gordon, 1903, p. 241.

[24] Pollard, pp. 543–44.

[25] Gordon, 1903, pp. 264–66.

[26] *American Heritage*, 1960, p. 458.

[27] Miller, 1911, pp. 64–66.

[28] Gordon, 1903, pp. 278–79.

[29] Gordon, 1903, pp. 385, 386, 387.

[30] Gordon, 1903, p. 389.

[31] Gordon, 1903, p. 394.

[32] Tankersley, 1955, pp. 183–85.

[33] Chamberlain, 1901.

[34] Gordon, 1900, pp. 15–16.

[35] Gordon, 1903, pp. 318–19.

[36] Tankersley, 1955, pp. 69–70.

[37] Tankersley, 1955, p. 98.

[38] Tankersley, 1955, pp. 94–95.

[39] Tankersley, 1955, p. 99.

[40] Vandiver, 1970, p. 304.

[41] Weiss, 1988, p. 9.

[42] Weiss, 1988, p. 58.

[43] In the book, *Wearing of the Gray* (1867) by John Esten Cooke (of Gen. JEB Stuart's staff), I found that Gen. Gordon enjoyed cigars also. Cooke writes: "We reached General Gordon's and were shown to the General's chamber. General G's cheery voice as he smoked his cigar and discussed the events of the day, did not make my companion smile." Cooke's companion was General Pegram who would die in battle the very next day.

[44] Tankersley, 1955, p. 372.

[45] All quotes in the last two paragraphs, Gordon, 1903, pp. 341–42.

[46] Gordon, 1903, pp. 349–50.

[47] Gordon, 1903, pp. 437–38.

[48] Worsham, 1912, p. 193.

[49] Tankersley, 1965, p. 16.

[50] Field, 1886, p. 33–35.

[51] Jeremiah Williams to John B. Bachelder, 18, June 1880, Bachelder Papers, New Hampshire Historical Society.

[52] Miller, 1993, p. 143.

[53] Tankersley, 1955, pp. 14–15.

[54] Tankersley, 1955, p. 191, note #15.

[55] Patton, 1994, p. 246.

[56] Tankersley, 1955, p. 221 (from *Confederate Military History I,* 704).

[57] Gordon, 1903, pp. 60–61.

[58] Gordon, 1903, pp. 64–65.

[59] Gordon, 1903, p. 65.

[60] From www.ial.goldthread.com

[61] www.ial.goldthread.com

[62] Leek, 1974.

[63] *The Adventure of George the Dinosaur* (LA Adventura De Jorge Il Dinosaurio) by Doron W. Blake, David Gremard (Illustrator), Winafred B. Lucas (Editor)

[64] The Inuit living in the western Canadian Arctic call themselves *"Inuvial-uit"* or "real human beings." Their homeland stretches from the Alaskan border east to Amundsen Gulf and the western edge of the Canadian Arctic Islands.

[65] *The Good, The Bad & The Ugly: Original Motion Picture Soundtrack* [soundtrack] Ennio Morricone.

[66] Excerpt from Dr. Semkiw's website, www.johnadams.net

[67] Excerpt from Dr. Semkiw's website, www.johnadams.net

[68] Gordon, 1903, p. 145–46.

[69] "Not Yet" had been the original title of my book.

[70] Excerpt from Dr. Semkiw's website www.johnadams.net

[71] Source: FIND-A-GRAVE www.findagrave.com (Bio by D. Stewart)

[72] Excerpt from Dr. Semkiw's website www.johnadams.net

[73] Linguistic analysis supplied to author by Dr. Walter Semkiw.

[74] Mayor Giuliani received an honorary knighthood from Queen Elizabeth II. Commissioner Von Essen was bestowed with honorary title of Commander of the British Empire.

[75] Golay, 1994.

[76] Gordon, 1903, pp. 35–36.

[77] Gordon, 1993 edition, Introduction.

Bibliography

American Heritage Picture History of the Civil War. New York: American Heritage Publishing Co. Inc. 1960. (Catton, Brucetext).

Bailey, Ronald H. (and the Editor of Time Life Books) *The Civil War; The Bloodiest Day.* Alexandria VA: Time Life Books, 1984.

Chamberlain, Major Gen. Joshua Lawrence, *New York Times,* 5/4/1901.

Early, Gen. Jubal A., *Autobiographical Sketch and Narrative of the War Between the States.* Reprinted by the Nautical and Aviation Publishing Company, 1989.

Eckert, Ralph Lowell, *John Brown Gordon, Soldier, Southerner, American.* Baton Rouge, LA: Louisiana State University Press, 1989.

Evans, Clement A., ed., *Confederate Military History,* Extended Edition. Vol. 7. Georgia. Wilmington, NC: Broadfoot, 1987.

Field, Henry M., *Blood Is Thicker Than Water: A Few Days Among Our Southern Brethren.* New York: George Munro Publisher, 1886.

Gallagher, Gary, "Till the Sun Goes Down or Victory is Won: The Confederate Defense of the Sunken Road at Sharpsburg," *Civil War Quarterly,* Volume IX, June 1987.

Golay, Michael, *To Gettysburg and Beyond.* Sarpedon Publishers, 1994.

Gordon, John B., *Boyhood Sketch, Youth's Companion* LXXIV (1900) 5-16.

Gordon, Gen. John B., *Reminiscences of the Civil War.* New York: Charles Scribner's Sons, 1903; reprinted Louisiana State University Press, 1993.

Johnson, Pharris Deloach, ed., *Under the Southern Cross: Soldier Life with Gordon Bradwell and the 31st Georgia.* Macon, GA: Mercer University Press, Nov. 1999.

Lee, Robert E., *Lee's Dispatches: Unpublished Letters of General Robert E. Lee, C.S.A.* New York, London: G.P. Putnam's Sons, Edited by Douglas Southall Freeman, 1915.

Leek, Sybil, *Reincarnation the Second Chance,* New York: Stein andDay Publishers, 1974.

Miller, Francis Trevelyan, editor in chief, Lanier, Robert S., managing editor, *Photographic History of the Civil War—The Decisive Battles,* Vol. 3,. New York: Patriot Publishing Co., 1911.

Miller, William J., *Mapping for Stonewall.* Washington, DC: Elliott & Clark Publishing, 1993.

Murray, Alton J., *The True Wartime Experiences of the 26th Regiment, Georgia Volunteer Infantry, Lawton-Gordon-Evans Brigade, Confederate States Army.* St. Marys, GA: Alton J. Murray,1976.

Nichols, Pvt. G. W., *A Soldier's Story of His Regiment (61stGeorgia) and Incidentally of the Lawton-Gordon-Evans Brigade, Army of Northern Virginia.* Kennesaw, GA: Continental BookCo, 1961). (E559.5.61st.N53.1961.

Patton, Robert H., *The Pattons: A Personal History of an American Family.* Crown Publishing Group, Inc., 1994.

Pollard, Edward A., *Lee and His Lieutenants.*

Scaife, William R., *The Georgia Brigade.* Atlanta, GA: William R.Scaife, 1988.

Stephens, Robert Grier , Jr., ed., *Intrepid Warrior: Clement Anselm Evans.* Dayton, OH: Morningside House, Inc. 1992.

Tankersley, Allen P., *John B. Gordon: A Study in Gallantry.* Atlanta, GA: Whitehall Press, 1965.

Vandiver, Frank E., *Their Tattered Flags.* New York: Harper & Row, 1970.

The War of the Rebellion: A Compilation of the Official Records of the Union and Confederate Armies (130 Vols.). Washington, DC. 1880-1901. XIX Part 1.

Weiss, Brian L., *Many Lives, Many Masters.* New York: Simon &Schuster Inc., 1988.

White, Gregory C., *This Most Bloody and Cruel Drama: A History of the 31st Georgia Volunteer Infantry.* Baltimore, MD: Butternut & Blue, 1997.

Worsham, John H., *One of Jackson's Foot Cavalry: His Experience and What He Saw During the War 1861-1865.* New York: Neale Publishing Company, 1912.

Who's Who, 1903-1905.

Biography

Jeffrey J. Keene was born in Danbury, Connecticut in 1947 and grew up in the town of Westport, CT, attending Staples High School. He joined the Air Force following his graduation in 1965. Following basic training, Keene served in Texas, Alabama, Florida, and New Jersey; he rose to the rank of sergeant, and received an honorable discharge in 1969. After returning to Westport, Keene joined the town's fire department in 1976. In his thirty-five years in the fire service, Keene studied Fire Science at Norwalk State Technical College and attended Delaware State Fire School, where he progressed to the Fire Instructor level. One of the state's first Hazardous Materials Technicians, he also developed a Mock Crash Program to educate local high school students on the dangers of drinking and driving, gaining recognition for his efforts from Mothers Against Drunk Driving (MADD). Jeffrey Keene is a decorated firefighter and retired in 2003 as an Assistant Fire Chief (Westport, Connecticut Fire Department). Asst. Chief Keene spent the last fifteen years as a shift commander and was charged with the development and implementation of Standard Operation Procedures for the department.

Jeff was filmed for a segment in the A&E documentary Beyond Death which first aired in April of 2001 and has continued to be shown over the years.

Independent film documentary; In Another Life aired 2003 Produced/directed by Stephen Sakellarios Mr. Keene tells his story of reincarnation at the gravesite of Confederate General John B. Gordon at Oakland Cemetery in Atlanta, Georgia (Circa 1997)

Mr. Keene's case was featured on Sci-Fi Channel's show, "Proof Positive," first airing November 2004.

Japanese program "Amazing Stories" Produced by: Fuji Television Network, Inc. Air Date: October 2006

"Weird or What" Hosted by William Shatner (Canada). Life After Death episode aired September 2011

History Channel's "The UnXplained" William Shatner Host, Season 1 Episode 6 titled Life Beyond Death aired Aug, 2019

Mr. Keene's book Someone Else's Yesterday was a finalist in the 2004 COVR visionary Awards (Coalition of Visionary Resources) held at the International New Age Trade Show in Denver Colorado in June 2004.

Through years of research and travel, Mr. Keene has amassed compelling evidence of a former life during the American Civil War; that of Confederate General John B. Gordon. Keene resides with his wife Anna in Trumbull, Connecticut; he has two children (Shannon and Samantha) and three stepchildren (Todd, Kathy and Adam).

Acknowledgements

Those who I cannot thank enough;
My two Earth Angels, Judy Goodman and Marianne Pestana
My Book Angel, Susan Veach
My Website Angel, Kandi Carter
Love you ladies, Jeff

"I regard Jeff Keene's reincarnation case as having extreme significance for the field of parapsychology. The various features—waking adult memories, birthmarks correlating with old battle wounds, and soul-group connections—all suggest to me new possibilities for validating the reincarnation hypothesis and for conducting further research. This book is a milestone."
—Jeffrey Mishlove, PhD
Host: NEWTHINKINGALLOWED.COM

"Never before have I run across such concrete evidence of reincarnation. Great book, the pictures are indeed haunting... the resemblance...very uncanny. "
—Laura M. Wandrie, New Age Journal

"One of the most profound books on reincarnation that sheds light into the nature of existence after death, our consciousness, and the soul's reincarnation journey through time."
—Marianne Pestana, Radio Show Host of
Moments with Marianne

"A fascinating look into the possibilities of rebirth and survival of the Soul. Jeffrey Keene takes us on an exciting journey into the realm of reincarnation."
—Robert L. Snow, (Capt. PD ret.) author of
Portrait of a Past-Life Skeptic:
The True Story of a Police Detective's Reincarnation

Made in the USA
Coppell, TX
27 August 2022

82169709R00193